Praise for Christopher Benfey's
A Summer of Hummingbirds

"[A] tender, suspenseful and informed meditation on action and thought in the cultivated realms of East Coast America following the Civil War."
—Mindy Aloff, *The Washington Post Book World*

"[Benfey] leads us to encounter the complexity and passions of a forgotten age and a group of fascinating people who seemed fated to obscurity."
—Bob Hoover, *Pittsburgh Post-Gazette*

"[Benfey] presents sensitive critiques of literature and art alongside tales of illicit love and broken, bent, or triumphant lives, all of which makes for compelling reading for specialist and nonspecialist alike."
—Trygve Thoreson, *Booklist*

"*A Summer of Hummingbirds* has an operalike tone and form—or maybe an operetta—shifting from scene to evanescent scene, almost sung rather than read or written, folding back and forth upon itself, but always coming back to the hummingbird, the trailing arbutus, the transit of Venus."
—Ann La Farge, *The Independent* (Massillon, Ohio)

"In Christopher Benfey's [*A Summer of Hummingbirds*], intellectual and personal plotlines intersect, intertwine, collide, and finish by creating a delicate pattern. It was a relatively small world in the nineteenth century so perhaps it is not too surprising that the lives of the American intelligentsia of the time were so interconnected. But it is fascinating—and Benfey's neatly pieced-together book makes for lively and moving reading."
—*The Christian Science Monitor*

D0360362

"A whimsical group biography of Emily Dickinson and her peers aims for the feeling, as well as the facts, of an artistic era. . . . [Benfey's] latest book, which rambles gracefully from anecdote to anecdote, is his most unconventional effort to date. Through a web of friendships and chance encounters, it attempts to describe what Benfey calls 'an informal cult of hummingbirds' that he believes took shape in the years following the Civil War."
—*The Chronicle of Higher Education*

"The years during and following the Civil War saw momentous social, political, religious, scientific, and artistic ferment. . . . Christopher Benfey explores this phenomenon in his engaging *A Summer of Hummingbirds: Love, Art, and Scandal in the Intersecting Worlds of Emily Dickinson, Mark Twain, Harriet Beecher Stowe, and Martin Johnson Heade*. Benfey skillfully explores the personal histories as well as the work of his primary subjects. . . . [He] adroitly presents this group in vivid scenes that re-create what it must have been like during a time of great cultural transformation."
—*BookPage*

"For the past quarter century, readers have been learning through myriad accounts about the frenetic whirl of sexual activity that surrounded—and even occasionally took place within—the hothouse world of Emily Dickinson. . . . Benfey knows this terrain—geographical as well as atmospheric—and visits it anew. . . . His unique contribution is finding a unifying force in the cult of the hummingbird, an evocative image of daring and freedom in a restrictive time. In so doing, he brings a fresh perspective to this too-often overheated topic, providing new contexts, insights, and depth."
—TheAtlantic.com

PENGUIN BOOKS

A SUMMER OF HUMMINGBIRDS

Christopher Benfey is Mellon Professor of English at Mount Holyoke College. He is a prolific critic and essayist who writes for *The New York Times Book Review, The New Republic,* and *The New York Review of Books.* He also serves as a regular art critic for the online magazine *Slate.* Benfey has published three books set in the American Gilded Age: *The Double Life of Stephen Crane; Degas in New Orleans;* and *The Great Wave: Gilded Age Misfits, Japanese Eccentrics, and the Opening of Old Japan.* He has held fellowships from the Guggenheim Foundation, the National Endowment for the Humanities, and the American Council of Learned Societies. He lives in Amherst, Massachusetts, with his wife, Mickey Rathbun, and their two sons.

A Summer of Hummingbirds

LOVE, ART, AND SCANDAL IN THE

INTERSECTING WORLDS OF EMILY DICKINSON,

MARK TWAIN, HARRIET BEECHER STOWE,

AND MARTIN JOHNSON HEADE

CHRISTOPHER BENFEY

PENGUIN BOOKS

PENGUIN BOOKS

Published by the Penguin Group
Penguin Group (USA) Inc., 375 Hudson Street, New York, New York 10014, U.S.A.
Penguin Group (Canada), 90 Eglinton Avenue East, Suite 700, Toronto,
Ontario, Canada M4P 2Y3 (a division of Pearson Penguin Canada Inc.)
Penguin Books Ltd, 80 Strand, London WC2R 0RL, England
Penguin Ireland, 25 St Stephen's Green, Dublin 2, Ireland (a division of Penguin Books Ltd)
Penguin Group (Australia), 250 Camberwell Road, Camberwell,
Victoria 3124, Australia (a division of Pearson Australia Group Pty Ltd)
Penguin Books India Pvt Ltd, 11 Community Centre, Panchsheel Park, New Delhi – 110 017, India
Penguin Group (NZ), 67 Apollo Drive, Rosedale, North Shore 0632,
New Zealand (a division of Pearson New Zealand Ltd)
Penguin Books (South Africa) (Pty) Ltd, 24 Sturdee Avenue, Rosebank, Johannesburg 2196, South Africa

Penguin Books Ltd, Registered Offices:
80 Strand, London WC2R 0RL, England

First published in the United States of America by The Penguin Press,
a member of Penguin Group (USA) Inc. 2008
Published in Penguin Books 2009

1   3   5   7   9   10   8   6   4   2

THE LIBRARY OF CONGRESS HAS CATALOGED THE HARDCOVER EDITION AS FOLLOWS:
Benfey, Christopher E. G., 1954–
A summer of hummingbirds : love, art, and scandal in the intersecting worlds of Emily Dickinson, Mark Twain, Harriet
Beecher Stowe, and Martin Johnson Heade / Christopher Benfey.
p. cm.
Includes bibliographical references and index.
ISBN 978-1-59420-160-8 (hc.)
ISBN 978-0-14-311508-3 (pbk.)
1. Dickinson, Emily, 1830–1886—Criticism and interpretation.   2. Twain, Mark, 1835–1910—Criticism and
interpretation.   3. Stowe, Harriet Beecher, 1811–1896—Criticism and interpretation.   4. Heade, Martin Johnson,
1819–1904—Criticism and interpretation.   5. Women and literature—United States—History—19th century.
6. Literature and society—United States—History—19th century.   7. Literature and history—United States—
History—19th century.   8. Florida—In art.   9. United States—History—1865–1898.   I. Title.
PS1541.Z5B46   2008
811'.4—dc22   2007036512

Printed in the United States of America
Designed by Claire Naylon Vaccaro

TO MICKEY

I have wasted my life with mineralogy, which has led to nothing. Had I devoted myself to birds, their life and plumage, I might have produced something myself worth doing. If I could only have seen a hummingbird fly, it would have been an epoch in my life.

—*John Ruskin*

Contents

PART THREE: TRANSITS OF VENUS

Dramatis Personae

HENRY WARD BEECHER (1813–1887): Amherst College graduate (1834) and preacher at the Plymouth Church in Brooklyn from 1847 until his death. Collector of gems and hummingbirds as well as paintings by Martin Johnson Heade. Known for his abolitionist views and his endorsement of evolution. Trial for adultery receives national attention.

LORD BYRON (1788–1824): Romantic poet, wildly popular in nineteenth-century New England, known for his subversive religious views and his seductions of women. In 1869, Harriet Beecher Stowe publicly accuses him of having had sexual relations with his half-sister, Augusta Leigh.

JOSEPH CORNELL (1903–1972): twentieth-century American artist, best known for his surrealist boxes. During the 1950s, develops a passion for the poetry of Emily Dickinson and constructs many boxes and collages inspired by her work.

AUSTIN DICKINSON (1829–1895): older brother of Emily Dickinson and art collector. Leading attorney in Amherst and treasurer of Amherst College, his alma mater (class of 1850). Has an adulterous affair with Mabel Loomis Todd.

EMILY DICKINSON (1830–1886): poet. In September 1882, sends a hummingbird poem to Mabel Loomis Todd in exchange for a painting of Indian pipes.

HENRY MORRISON FLAGLER (1830–1913): a founder of the Standard Oil Company, develops St. Augustine, Florida, as a destination for Yankee migrants, building railroads and the Ponce de Leon Hotel. Hires Martin Johnson Heade as painter-in-residence for the hotel.

MARTIN JOHNSON HEADE (1819–1904): painter of hummingbirds. Visits Amherst during the summer of 1882 in pursuit of his pupil Mabel Loomis Todd.

THOMAS WENTWORTH HIGGINSON (1823–1911): abolitionist, secret supporter of John Brown, and Emily Dickinson's literary mentor. Leads the first black regiment during the Civil War, fights along the St. Johns River, and occupies Jacksonville, Florida.

EBEN LOOMIS (1828–1912): statistician at the National Almanac Office, nature writer, and father of Mabel Loomis Todd. Martin Johnson Heade's best friend and agent after Heade settles in Washington, D.C., during the winter of 1881.

OTIS LORD (1812–1884): Amherst College graduate (1832), Whig politician, and justice of the supreme judicial court of Massachusetts. Falls in love with Emily Dickinson during the late 1870s and proposes marriage. Commencement speaker at Amherst College in 1862, opposite his intellectual rival, Henry Ward Beecher.

PEDRO II (1825–1891): last emperor of Brazil. Amateur naturalist and astronomer, supports Martin Johnson Heade's projected album of Brazilian hummingbirds. Travels to the United States in 1876 to meet Longfellow and view the northern sky.

HARRIET BEECHER STOWE (1811–1896): author of *Uncle Tom's Cabin*, settles in Mandarin, Florida, on the St. Johns River, after the Civil War, where Colonel Higginson had fought during the war and where Martin Johnson Heade visits her during the winter of 1883. Her daughter Georgiana, a morphine addict, marries the minister of the Episcopal church in Amherst. Her son Fred is wounded at Gettysburg and disappears in San Francisco.

DAVID TODD (1855–1939): Amherst College graduate (1875) and astronomer, discovers Phobos, the second moon of Mars. Todd's photographs of the Transit of Venus of 1882 excel all others. As a child, attends Beecher's Plymouth Church and admires its organ. Husband of Mabel Loomis Todd. Dies insane.

MABEL LOOMIS TODD (1856–1932): virtuoso writer, painter of flowers and birds, lecturer, and mistress to Austin Dickinson. Studies painting with Martin Johnson Heade. Edits Emily Dickinson's poetry with Thomas Wentworth Higginson.

MARK TWAIN (1835–1910): novelist, essayist, and travel writer. Travels through Nicaragua a few months after Heade. Admires Heade's paintings and buys one of his Florida landscapes to decorate his Hartford house. Friend of Henry Ward Beecher and neighbor of Harriet Beecher Stowe.

A Place in the Sky Where
a Cloud Has Been

I.

D URING THE SPRING of 1882, Mark Twain, Missouri river rat turned respectable Connecticut Yankee, traveled down the Mississippi River to refresh his memories of the lost world of his childhood. He had reached an impasse in the novel he was writing, about a white boy and a black man adrift on the river, both of them in search of freedom. Twain's riverboat journey down to New Orleans served as a stark reminder of the transformation of the country during the twenty years since he had left the South in 1861, after his mercifully brief service in a ragtag Confederate militia. "The river is so thoroughly changed that I can't bring it back to mind even when the changes have been pointed out to me," he wrote. "It is like a man pointing out to me a place in the sky where a cloud has been."[1]

The Civil War was the devastating storm that had swept the sky clean. Like so many Rip Van Winkles, Americans awoke to a new world and rubbed their eyes in disbelief. For Southerners, Twain noticed, "the war is what A.D. is elsewhere: they date from it. . . . It shows how intimately every individual was visited, in his own person, by that tremendous episode."[2] The

Martin Johnson Heade, Approaching Thunder Storm
(The Metropolitan Museum of Art)

transformation was evident in the North as well. The war had decimated a generation of young men on both sides, and touched their families and friends in ways that endured for generations.

This book is about a cluster of American artists and writers adrift during the seismic upheaval of the Civil War and its wrenching aftermath. It is about a pre-Civil War mind-set and a post-Civil War need. Social arrangements and practices that seemed natural before the war, from slaveholding to churchgoing, did not survive the carnage on the killing fields of Antietam and Gettysburg. Scarred sensibilities did not remain the same either, as people tried desperately to hold on to familiar attitudes and emotions that no longer fit new realities. As he began his second term in office, President Abraham Lincoln called on all Americans "to bind up the nation's wounds"; six weeks later, killed by an assassin's bullet, he joined the mounting list of casualties, and others took up the difficult task of healing.

The quest for psychic wholeness played out in kindred ways among the central characters of this book, all of whom were connected by ties of friendship and family. Three are among the best-known American writers: Mark Twain, the vagrant humorist; Emily Dickinson, the stay-at-home visionary; and Harriet Beecher Stowe, whose electrifying antislavery novel, *Uncle Tom's Cabin*, ignited the war, according to Lincoln. Martin Johnson Heade, itinerant painter of hummingbirds and salt marshes, is now regarded as one of the handful of significant American painters of the postwar era. (His best-known painting, *Approaching Thunder Storm*, has been thought by some to anticipate the impending national cataclysm.) Three other figures complete the circle: Stowe's brother, the charismatic preacher Henry Ward Beecher; Dickinson's literary mentor, the Civil War colonel Thomas Wentworth Higginson; and the painter and musician Mabel Loomis Todd, who studied under Heade, fell in love with Dickinson's brother, and brought Emily Dickinson's poetry to the world.

2 .

They seem at first glance a motley assemblage for a single stage. Who could have less in common than Mark Twain, adrift on the Mississippi, and Emily Dickinson, secluded in her father's house on Main Street in Amherst, Massachusetts? In the Homestead, as the imposing brick mansion was called, Dickinson wrote her enigmatic poems and cryptic letters, a verbal thicket against intruders. She never left the house except to tend the hyacinths and heliotrope in her garden, or to cut back the cascading honeysuckle, which, as her niece next door observed, "lured the hummingbirds all day."[3] Her hermit ways did not go unremarked. When asked why she shunned men and women, Emily Dickinson explained, "because they talk of hallowed things—aloud—and embarrass my dog."[4]

And yet, the geographical distance from Hartford—where Stowe and Twain were next-door neighbors—to Amherst, meandering up the bends of the Connecticut River that Heade loved to paint, is a short one. So, it would seem, is the temperamental distance among these remarkable creative minds, who survived the war and the loss of so many certainties, and changed forever the ways in which Americans think and feel.

These gifted men and women felt themselves distinctively different in taste and temperament from the pre—Civil War world in which they had come of age. In one sense, they had lost their bearings; the rigid old arrangements were gone with the wind. But with these losses came a counterbalancing opening of possibility. Their sense of liberation was religious, political, aesthetic, and erotic. They had grown up under the harsh regime of a dour Calvinist faith, embracing infant damnation, human depravity, and predestination. With Harriet Beecher Stowe and Henry Ward Beecher leading the way, they embraced a more dynamic order based on love and the human capacity for self-transformation. We can see in their paintings and poems, in their love of nature and music, a poignant effort to find a redemptive order amid traumatic circumstances. Adrift in a new world of often devastating change, they found meaning in the shifting light on a river at dawn, or the evanescent flash of a hummingbird's flight.

3 ·

This book had its origins in a confluence of hummingbirds. In July 1882, Martin Johnson Heade, most famous of all hummingbird painters, came to Amherst in pursuit of his pupil Mabel Todd, the dazzling young wife of the Amherst College astronomer.[5] Heade's timing could hardly have been worse; he arrived just in time to witness Mabel falling in love with another man: Emily Dickinson's married brother, Austin. A few weeks later, Mabel Todd was invited to play the piano at the Dickinson Homestead. After the recital, Emily Dickinson, in gratitude, sent Todd a mysterious poem about a hummingbird, in which she described the hummingbird's flight as "a route of evanescence."

The vivid exchange gives rise to a host of questions. Was it entirely by coincidence that Dickinson gave Mabel a poem about a hummingbird so soon after Heade's visit? Was Dickinson aware of Mabel's close relationship with Heade, and was the poem a way of commemorating it? It was in pursuit of answers to these riddles that I first began to trace the often dizzying relationships that connect the figures in this book.

I soon discovered that almost all the actors I had begun to assemble on my little stage—Mabel Todd and Martin Heade, Emily Dickinson and Thomas Wentworth Higginson, Henry Ward Beecher and Harriet Beecher Stowe—were fanatical about hummingbirds. They wrote poems and stories about hummingbirds; they painted pictures of hummingbirds; they tamed wild hummingbirds and collected stuffed hummingbirds; they set music to the humming of hummingbirds; they waited impatiently through the winter months for the hummingbirds' return.

My attempts to trace the origins of this informal cult of hummingbirds kept leading back to the Civil War. The national upheaval, claiming so many lives and forever unsettling so many others, brought a new set of feelings and convictions in its wake. But why did hummingbirds in particular elicit such a powerful attraction, rising at times to the level of an obsession? The short answer—the string on which the ten chapters of this book are strung—is that Americans during and after the Civil War gradually left behind a static view of existence, a trust in fixed arrangements and hierarchies. In science and in art, in religion and in love, they came to see a new dynamism and movement in their lives, a brave new world of instability and evanescence. This dynamism, in all aspects of life, found perfect expression in the hummingbird.

· 4 ·

Long before the coming of the Europeans, the Aztecs of Mexico worshipped the hummingbird, in the guise of their warrior-god and wizard-god, Huitzilopochtli.

Christopher Columbus was mesmerized by whirring hummingbirds, which he first took to be insects, on his arrival at San Salvador. Hummingbirds are strictly New World birds, with a handful of species in North America and the rest—more than three hundred species—concentrated in Central and South America.

As Europeans ventured into the American wilderness during the eighteenth century, they were astonished by the profusion of flora and fauna they encountered. The French writer Chateaubriand, exiled in Philadelphia after the French Revolution, marveled at the "New Eden" east of the Mississippi River, teeming with woodpeckers and hummingbirds:

> A host of animals placed by the Creator's hand in these retreats radiate gladness and life. Down avenues of trees, bears may be seen drunk with grapes, and reeling on the branches of the elm trees; caribou bathe in the lake, black squirrels frolic in the thick foliage; mocking birds and Virginia doves no larger than sparrows fly down to grass patches red with strawberries; green parrots with yellow heads, crimson-tinged woodpeckers and fire-bright cardinals spiral up to the tops of the cypresses; hummingbirds sparkle on the jasmine of the Floridas, and bird-catching serpents hiss as they swing, like lianas, from the forest domes.[6]

This was a period when, as the historian Henry Adams observed, America had "an ornithology more creditable than anything yet accomplished in art or literature."[7] Artists vied with one another to paint the luminous hummingbird, first as isolated species and then as part of the subtle weave of natural interaction. "The richest pallet of the most luxuriant painter could never invent any thing to be compared to the variegated tints with which this insect-bird is arrayed," wrote the French immigrant writer J. Hector St. John de Crèvecoeur in 1782.[8] When Audubon came to England during the late 1820s to find patrons for his *Birds of America*, his delicate rendition of the rubythroat competed for attention with such outlandish creatures as the turkey buzzard and the roseate spoonbill.

5.

As word of the miraculous features and astonishing variety of humming-birds reached Europe during the early decades of the nineteenth century, popular curiosity was piqued and primed to the utmost. But these athletic birds, capable of traveling hundreds of miles without respite while losing as much as two-thirds of their body weight in flight, did not travel well in captivity. John Gould, the English ornithologist who had helped Charles Darwin identify variations in Galápagos finches, was particularly eager to import a live hummingbird. The greatest of British hummingbird collectors and artists, Gould had amassed more than five thousand stuffed specimens, sent to him by hunters in Brazil and Peru. But the live bird he managed to have imported to England (he never went to America himself) died on the second day after it arrived at his house.[9]

Such disappointments didn't hinder Gould from staging dramatic reen-actments of hummingbirds in flight. With invisible wire and illuminated revolving cases, he put on a dazzling display for the seventy-five thousand visitors who crammed into London's Zoological Gardens in 1851. "They hang amidst *fuchsia* flowers, or float over beds of *bromelia*," wrote Charles Dickens. Queen Victoria herself was astonished at "their variety and the extraordinary brilliancy of their colours."[10]

Gould's mummified specimens, dusted with arsenic for preservation and displayed in glass cases, seemed more like jewels than living things. Never having witnessed hummingbirds in the wild, he compared them to gem-stones in the many names he bestowed on the birds: sapphire and emerald, topaz and amethyst. With the publication of Darwin's *The Origin of Species* in 1859, hummingbirds became almost as central to the debate on evolution as apes and monkeys.[11] Opponents of natural selection (including Gould) ridiculed the idea that these gorgeous birds in all their variety were the result of chance rather than God's delight in creating things of beauty.

For Americans around the time of the Civil War, hummingbirds were closely associated with an awakened interest in the tropics. Steamship and railroad travel brought the exotic regions of Mexico and Brazil closer to a restless and curious public. After the Romantic travels of Alexander von Humboldt and others, it was widely believed that the biblical Eden lay somewhere in the rainforests of Brazil and Peru. Darwin provided a more scientific narrative of the origins of life, and introduced seductive metaphors of sex and the battle for survival that appealed to American artists and intellectuals. Travelers in the tropics such as Mark Twain and Martin Heade (who sought to supplant Gould as the supreme painter of hummingbirds) found an uneasy world of peril and procreation. The tropics, with their great sugar plantations and thriving trade in human labor, were also linked in the American mind with slavery. For Harriet Beecher Stowe and others, hummingbirds were images of freedom in a world of captivity.

6.

The three sections of this book represent the three main stages of my story. The first, "An Oblique War," evokes the traumatic experience, direct and indirect, of the Civil War. The narrative registers a new sense of precariousness in the lives of artists and writers, and the ways in which art served as temporary anchorage amid uncertainty. This was a period in which art and activism were closely allied. Many of Emily Dickinson's closest literary contacts had ties to the abolitionist hotbed of Newburyport, Massachusetts. Both Higginson and Heade worked in Newburyport, the hometown of the leading abolitionist William Lloyd Garrison. Exquisite objects—flowers and hummingbirds and precious gems—were part of a shared emotional language with political implications. Like members of a secret society, the Beechers and Dickinsons passed favorite poems and objects from pocket to pocket like samizdat. Superior sensibility and human feeling were thought to guarantee right conduct during a time of national crisis.

The second section, "At the Hotel Byron," carries this search for new spiritual and aesthetic bearings from the 1860s up to the 1870s. Particular places of happiness or doom took on a luminous importance for these writers and artists. They were transfixed by the Castle of Chillon on Lake Geneva, where a fighter for Swiss independence had been imprisoned in a dungeon, and memorialized in a poignant poem by Lord Byron. Byron, the great poet of romantic scandal and heroic solitude, was a controversial focal point for American artists and poets. Under Byron's dangerous spell, old assumptions about the fixed world of marriage yielded to a new sense of the fluidity of human attraction. Artists were also drawn to earthly paradises in the New World. Martin Johnson Heade spent part of the Civil War years painting hummingbirds in Brazil, where his sponsor was another Newburyport abolitionist, Reverend James Fletcher. For many writers and artists, the quest took the form of incessant travel. For Heade and Mark Twain, a parallel journey through tropical Nicaragua was decisive in shaping a new vision.

The third section delves deeply into the summer of 1882, a summer of love, when so many paths crossed in and around Amherst. Emily Dickinson found the love and recognition she had sought for two decades. Mabel Todd exploded the placid social world of Amherst. Martin Heade came to Amherst in search of love. And the Transit of Venus, when the planet of love passed like a beauty spot across the sun's face, seemed to preside over the summer's passions.

The story then follows Heade and Stowe into what Henry James called the "hotel world" of Florida. In the sparsely settled state of flowers and the Fountain of Youth, New Englanders found an earthly paradise closer to home. It was during the Gilded Age that Florida, long dismissed as a pestiferous land of alligators and mosquitoes, became the favored destination for New Englanders, displacing Newport and Saratoga. Harriet Beecher Stowe had settled near St. Augustine right after the Civil War, establishing an orange plantation on the St. Johns River for her shell-shocked son, Fred. Martin Johnson Heade headed for St. Augustine in 1883, where he became the favored painter of Henry Flagler, the great developer and railroad magnate who turned Florida into a tourist destination.

The book closes with an unexpected epilogue: the twentieth-century artist and collagist Joseph Cornell's rediscovery of Emily Dickinson as poet of hummingbirds and hotels, solitude and romantic love.

The three sections of the book follow a progression from conflict to confinement to release. Each section has a dominant central image: the first is war; the second is prison; and the third is flight, or escape. Each section, in turn, has its dominant picture of divinity. For the years leading up to the Civil War, God is a vengeful God, the punitive deity of "The Battle Hymn of the Republic," who tramples on the grapes of wrath. In the postwar section, God becomes a God of love, with all the concomitant entanglements of desire. In the third phase, circa 1882, God is a Darwinian deity of anarchic energy, permeating the vegetable, mineral, and animal realms.

Dickinson's word *evanescence* aptly describes the new sense of evolution as metaphor and reality for this generation of writers and thinkers, as they learned to leave behind the fixed hierarchies of both science and society and embraced a new world of fluidity and flux. They found the words and images for this new world. It was a route of evanescence, a place in the sky where a cloud has been. In this final phase, which remains our own, the best picture of God is the hummingbird.

Part One

An
Oblique
War

❧❧

Chapter One

A TEA ROSE

I shall have no winter this year—on account of the soldiers—Since I cannot weave Blankets, or Boots—I thought it best to omit the season . . . I've got a Geranium like a Sultana—and when the Humming birds come down—Geranium and I shut our eyes—and go far away.

✎ EMILY DICKINSON, *August 1861*[1]

I .

*I*T WAS THE silence that most unnerved Colonel Thomas Wentworth Higginson as the fleet of three vessels under his command steamed up the St. Johns River on the sun-drenched morning of March 10, 1863, toward the Rebel stronghold of Jacksonville. Higginson led an occupying force of nine hundred African-American soldiers, many of whom were former slaves from this part of Florida. Liberated by Lincoln's Emancipation Proclamation of January first of that year, they took particular pleasure—were indeed "wild with delight," according to their commander—in returning to their former homes as free men.[2] Colonel Higginson had hoped to capture the city in a raid at dawn, surprising the inhabitants in their beds. But the shifting sands of the glassy river were deceptive, and Higginson began to feel beneath the keel, as he noted in his memoir, "that ominous, sliding, grating, treacherous arrest of motion which makes the heart shudder, as the vessel does."[3]

The St. Johns flows north, like the Nile, and so slowly, and with such wide expanses, that the Indians had believed it was a series of interconnected lakes. The sunlit shores of the river were wooded right up to the water's edge, Higginson noted, "with sometimes an emerald meadow, opening a vista to some picturesque house." The landscape was unlike any that Higginson had seen in the South, reminding him instead of the tidal rivers of coastal Maine, where he had loved to swim as a boy.

The ships passed an occasional ruin, a burned sawmill from an earlier invasion, "but nothing else spoke of war, except, perhaps, the silence." Even at eight o'clock, as they rounded the point below the city, its streets were silent, "though none knew what perils might be concealed behind those quiet buildings." The boats approached the wharves, in sight of brick warehouses, charming white cottages, and overshadowing trees, "and the pretty town was our own without a shot."[4]

The occupation of Jacksonville by Higginson's troops, and the subsequent burning of the town, does not loom large in the history of the Civil War. Even in the history of the Civil War in Florida it figures as a minor episode at best, rendered more piquant by the black soldiers involved. It was the third occupation of the city by Union troops, and another would soon follow. It is to be presumed that the inhabitants—some three thousand at the start of the war reduced to a mere five hundred when Higginson and his men entered the city—had had some practice in leaving their homes in a hurry. Colonel Higginson's orders from his superior officer were vague as to both scope and tactics: "to occupy as much of the State of Florida as possible with the forces under your command; and to neglect no means consistent with the usages of civilized warfare to weaken, harass, and annoy those who are in rebellion against the Government of the United States."[5]

An officer of harsher temperament might have seen in this order an invitation to subdue and humiliate what remained of the local populace. But Colonel Higginson's dedication to what he called "the usages of civilized warfare" was absolute. He engaged in no major battles during his expedition to capture Jacksonville, and he seems neither to have inflicted great damage nor to have suffered any. Higginson's various written accounts of the episode are notable for the literary rather than the military skill of the dashing commander, as well as for a certain ghostly quality pervading the proceedings.

2 .

Colonel Higginson was a few months shy of forty when he led his expedition up the St. Johns River. Descended from several strands of distinguished New England families, including the Higginsons of Salem, he had already made his mark as a literary man and an activist in political causes. He combined, in a peculiar way, the instincts of the shade-seeking hermit and the heroic man of action. Like his idol, Emerson, he had begun his life after Harvard as a Unitarian minister, receiving a call to preach at the seaport and factory town of Newburyport on the North Shore of Boston. The home of William Lloyd Garrison and, in neighboring Amesbury, the Quaker poet John Greenleaf Whittier, Newburyport was a hotbed of abolitionist sentiment, and Reverend Higginson was eager to preach on the evils of slavery. When he did so, however, he quickly discovered that his congregation, led by conservative factory owners and shipping merchants with commercial ties to the South, was not of one mind on the matter. When the young minister refused to moderate his message, he was asked to leave the pulpit, which he did, seemingly with no regrets, after serving for two and a half years. At Whittier's urging, he briefly tried a career in politics, but failed in his attempt to be elected to Congress.

Upon assuming his position in Newburyport, Higginson was drawn to other radical causes. He embraced what he called "the Sisterhood of Reforms," a cluster of "social and physiological theories of which one was expected to accept all, if any." Higginson committed himself to temperance agitation, social reform, and the women's rights movement—"this last-named," he remarked, "seems to me the most important."[6] After leaving the ministry, Higginson set up a class in reading and study for factory girls, enlisting the help of promising young women in the neighborhood, including the gifted Harriet Prescott Spofford. Higginson shepherded Spofford's precocious career, finding space in *The Atlantic* for her vivid poems about birds and flowers and her gothic tales of women in danger. Convinced that Spofford was a worthy successor to Harriet Beecher Stowe, Higginson was disappointed when, at a dinner convened by *The Atlantic Monthly*, they found nothing to say to each other.

Higginson embraced a combination of political causes and aesthetic concerns. As Garrison's lieutenant, he joined other Boston radicals in seeking to free from police custody a fugitive slave named Anthony Burns; he was clubbed by the police in the riot that ensued. But if Higginson was willing to embrace civil disobedience in a just cause, his heroes were sticklers for decorum. He praised John Brown of all people for his orderly leadership: "He was so strict as to the demeanor of his men that his band was always kept small."[7] In 1858, Higginson personally raised money for Brown's vague plan of rounding up fugitive slaves in Virginia and then holing up as guerrilla fighters in the fastnesses of the Allegheny Mountains. This fantasy, redolent of Sir Walter Scott's highland scrimmages, had a certain charm for Higginson. When the postponement of the plan had, as Higginson commented, "somewhat disturbed the delicate balance of the zealot's mind," Brown shifted his sights to the federal arms depot at Harper's Ferry.[8]

It was Higginson who behaved decorously, and bravely, in the wake of the bloody events that transpired the following year. He served as a witness for the defense in Brown's trial when other supporters fled the scene, and he personally visited and cared for Brown's wife and family. With naïve confidence, Higginson continued to believe in John Brown's essential humanism, viewing Brown's moments of descent into murderous butchery—first in Kansas and then at Harper's Ferry—as mere "disturbances" of his heroic "balance." Higginson displayed on this occasion, as on many others, his blithe capacity for keeping valiant ends separate in his mind from violent means. Two years after the raid on Harper's Ferry, Higginson enlisted in the army. He described his mood of exaltation: "To call it a sense of novelty was nothing; it was as if one had learned to swim in air, and were striking out for some new planet."[9]

3.

Even as he became increasingly enmeshed in the national struggle for abolition, Higginson wrote essays in a completely different vein. He had always loved the plants and animals of his native New England; his naturalist writings, reminiscent of Thoreau, find moral meaning in the hidden life of the woods. Higginson's *Outdoor Essays* were written during the months that preceded the outbreak of the Civil War. In "The Life of Birds," first published in *The Atlantic* in September 1862, he struck a surprisingly melancholy note, imagining birds as exiles from another, better world:

> When one thinks of a bird, one fancies a soft, swift, aimless, joyous thing, full of nervous energy and arrowy motions,—a song with wings. So remote from ours their mode of existence, they seem accidental exiles from an unknown globe, banished where none can understand their language; and men only stare at their darting, inexplicable ways, as at the gyrations of the circus . . . this bird that hovers and alights beside me, peers up at me, takes its food, then looks again, attitudinizing, jerking, flirting its tail, with a thousand inquisitive and fantastic motions,— although I have power to grasp it in my hand and crush its life out, yet I cannot gain its secret thus, and the center of its consciousness is really farther from mine than the remotest planetary orbit.

Higginson quoted Darwin on "how profoundly ignorant we are of the condition of existence of every animal."

Higginson opened "The Life of Birds" with an extended account of the hummingbird. He drew a veiled self-portrait in his poignant account of this "mysterious, almost voiceless" bird, "smallest of feathery things, and loneliest, whirring among birds, insect-like, and among insects, bird-like, his path untraceable, his home unseen." The hummingbird, in Higginson's view, was

> an image of airy motion, yet it sometimes seems as if there were nothing joyous in him. He seems like some exiled pygmy prince, banished, but still regal, and doomed to wings. Did gems turn to flowers, flowers to feathers, in that long-past dynasty of the Humming-Birds? It is strange to come upon his tiny nest, in some gray and tangled swamp, with this brilliant atom perched disconsolately near it, upon some mossy twig.[10]

For Higginson, the hummingbird's only consolation was family life. Wishfully and inaccurately, he imagined the male hummingbird as a model father, sharing domestic tasks with his mate: "Among all the created things, the birds come nearest to man in their domesticity. Their unions are usually in pairs, and for life; and with them . . . the male labors for their young." As for other conjugal pleasures, Higginson quoted his protégée Harriet Spofford: "When a Humming-Bird, a winged drop of gorgeous sheen and gloss, a living gem, poising on his wings, thrust his dark, slender, honey-seeking bill into the white blossoms of a little bush beside my window, I should have thought it no such bad thing to be a bird."

In a pendant essay called "The Procession of the Flowers," Higginson followed the seasons of New England from the first flowering arbutus among the lingering snows of April to the late-blooming fall blossoms heralding the coming of winter. Again, the melancholy mood was unmistakable, and again Higginson opened the essay with a hummingbird, as a stand-in for himself:

> In Cuba there is a blossoming shrub whose multitudinous crimson flowers are so seductive to the humming-birds that they hover all day

around it, buried in the blossoms until petal and wing seem one. At first upright, the gorgeous bells droop downward, and fall unwithered to the ground, and are thence called by the Creoles "Cupid's Tears." Fredrika Bremer relates that daily she brought home handfuls of these blossoms to her chamber, and nightly they all disappeared. One morning she looked toward the wall of the apartment, and there, in a long crimson line, the delicate flowers went ascending one by one to the ceiling, and passed from sight. She found that each was borne laboriously onward by a little colorless ant much smaller than itself: the bearer was invisible, but the lovely burdens festooned the wall with beauty.

For Bremer, an ardent abolitionist from Sweden, Cuba was a jarring clash of slavery and seductive natural beauty. Higginson found in her "march of flowers" an image of what he called "the ceaseless motion" of the natural world, in which "the apparent stillness, like the sleeping of a child's top, is in truth the very ecstasy of perfected motion."[11]

Toward the end of the essay on flowers, Higginson quoted Harriet Spofford to the effect that "some souls are like the Water-Lilies, fixed, yet floating." The phrase captures Higginson's own temperament, which combined firmly held political convictions with a romantic distance on the harsher realities of life.

4 ·

Colonel Higginson was a stickler for rules and regulations, for proper comportment before all else. Fastidious in his own dress and manners, he demanded the same from his troops, and was quick to discipline any shortcomings. There were reasons, beyond military necessity, for such an exacting policy. The First South Carolina Regiment was a military force, but it was also a demonstration: an unfolding proof in the face of skepticism and outright hostility that black soldiers could perform up to the same standards of military efficiency and decorum as whites. Higginson knew that to satisfy skeptical observers his troops would have to exceed those standards. Photographs intended for the Northern press of the regiment drilling were part of the campaign, as were Higginson's own published letters, journals, and reports. President Lincoln's response to the news of the capture of Jacksonville, on April 1, 1863, stresses the importance of black troops in such a place at such a time: "I am glad to see the account of your colored force at Jacksonville," Lincoln told Higginson. "I see the enemy are driving at them fiercely, as is to be expected. It is important to the enemy that such a force shall not take shape and grow and thrive in the South, and in precisely the same proportion it is important to us that it shall."[12]

The fierceness to which Lincoln alludes is otherwise missing from the historical record of the occupation of Jacksonville. Emptiness, instead, is the dominant theme. Colonel Higginson took as his headquarters the handsome brick house of a Confederate colonel named Sunderland, who had left without a trace. "There was a neat office with ample bookcases and no books, a billiard-table with no balls, gas-fixtures without gas, and a bathing-room without water." Suspecting that his own military force was too small to hold the town, Higginson resorted to subterfuge: "Judicious use was made, here and there, of empty tents." To barricade the approaches to the main streets, Higginson had many trees cut down—a blow to his sensibilities. "It went to my heart to sacrifice, for this purpose, several of my beautiful lindens," he wrote, "but it was no time for aesthetics."[13]

And yet, aesthetic considerations pervade Higginson's account, which draws heavily on the romantic renderings of Sir Walter Scott. For Higginson, war—at least the St. Johns campaign—was a matter of bloodless skirmishes and dashing bravado, interspersed with jokes and high jinks. In the midst of the bloodiest war in American history, Higginson managed to create and occupy an alternative world of his own imagination. And such were the surreal touches of the landscape along the St. Johns River—with its alligators, orange groves, and gothic moss hanging like beards from rotting branches—that nature seemed to align itself with his vision.

Once Jacksonville was secured, Higginson dispatched raiding parties up the river and behind the town in search of enemy hideouts. One day, intelligence arrived of a Rebel camp four miles distant with twenty-two tents. Higginson set out through the pinewoods with two hundred picked men. "We went three or four miles out, sometimes halting to send forward a scout, while I made all the men lie down in the long, thin grass and beside the fallen trees, till one could not imagine that there was a person there. I remember how picturesque the effect was, when, at the signal, all rose again . . . and the green wood appeared suddenly populous with armed life." Higginson divided his troops "to flank the unsuspecting enemy," with his main force stealing through the dense woods. At his order, all "swooped down at last in triumph upon a solitary farmhouse,—where the family-washing had been hung out to dry."[14] This innocuous domestic scene was the supposed Rebel camp, a phantom clash quickly dubbed the Battle of the Clothes-Lines.

A later encounter along the railroad, in which Higginson's troops fired guns from a handcar toward what seemed to be cannonballs launched from a locomotive, seems only slightly more momentous. Higginson never saw the locomotive, if indeed there was one, and the exchange of fire seems barely more substantial than tilting with clotheslines.

AND THEN, ABRUPTLY, came orders on March 28 to evacuate the town so easily taken. No reason for evacuation was given. Some white troops had arrived as reinforcements, rendering the orders to retreat even more puzzling. It was these white soldiers, according to Higginson, who were responsible for an outrage perpetrated on the final morning of the occupation. Fires were set in the sector of town comprised of wooden structures, and not, Higginson insisted, in the brick part held by the black troops. Some twenty-five buildings were burned to the ground. "The sight and roar of the flames, and the rolling clouds of smoke, brought home to the impressible minds of the black soldiers all their favorite imagery of the Judgment-Day."[15]

But Colonel Higginson was possessed by a different sentiment altogether.

"The only time since I entered the service when I have felt within the reach of tears," he wrote in his *War Journal*, was after his men were all onboard and prepared to depart Jacksonville. Higginson felt himself irresistibly drawn to the deserted streets.

> I walked back among the burning buildings (set on fire by the white soldiers, not by mine) & picked a tea rose bud from the garden of my Headquarters. To think that this was the end of our brilliant enterprise & the destruction of my beautiful city was a sadder thing than wounds or death . . . and [with] the apparent aimlessness of the evacuation, it was doubly hard. But this did not last long—"tomorrow to fresh fields & pastures new."[16]

Plucking the tea rose—a cultivated Chinese rose thought to smell like tea—was a poignant gesture, perfectly in keeping with Higginson's temperament. The twentieth-century Southern novelist James Branch Cabell, who blamed Higginson for burning the city, came down hard on this sentimental moment. But Higginson, for better or worse, was no Sherman. Floating back down the St. Johns River, with his tea rose in his lapel and the line from Milton's "Lycidas" reverberating in his head, he was lucky to be spared the harsher phases of the war yet to come, where none of his romantic dreams, no matter how deeply held, could have possibly survived.

A few weeks later, on June 10, 1863, Higginson was back at his regimental base on Hilton Head, off the coast of South Carolina. He wrote to his wife, Mary Channing Higginson, that he was still baffled by the order to abandon Jacksonville: "As for Florida, nothing seems to come to a head—still a general impression that it is to be re-occupied, though I doubt it, at present. Now that it is found colored troops can operate in this region [i.e., South Carolina] just as well, I think it quite as likely that we may stay here, & perhaps make Expeditions hereabouts." In the meantime, he reported, a ship had arrived from the North with Higginson's mail. He listed his correspondents for his wife: "Emeline Everett, Mary Curson, Barbara [Channing], Ade' May, Emily Dickinson & Charlotte [Hawes]"—"as usual," he added, "all female, so much the better, they write so much more entertainingly."[17]

5 .

Women were drawn to Higginson for a number of reasons; he was a dashing and influential man who took a particular interest in women's education. "Ought Women to Learn the Alphabet?" was the ironic title of one of his polemical essays. But it was his friendly column of advice, "Letter to a Young Contributor," published in *The Atlantic Monthly* in April 1862, that had first inspired Emily Dickinson to write to Higginson. She can hardly have been moved by his distaste for "slovenly" manuscripts and his pedestrian injunction to "use good pens, black ink, nice white paper and plenty of it"—precisely the kind of decorous behavior he urged on his troops.[18]

What caught Dickinson's attention was Higginson's insistence that editors were always looking for a fresh voice. He denied that there was "the slightest foundation for the supposed editorial prejudice against new or obscure contributors. On the contrary, every editor is always hungering and thirsting after novelties. To take the lead in bringing forward a new genius is as fascinating a privilege as that of the physician who boasted to Sir Henry Halford of having been the first man to discover the Asiatic cholera and to communicate it to the public."[19]

A fresh voice was what Emily Dickinson had assiduously cultivated during the first three decades of her life. Audacity marked her career from the beginning—if *career* is the right word for her improbable persistence in the face of patronizing advice and general incomprehension. She was born in 1830, the middle child of three. Her privileged childhood as a lawyer's daughter in Amherst, Massachusetts, gave her the time and literary education, as well as the confidence, to try her hand at writing verse. Her father, she noted affectionately, was "too busy with his Briefs—to notice what we do—He buys me many Books—but begs me not to read them—because he fears they

*Daguerreotype of Emily
Dickinson at age seventeen
(Amherst College, Archives and
Special Collections)*

joggle the Mind." After a solid course of study at the private Amherst Academy, Dickinson spent a year at the Mount Holyoke Female Seminary a few miles away in South Hadley. Though she found the religious rigor of the formidable founder Mary Lyon's regimen somewhat oppressive, she enjoyed her fellow students, who were not as "rough & uncultivated" as she snobbishly expected.[20]

In Dickinson's letters home we can already see her imaginative way of making national events her own. "Won't you please to tell me when you answer my letter who the candidate for President is?" she wrote her brother, Austin, in the fall of 1847, when she was sixteen.

> I have been trying to find out ever since I came here & have not yet succeeded. I don't know anything more about affairs in the world, than if I was in a trance. . . . Has the Mexican war terminated yet & how? Are we beat? Do you know of any nation about to besiege South Hadley? If so, do inform me of it, for I would be glad of a chance to escape, if we are to be stormed. I suppose Miss Lyon would furnish us all with daggers & order us to fight for our lives, in case such perils should befall us.[21]

The "mind-joggling" intellectual debates of her time, such as religious revivalism versus the inroads of modern science, elicited a similarly wry and idiosyncratic response from her, as in this early verse epigram:

"Faith" is a fine invention
When Gentlemen can see—
But Microscopes are prudent
In an Emergency.[22]

During her twenties, as she settled into her life in her family's capacious and conspicuous brick house on Main Street (hardly the frontier outpost suggested by its nickname, "The Homestead"), Dickinson was part of a lively circle of friends with literary tastes that included the vivacious Susan Gilbert. When Susan married Austin Dickinson in 1856, they moved next door into the Italianate villa known as the Evergreens, and the circle became even tighter. Dickinson wove snatches of verse and even complete poems into her lyrical correspondence with Susan and other correspondents.

Emily Dickinson turned thirty in 1860. She had never formally submitted poems for publication, though Susan had sent some of Dickinson's poems to friends like Samuel Bowles, the handsome and worldly editor of the nearby *Springfield Daily Republican*. On March 1, 1862, the following poem by Dickinson appeared in the newspaper:

Safe in their alabaster chambers,
Untouched by morning,
And untouched by noon,
Sleep the meek members of the Resurrection,
Rafter of satin, and roof of stone.

Light laughs the breeze
In her castle above them,
Babbles the bee in a stolid ear,
Pipe the sweet birds in ignorant cadence:
Ah! What sagacity perished here![23]

Susan had initially criticized the second stanza of this now famous poem, and Dickinson sent her an alternative, substituting planetary and political cycles for the birds and bees. Susan liked this ending even less, and advised Dickinson to cut her losses and treat the first stanza as a complete poem.

Emboldened by the publication of the poem, and frustrated with Susan's tepid response, Dickinson was ready to aim for a wider and more sophisticated audience. So it was that on April 15, 1862, six weeks after the appearance of "Safe in their alabaster chambers," she enclosed it (with the ending Susan liked least) and three others in a letter to Higginson. It was surely with the hope that Higginson might recognize in her efforts a new genius of the kind he had described in his "Letter to a Young Contributor" that Dickinson sent the poems to him, along with the following cover letter:

> Mr Higginson,
> Are you too deeply occupied to say if my Verse is alive?
> The Mind is so near itself—it cannot see, distinctly—and I have none to ask—
> Should you think it breathed—and had you the leisure to tell me, I should feel quick gratitude—
> If I make the mistake—that you dared to tell me—would give me sincerer honor—toward you—
> I enclose my name—asking you, if you please—Sir—to tell me what is true?
> That you will not betray me—it is needless to ask—since Honor is its own pawn—[24]

She enclosed, in place of a signature, a card in a separate envelope on which she had written her name.

It was at this perilous juncture that Emily Dickinson's courage as a poet was confirmed, for Higginson was not encouraging. Her elaborate introduction seems not to have elicited quite the response she had hoped for. Since Higginson's letters have not survived, we can only surmise the tenor and tone of his strictures from Dickinson's wounded appeals. She thanked him, twice, for his "surgery—it was not so painful as I supposed"—but didn't change a thing in her poems. She magisterially deflected the words that must have hurt:

> You think my gait "spasmodic"—I am in danger—Sir—
> You think me "uncontrolled"—I have no Tribunal.

And to his most sweeping piece of advice, she was even more imperious: "I smile when you suggest that I delay 'to publish'—that being foreign to my thought, as Firmament to Fin."[25]

It is difficult to separate the defiance from the defensiveness in Dickinson's early letters to Higginson. The wonder is that with so little encouragement, Dickinson had the inner strength and ambition to keep at her task, and the confidence to know that her eccentricities of language—"spasmodic," "wayward," "uncontrolled"—were in fact her strengths. Rather than feeling discouraged, she seems to have taken provocation from her correspondence with Higginson. The following year, 1863, was her most productive; she wrote or arrived at finished versions of nearly three hundred poems—many of them among her best—during that year alone.

Higginson was intrigued by his mysterious female correspondent, though his curiosity centered on her life rather than on her poetry. She refused to send him the photograph he asked for, and she parried his prying questions with a smoke screen of riddles:

> You ask of my Companions Hills—Sir—and the Sundown—and a
> Dog—large as myself, that my Father bought me—They are better than
> Beings—because they know—but do not tell—and the noise in the
> Pool, at Noon—excels my Piano.

Her reckless poems evidently reminded Higginson of two other writers. "You speak of Mr. Whitman—I never read his Book—but was told that he was disgraceful," she wrote. As for Higginson's protégée Harriet Prescott Spofford, and her gothic tale of a woman attacked by a leopard in the forest, who sings hymns to postpone the inevitable, Dickinson wrote with guarded enthusiasm: "I read Miss Prescott's 'Circumstance,' but it followed me, in the Dark—so I avoided her."

After a flurry of letters, in which Dickinson continued to send poems to Higginson in exchange for his patronizing advice, the correspondence languished for a few months, only to be reignited by the news, gleaned from the *Springfield Republican*, that Higginson was in South Carolina with his Negro regiment. "I should have liked to see you, before you became improbable," Dickinson wrote in February 1863. "War feels to me an oblique place."[26]

BY THIS TIME, Dickinson had all but memorized Higginson's *Outdoor Essays*, and she had written several poems inspired by his descriptions of spring flowers and hummingbirds.

> *Within my Garden, rides a Bird*
> *Upon a single Wheel—*
> *Whose spokes a dizzy Music make*
> *As 'twere a traveling Mill—*
>
> *He never stops, but slackens*
> *Above the Ripest Rose—*
> *Partakes without alighting*
> *And praises as he goes*[27]

That February of 1863, she told Higginson that she hoped his "Procession of the Flowers" essay was not "a premonition"—a premonition, that is, of a flower-decked funeral procession. She faced with uneasy flippancy Higginson's proximity to death: "Should you, before this reaches you, experience immortality, who will inform me of the Exchange?"[28]

Higginson received another letter from Dickinson, written about the same time, which included a remarkable poem:

The possibility to pass
Without a Moment's Bell—
Into Conjecture's presence—
Is like a face of steel

That suddenly looks into ours
With a Metallic Grin—
The Cordiality of Death
Who Drills his welcome—in—[29]

Death's metallic "cordiality" is a nightmare version of the courtly suitor, conspicuous for his "civility," in her great poem "Because I could not stop for Death." The immediacy of such lines shows how urgently Dickinson, in remote Amherst, felt the progress of the war.

6.

During the perilous months of 1863, as his regiment moved into closer proximity with the enemy, Higginson had a growing sense of his own personal danger, and he discerned death's metallic grin everywhere. Death's nearness is palpable in the strangest and most powerful thing that he ever wrote about the war, an essay titled "A Night in the Water," later collected in his *Army Life in a Black Regiment*. The essay began as a description of a late-night swim and turned into something else entirely. In its combination of narrative verve and disembodied hallucination, it perfectly captures Higginson's ambiguous relation—by turns intimate and estranged—with the war around him.

After his return to his base in South Carolina, Higginson received official orders to acquire all possible information regarding the Rebel outposts on the mainland, across the tidal river from the island of Hilton Head where his troops were stationed. "To those doing outpost-duty on an island, however large, the mainland has all the fascination of forbidden fruit," he wrote. "Every grove in that blue distance appears enchanted ground."[30] Since even the quietest boat on the darkest night was vulnerable to enemy scouts, Higginson decided to try what he called "a personal reconnaissance," by swimming toward the enemy positions. An experienced swimmer from his youth along the New England shore, Higginson wrote that "water was my ground, where I, too, had been at home from boyhood."

It was a "warm, breathless Southern night" when Higginson informed his pickets that he was going for a swim.

> I do not remember ever to have experienced a greater sense of exhilaration than when I slipped noiselessly into the placid water, and struck out into the smooth, eddying current for the opposite shore. The night was so still and lovely, my black statues looked so dream-like at their posts behind the low earthwork, the opposite arm of the causeway stretched so invitingly from the Rebel main . . . that I seemed floating in some concave globe, some magic crystal, of which I was the enchanted center. With each little ripple of my steady progress all things hovered and changed; the stars danced and nodded above; where the stars ended the great Southern fireflies began; and closer than the fireflies, there clung round me a halo of phosphorescent sparkles from the soft salt water.

This is the ecstatic version of Higginson's night in the water, a dissolution of all things solid into pure light and motion. But as he nears the opposite shore, he becomes hyperaware of his "unfortunate head" exposed above the water. As if in a story by Poe, the head takes on a hallucinatory shape: "The outside of this member gradually assumed to its inside a gigantic magnitude," accompanied by "a physical feeling of turgescence and congestion" and "animal bigness." The whole image is astounding: the outsize head swelled to surreal dimensions, with stars and fireflies yielding to one another, as in an Escher drawing. The fantasy is palpably sexual, a man's feeling of heightened excitement twinned with anxious vulnerability.

Suddenly a dog barks, breaking the spell.

Higginson makes a few hurried observations concerning the shoreline, confirming some details he has learned from fugitive slaves. Then he allows himself to sink below the surface and swims downstream as far as he can underwater. His aim is to distance himself from dog and master, and learn a bit more about the enemy position. But as he swims downstream, he finds it difficult to keep his bearings: "everything appeared to shift and waver, in the uncertain light." Suddenly, when he least expects it, he feels "a sensation as of fine ribbons drawn softly across my person, and I found myself among some rushes. But what business had rushes there, or I among them?" He realizes that he has lost his way, each marshy islet "strangely out of place." And then, to crown the horror, he determines from the movement of the shadowy shapes onshore that he is in a powerful current, "and that this current set *the wrong way*." "I can distinctly remember that for about one half-minute the whole vast universe appeared to swim in the same watery uncertainty in which I floated. I began to doubt everything, to distrust the stars, the line of low bushes for which I was wearily striving, the very land on which they grew, if such visionary things could be rooted anywhere."

Amid this nightmare sensation, the man in the water looks for his customary place in the universe and finds nothing.

It was as if a fissure opened somewhere, and I saw my way into a madhouse; then it closed, and everything went on as before. . . . I had no well-defined anxiety, felt no fear, was moved to no prayer, did not give a thought to home or friends; only it swept over me, as with a sudden tempest, that, if I meant to get back to my own camp, I must keep my wits about me. I must not dwell on any other alternative, any more than a boy who climbs a precipice must look down. Imagination had no business here. That way madness lay.

And then, with almost unbearable delay, a light gleams in the distance, a ruined plantation building looms, and Higginson knows where he is. The tide had turned as he swam; he had come much farther downstream than he had calculated; here was his own haven, "where the great gnarled branches of the live-oaks hung far over the muddy bank." Back onshore after his ordeal, with dawn still far off, Higginson learns that his nocturnal swim, which had seemed to last an eternity, had barely consumed a single hour.

Higginson's nightmare night in the water is his deepest sounding of the experience of the Civil War. These paragraphs capture the drift and disorientation of his months in active service, where all certainties were lost. Downstream and upstream, friend and foe, were indistinguishable. To the man in the water who had lost his moorings, all was flux and fluidity. What happened next only confirmed the trauma.

7.

A month after reading Emily Dickinson's letters, Colonel Higginson led another flotilla of three boats up a tidal river, the South Edisto in South Carolina, and on July 10 came under enemy fire. One of the boats, the *Milton,* had to be abandoned after it caught on posts erected to obstruct passage. It was during an ensuing attack on the remaining two vessels that Colonel Higginson experienced something like and unlike a wound, a fitting end to his ghostly war:

> As I stood on the deck, while we were in action with a shore battery, I felt a sudden blow in the side, doubling me up as if a Sullivan or a Fitzsimmons had struck me. My clothes were not torn, but very soon a large purple spot, called "ecchymosis" by the surgeons, covered the whole side, and for weeks I was confined to bed. I had supposed it to have been produced by the wind of a ball, but the surgeons declared that there could be no ecchymosis without actual contact, and that I must have been grazed by a grapeshot or an exploded shell. This was to have found myself only half an inch from death, yet, in Mercutio's phrase, it was enough.[31]

When the wound refused to heal, Higginson traveled north to recuperate.

Emily Dickinson wrote to him again in early June 1864. In her previous letter, she had suggested that both she and Higginson were participants in an "oblique war." Now she implied that both were wounded survivors. She wrote from her Norcross cousins' house in Cambridge:

> Are you in danger—
> I did not know that you were hurt. Will you tell me more? Mr
> Hawthorne died.
> I was ill since September, and since April, in Boston, for a
> Physician's care—He does not let me go, yet I work in my Prison,
> and make Guests for myself—

She assured him that "Knowledge of your recovery—would excel my own."[32]

Dickinson was being treated in Cambridge for an alarming eye disorder. During her nearly seven months of sometimes painful treatment, with a later follow-up visit, she was required to spend long periods immobilized in darkness. Writing to her sister-in-law, Susan Dickinson, she identified her location as "At Center of the Sea." Her only relief was literature, especially Shakespeare, read to her by visitors. When she learned that Robert Browning had published a new collection of poems, she claimed to have been "astonished—till I remembered that I, myself, in my smaller way, sang off charnel steps."[33] In other words, she too was a poet of war and death. During the months that followed, as she lay in self-imposed paralysis, her own view of the "oblique war" crystallized in her mind and in her poetry.

Already, in her year at Mount Holyoke, Dickinson had shown her intellectual honesty in her refusal to count herself among the "saved." She told Higginson that the members of her family "are religious—except me—and address an Eclipse, every morning—whom they call their 'Father.'[34] The overwhelming impression conveyed in Dickinson's letters to Susan Dickinson and to her other correspondents is of someone who couldn't stand—who had a visceral shudder in the presence of—the flatulent rhetoric of church and state around her. Hollow religious language disgusted her:

"He preached upon 'Breadth' till it argued him narrow . . . The Truth never flaunted a Sign—/Simplicity fled from his counterfeit presence/As Gold the Pyrites would shun."[35] Dickinson was out to purge her own language of deadness and counterfeit emotion.

Dickinson was immune to the war fever around her. Her greatest outpouring of verse coincided with the Civil War, but her inspiration during those years seems to have been resistance to high rhetoric. While Julia Ward Howe was writing her saber-rattling "Battle Hymn of the Republic," published in the same issue of *The Atlantic* as Higginson's "Letter to a Young Contributor," Dickinson was quietly demolishing myths of heroic pomposity:

> *Finding is the first Act*
> *The second, loss,*
> *Third, Expedition for the "Golden Fleece"*
>
> *Fourth, no Discovery—*
> *Fifth, no Crew—*
> *Finally, no Golden Fleece—*
> *Jason, sham, too—*[36]

In May 1865, under her eye doctor's care again, Dickinson wrote of her pleasure in the capture of Jefferson Davis, and the rumor that he had been disguised in a woman's skirt. "The Tea Rose I gave Aunt Lavinia," she added, "has a flower, now."[37]

AFTER HIS OWN brush with death, Higginson spent weeks in an army hospital, traveled north on furlough, returned to his regiment in South Carolina, and finally resigned from the army in the fall of 1864, never fully recovering from his mysterious wound—an affliction that would now be diagnosed as post-traumatic shock. He moved with his invalid wife to a rooming house in Newport, Rhode Island, where he began to assemble his memories of the war and continued to encourage young women writers. One of these was the talented young Jewish poet Emma Lazarus, author of the sonnet "The New Colossus," which was later inscribed on the pedestal of the Statue of Liberty. Another was Helen Hunt (later a successful novelist under the name Helen Hunt Jackson), who lived in the same Newport establishment as the Higginsons; it turned out that she had grown up in Amherst and had known Emily Dickinson as a child. Higginson showed her some of the poems that Dickinson had sent him, and Hunt never forgot them.

8.

Despite his valor under enemy fire, and the lingering effects of the war on his mental and physical health, Colonel Higginson ultimately seems less a martyr than a martinet. His fastidious determination that no houses in Florida should be destroyed or plundered along the way ("Sherman's 'bummers' not having yet arrived," as he noted proudly) seems to date from another era. So does the tea rose in his lapel.[38] Lost in a dream of valiant raids and gentlemanly gestures, Higginson floated through the war on the current of his own imaginings.

The grim conditions of the final stages of the war put an end to such genteel sentiments, as Lincoln found the implacable generals who understood that victory was a matter of superior numbers and technology. General William Tecumseh Sherman, in his decisive march to the sea with his scavenging "bummers," knew that he couldn't compete with the young hotheads of the South according to their own methods. "War suits them," he wrote, "and the rascals are brave, fine riders, bold to rashness, and dangerous subjects in every sense. . . . These men must be killed or employed by us before we can hope for peace."[39]

It would be misleading, however, to plot the progress of the Civil War as the inevitable victory of realism over romance. If Lincoln's plainspoken speeches touch us more deeply today that those of Daniel Webster or Henry Clay, the great masters of oratory and compromise during the prewar period, it is not because we can no longer value great rhetoric. It is rather because Lincoln found the tone and sensibility for a new time. The Civil War reversed these reputations as it did so many others. And when an unknown poet named Emily Dickinson, daughter of a congressman who campaigned for Clay, wrote to Higginson for advice about her poetry, he couldn't quite make out the words on the page. He couldn't see that Emily Dickinson, so far from the action of the war, had internalized its significance better than he, in his proximity, had managed to do.

A man of an earlier time, Higginson has suffered in the eyes of posterity for his obtuseness. Nonetheless, he was instrumental in Dickinson's success. She told him, twice, that he had saved her life. She knew his essays, every word and comma, by heart. And in his very disorientation amid new conditions, he demonstrated how much a new sensibility was needed for changed circumstances. As a soldier, Higginson was often ill at ease; as a writer, he was perhaps too comfortable. When he wrote that birds were "accidental exiles from an unknown globe, banished where none can understand their language," he could have been writing about himself. He knew that he and his kind were destined for irrelevance. That was his burden and his tragedy.[40]

One might have expected that a radical abolitionist like Higginson, with his demonstrated commitment to the basic human rights of African-Americans, would work zealously after the Northern victory for the cause for which he had risked his life and permanently harmed his psychic health. But like many intellectuals of his class, Higginson seemed to have spent his energies by war's end. When he returned in 1878 to the St. Johns River and the other places where he had served in the South, he was inclined to think that it was a good thing that the policies of Reconstruction should be lifted. He trusted that Southern gentlemen, a class with whom he shared a certain sensibility, would keep order; if blacks found life unbearable, he complacently believed, they would leave for greener pastures in the North.

In his perfectly titled autobiography, *Cheerful Yesterdays*, Higginson regarded race relations as a minor problem essentially solved by the war. His commitment to women's rights, and to young women writers, seemed more pressing than his service along the St. Johns. After the war, it was left to others, most notably to Harriet Beecher Stowe and her friends and formidable family, to adopt Florida as their own, and to take up the cause of that very same river—its birds and its flowers, along with the black and white folk who made it their home.

Chapter Two

THE PRODIGAL

One of the ones that Midas touched
Who failed to touch us all
Was that confiding Prodigal
The reeling Oriole—

So drunk he disavows it
With badinage divine—
So dazzling we mistake him
For an alighting Mine—

☞ EMILY DICKINSON[1]

I.

CAPTAIN FREDERICK STOWE was standing in the graveyard above Gettysburg on July 3, 1863, when an artillery shell entered his ear like a summons from the dead beneath his feet. Two days earlier, Captain Stowe had run in terror through the streets of the little crossroads town as screaming rebels pursued the Union troops up into the hills. The Union forces managed to hold the high ground—Cemetery Ridge, an ominous position. Everyone knew that the Confederate troops would storm the position. Everyone knew that it was just a matter of time. No one knew amid the mayhem that Gettysburg would become the most famous battlefield of the war.

The assault was expected during the morning of the third day of battle. For two long days, the corpses and wounded men had spilled down the hillside, like some nightmare vision of the Last Judgment. For the moment, the Union soldiers were away from the fighting, the sporadic gunfire and screams of bayoneted men. The midsummer sun filtered through gathering storm clouds. It was hot and muggy in the graveyard, and the men were sweating profusely in their woolen blue uniforms.

But General James Longstreet, Robert E. Lee's chief lieutenant, still hesitated to give the order to fire. He did not begin his artillery onslaught on the Union positions until after one o'clock. Once begun, however, the guns kept up their deafening barrage for two solid hours. It is said that the din of three hundred guns—"a clangor of death, such as had never been heard upon this continent"—was so loud that it could be heard across the state in Pittsburgh, 180 miles away.[2]

Longstreet's aim was high, however, and the damage done to the Union force was insufficient preparation for his next move. At three o'clock came the order for General George Pickett's doomed Confederate charge. Pickett's men fell to Union sharpshooters "like leaves in an autumn wind," and the Union troops—especially a hardy regiment of Maine farmers—held their positions in hand-to-hand combat on the high ground.[3] Neither side escaped unscathed from Gettysburg. The Union casualties were twenty-three thousand men dead or wounded. Altogether, fifty-one thousand men were dead, missing, or wounded in the most stunning carnage of the war.

But if Longstreet's artillery barrage overshot the ridge, it fell squarely on the cemetery beyond, on the back side of the hill. "In the burial-ground on the head of Cemetery Ridge fell the iron hail, rending the graves and splintering the monuments," wrote Henry Ward Beecher, Fred Stowe's uncle. "Flowers growing on graves were rudely picked by hurtling iron."[4] For Captain Stowe and the other unlucky officers who had sought cover in the graveyard, the effect was ghoulish; men fell where others were already buried.

The following day was July 4, Independence Day. A hard rain fell all day on the wounded and the dead in the cornfields and the cemetery of Gettysburg. For reasons still not fully clear, the Union troops did not pursue the retreating Confederate force. The sheer trauma of three days of carnage, and relief that it was momentarily past, may have cooled the Union response. Casualties were loaded on wagons to be hauled to hospitals or graves.

HARRIET BEECHER STOWE received news of her fallen son in a letter from the army chaplain dated July 11: "Among the thousands of wounded and dying men on this war-scarred field, I have just met with your son, Captain Stowe. If you have not already heard from him, it may cheer your heart to know that he is in the hands of good, kind friends. He was struck by a fragment of a shell, which entered his right ear. He is quiet and cheerful, longs to see some member of the family, and is, above all, anxious that they should hear from him as soon as possible. . . . I know that, to a mother's anxious heart, even a hasty scrawl about her boy will be more than welcome."[5] There was no indication of where Fred would be transported for medical help.

When Fred's father, Calvin Stowe, saw his son's name in the newspaper on a list of wounded men in New York City, he immediately boarded a train. He got as far as Baltimore, only to find his pocket had been picked of his money and letters to Fred. After this feckless adventure, the Stowes sought in vain for further news of their son. The mail was disrupted during the violent draft riots in New York City, beginning on July 13, and Harriet was afraid that Fred had been "torn limb from limb" by marauding "wild beasts" there.[6] She appealed directly to Secretary of War Edwin Stanton for assistance. She finally saw her son on November 26 in New York. His wound, the source of excruciating pain, had not healed; a year later it was still no better.

2 .

Harriet Beecher Stowe had followed her second son's military career with pride mingled with dread. Fred had become a soldier almost by accident, as a way to atone and give focus to a scattered early life. He was born in 1840 in Ohio, where the Beecher family had moved, from its Connecticut origins, to shore up the western church against the twin depredations of slavery and backwoods dissipation. His grandfather, the famous preacher Lyman Beecher, was head of the Lane Theological Seminary, and his father, Calvin, taught Hebrew there. Fred spent his first months of existence with a wet nurse in Cincinnati as his mother recovered in bed from a difficult childbirth. The pattern of separation continued when Stowe suffered a series of miscarriages and illnesses. Then came another crisis, when her brother George committed suicide in 1843. While enduring these personal losses, she developed a profound identification with the suffering of the slaves, especially the slave mothers.

A great epic story began to take shape in her imagination, in which mothers carried the burdens of a struggling nation. A noble slave named Uncle Tom, sold down the river to an evil master, would sacrifice himself so that a future generation of black people—courageous mothers and their children—could escape to the North and freedom. Feeling as though she were taking dictation from God, she began to write her novel.

The astonishing worldwide success of *Uncle Tom's Cabin* in 1851 made Fred's mother a celebrity; she traveled to England in 1853 to enlighten the Old World about the horrors of slavery. Fred was left behind. Meanwhile, Calvin Stowe, offered a position at Bowdoin College in 1850 and later at Andover Theological Seminary, had moved the family back east, and Fred entered Andover Academy. There, Fred distinguished himself primarily by his drinking, much to the shock of his mostly abstemious family.[7] While Harriet continued her travels in Europe, Fred was farmed out to an uncle,

Reverend Thomas Beecher, who ran a storefront "water cure" in Elmira, New York, catering to reformed alcoholics and prostitutes. The water cure, or "hydropathy," was a popular alternative to doctors and drugs; the aim was to cleanse the body of "sickly matter" by means of baths and drinking water. And then, in 1857, another family tragedy occurred: Henry Stowe, Fred's handsome and talented older brother, drowned while swimming with friends in the Connecticut River near Dartmouth College. It was suspected that alcohol was a factor in the drowning.

Fred Stowe joined part of his family for an extended tour of Europe, beginning during the summer of 1859, and resolved to bring some order to his life. He wrote to his father from Rome in March 1860 that he had been "a very troublesome thing . . . for a long while," but felt that he had "changed a great deal" during his travels.[8] He had decided to train as a medical doctor instead of pursuing the family business in the ministry, and entered Harvard Medical School the following fall. Abraham Lincoln's call for volunteers during the spring of his first year interrupted his studies—for good, as it turned out. He joined Company A of the First Massachusetts Volunteers, and drilled on Boston Common before cheering crowds.

Harriet Beecher Stowe visited her son several times before he saw action. Fretting about the "temptations and dangers" of camp life, she attended the official leave-taking on Boston Common. She found her son "mysteriously changed," his face wearing "an expression of gravity and care." "So our boys come to manhood in a day," she wrote.[9] This was the second time in two years that Fred seemed "changed," but a photograph of him in battle dress hardly seems to represent a grown man. He looks awkward, scared, and tentative, his rifle held behind him with the bayonet pointed down, his paunchy coat and bunched pants looking one size too large. His expression is wary, his hat askew on his recently trimmed hair. His left ear is turned toward the camera as though listening intently for an order, or for an incoming shell.

In the middle of June, while visiting her brother Henry Ward Beecher in Brooklyn, Harriet managed to see her son again, when his boat docked

Portrait of Fred Stowe in military uniform, ca. 1863 (The Schlesinger Library, Radcliffe Institute, Harvard University)

in Jersey City. She described Fred as in high spirits—"bristling with knapsack and haversack, and looking like an assortment of packages." She filled his pockets with fresh oranges.[10]

IT WAS ANOTHER year and a half before she saw him again. Fred had taken part in the skirmishing in northern Virginia leading up to the stunning Union defeat at Bull Run on July 18. For his bravery in action, he was promoted to sergeant and then to second lieutenant. But by the fall, the First Massachusetts was no longer in the thick of action, and was guarding forts near Washington, D.C., instead. On September 17, 1862, Fred complained to his mother, with his usual haphazard spelling, that "My regt will neaver go into action and so long as I remain here I shall neaver be advanced."

Fred wanted his famous mother to pull strings in order to put his life in greater danger. Meanwhile, she had her own worries about her wayward son. "I *must* see Fred," she told one of her daughters. "Since I heard that his physician was prescribing whiskey for his ague I have had no rest—God only knows what the temptations of soldiers are in so cold & comfortless a life as theirs."[11] Her fears were compounded when her nephew Harry Beecher, Henry Ward Beecher's son and Fred's first cousin, was dismissed from his regiment outside Washington for an unspecified breech of morality, apparently involving prostitutes and alcohol.[12]

Stowe's opportunity came in November, when she was invited to Washington to attend a Thanksgiving dinner in honor of fugitive slaves gathered there. She was deeply moved by the occasion, especially a heartfelt rendition of "Go Down, Moses." She had spent the summer lobbying hard for emancipation rather than preservation of the Union as the main goal of the war. It was known that Lincoln had already drafted his Emancipation Proclamation—primarily as a way to weaken the South—and was only waiting for a Union victory to put it into effect. On her way south, Stowe stopped first for a week in Brooklyn, and tried to persuade her brother Henry Ward Beecher, minister of the Plymouth Church there, to join her on her errand.

Harriet stopped at Fort Runyon, where Fred was stationed, and spoke to an old admirer, Brigadier General Adolph von Steinwehr, who commanded a division of the Eleventh Corps of the Army of the Potomac. Steinwehr promised to appoint Fred to his personal staff, with a promotion to the rank of captain. The position was technically a noncombat position, involving communications and reports, and Harriet Beecher Stowe may have hoped to protect her son in the midst of the military action he craved. It is also possible, as one biographer has suggested, that Harriet "feared the dullness of camp life and the lure of the bottle more than the dangers of battle."[13] It is grimly ironic that Stowe's efforts to protect her son, by giving him a position removed from battle, may actually have put him in harm's way, in the cemetery at Gettysburg.

At a reception in the White House on December 2, 1862, marked by unaccountable merriment on all sides, Lincoln delivered his famous line to Harriet Beecher Stowe: "So, you're the little woman who wrote the book that started this great war!" Apparently she got the assurances from the president that she sought: the Emancipation Proclamation became law on New Year's Day, 1863.

3·

During the fall of 1863, immediately after the battle of Gettysburg, Harriet Beecher Stowe began writing a series of essays concerning the home front. The essays were first published in *The Atlantic* and then collected in a popular series of volumes beginning with *House and Home Papers* (1864) and *The Chimney Corner* (1868). Stowe's main point in these essays, in which she assumed the voice of a meditative New Englander named Christopher Crowfield, was that the Northern families at home owed it to their soldier sons to be morally worthy of the sacrifices made in their name. As Stowe ranged across such domestic concerns as the decoration of houses and the proper clothing for young women, she kept one eye on the battles to the south. We can feel the emotional pressure of the war in the third of the *House and Home Papers*, called "What is a Home?" "Right on the threshold of all perfection lies *the cross* to be taken up," she writes. "Without labor and self-denial neither Raphael nor Michel Angelo nor Newton was made perfect. Nor can man or woman create a true home who is not willing in the outset to embrace life heroically, to encounter labor and sacrifice."[14]

In Stowe's view, simplicity and sunlight seemed to follow naturally from this moral creed. And self-denial, she aimed to show, was in perfect accord with good taste. Through her genial alter ego, Crowfield, she set out to prove that "the most beautiful things are always the cheapest." The expensive heavy drapes that make a room "close and somber as the grave" must yield to "sunshine and fresh air," which are free. She recommended paintings that would "light up the whole" of a room, and these too, she intimated, could be purchased cheaply: "For a picture, painted by a real artist, who studies Nature minutely and conscientiously, has something of the charm of the good Mother [Nature] herself,—something of her faculty of putting on different aspects under different lights."

Stowe knew just the right painter to meet the challenge. "We have that lovely golden twilight sketch of Heade's," she wrote. She seems to have expected her audience to be familiar with the name Martin Johnson Heade, and by this time, perhaps through Newport or Brooklyn circles, she apparently knew Heade himself. Heade was best known during the 1860s for his landscapes of salt marshes dotted with haystacks, along with his detailed paintings of hummingbirds. Stowe's brother Henry Ward Beecher owned at least two of Heade's paintings, a landscape with cows and a marine scene. By recommending Heade's work in her *House and Home* essay, Stowe found a way to draw Heade into the war effort. For Stowe, Heade provided an inspiring image of the serene and simple world that the Northern soldiers, including her son Fred, had been fighting heroically to secure.

When Stowe turned her attention from Victorian excess in household decoration to excessive personal adornment, she struck a similar note of heroic self-denial. "The genius of American life," she insisted, "is for simplicity and absence of ostentation."[15] The Quakers of Philadelphia achieved Stowe's ideal of proper dress: "The most perfect toilets that have been achieved in America have probably been those of the class familiarly called the gay Quakers,—children of Quaker families, who, while abandoning the strict rules of the sect, yet retain their modest and severe reticence, relying on richness of material, and soft, harmonious coloring, rather than striking and dazzling ornament."

Like the "gay Quakers," Stowe saw herself as a second-generation Puritan, softening the severities of her father's generation while upholding its instinctive modesty. She was even willing to compromise on the matter of ornament. "It is . . . neither wicked nor silly nor weak-minded to like beautiful dress, and all that goes to make it up," she wrote. "Jewelry, diamonds, pearls, emeralds, rubies . . . are as lawful and innocent objects of admiration and desire, as flowers or birds or butterflies, or the tints of evening skies. Gems, in fact, are a species of mineral flower; they are the blossoms of the dark, hard mine."

But the tastes of fashionable American women went beyond diamonds and pearls. While they did not wear sunsets in their hair, they did manage to wear almost everything else on Stowe's list. Stowe has Christopher Crowfield express his dismay that his own fashion-conscious daughters and their friends "wore on their hair flowers, gems, streamers, tinklers, humming-birds, butterflies, South American beetles, beads, bugles, and all imaginable rattle-traps, which jingled and clinked with every motion." Stowe is describing the taste for *actual* hummingbirds and real beetles. These young women are well brought up and well educated, according to Stowe, having "calculated eclipses, and read Virgil, Schiller, and La Fontaine." Despite their love of tropical flora and fauna, they are "the flowers of good, staid, sensible families,—not heathen blossoms nursed in the hot-bed heat of wild, high-flying, fashionable society." And yet, to Crowfield's dismay, all they talk about is feminine fashions. While his own ornithological name suggests plainness, Crowfield confers on each of the young women "the name of the bird under whose colors she was sailing": Pheasant, Dove, and so on. To the "most notoriously dressy individual in the little circle," and the most emphatic in her views, Crowfield gives the name "Humming-Bird."[16]

Humming-Bird keeps a close eye on the whirring change in fashions. "I'm quite worn out with sewing," she says, "the fashions are all *so* different from what they were last year." Humming-Bird wonders "who *does* set the fashions . . . they seem nowadays to whirl faster and faster." She herself is constantly in motion: "Taking care of my clothes and going into company is, frankly, *all* that I do." Humming-Bird has vaguely heroic aspirations: "During the war," she says, "I did so long to be a man! I felt so poor and insignificant because I was nothing but a girl." Nonetheless, she is appalled that a certain virtuous woman of her acquaintance, who visits the poor and gives to many charities, "wears such a fright of a bonnet."

Stowe's challenge in this essay is to establish a connection between good taste in dress and the sacrifices on the battlefield. She has Crowfield claim that extravagances in feminine dress are traceable, like so many other dangerous temptations in American life, to the French aristocracy and its courtesans: "A certain class of women in Paris . . . makes the fashions that rule the feminine world . . . They have no family ties; love, in its pure domestic sense, is an impossibility in their lot." The French are hurtling to perdition; fortunately, "We are across the Atlantic . . . far enough off to be able to see whither things are tending."

Crowfield provides the moral, linking self-denial in dress to self-denial in winning the Civil War. "We have just come through a great struggle, in which our women have borne an heroic part,—have shown themselves capable of any kind of endurance and self-sacrifice." In the postwar "reconstructive state," Americans "instead of following the corrupt and worn-out ways of the Old World . . . are called on to set the example of a new state of society,—noble, simple, pure, and religious; and women can do more towards this even than men, for women are the real architects of society." American women can "hold back their country from following in the wake of old, corrupt, worn-out, effeminate European society, and make America the leader of the world in all that is good."

In launching this gentle attack, Harriet Beecher Stowe was undoubtedly thinking of her own twin daughters, whose frolicsome parties stood in sharp contrast to Fred's hard life in the Union Army camps. "Hatty & Eliza . . . are dressed as usual in expense of the worst & most exaggerated fashion," she complained in a typical letter to Calvin. The Stowes worried that their daughters' education had been "too worldly" and Harriet fretted that they lived for "outward show" alone. And yet, she also "bought them silk dresses whenever she had a windfall of money and delighted like a schoolgirl in the fashions."[17]

Another of Stowe's pampered hummingbird daughters, Georgiana, had a serious beau during the summer of 1864; she was engaged to Reverend Henry Allen of the Episcopal church in Stockbridge, in the Berkshires. Georgie, as she was known, had exhibited manic-depressive symptoms as a vivid teenager; as a girl of sixteen, according to her mother, she was "a poor drooping bird half the time and then *too* excited and too frolicsome the rest."[18] Stowe encouraged her daughters to treat their various ailments with the popular cures of the time, and in the process of treating her own wildly fluctuating moods, Georgie had become addicted to morphine. Amid preparations for the wedding, the Stowes took a vacation at the seashore.

4 ·

One stormy day during that summer of 1864, while vacationing on the rocky seacoast of New Hampshire, Harriet Beecher Stowe found a wounded hummingbird in the rain. "The rose-bushes under the window hung dripping under their load of moisture," she wrote in a story based on the event, "each spray shedding a constant shower on the spray below it."[19] On one of the lower sprays, Stowe found "a poor little humming-bird, drawn up into the tiniest shivering ball, and clinging with a desperate grasp to his uncomfortable perch." He was, she observed, "a humming-bird in adversity." Held in the warm hollow of human hands, the bird slowly revived. "Then we bethought ourselves of feeding him, and forthwith prepared him a stiff glass of sugar and water, a drop of which we held to his bill."

Soon enough, the Stowe family—identified as Mr. A and Jenny as well as Stowe herself—had made room for the rescued bird in their modest apartment (and not the posh Atlantic House hotel nearby) at the summer resort of Rye Beach.

> Immediately he was pronounced out of danger by the small humane society which had undertaken the charge of his restoration, and we began to cast about for getting him a settled establishment in our apartment. I gave up my work-box to him for a sleeping-room, and it was medically ordered that he should take a nap. So we filled the box with cotton, and he was formally put to bed, with a folded cambric handkerchief round his neck, to keep him from beating his wings. Out of his white wrappings he looked forth green and grave as any judge with his bright round eyes.

One can see where Stowe's imagination is going, with the "small humane society," the "settled establishment," the workbox, and the medically mandated nap. She was in the business of domesticity and uplift, in the service of freed slaves, fallen women, and her own fallen son. The little wild bird is "domesticated," and given a proper home. "Hum has learned to sit upon my finger," she wrote, "and eat his sugar and water out of a teaspoon with most Christian-like decorum." The rescued bird could be Eliza herself, fetched from her perilous, ice-choked crossing of the Ohio River, and given a clean bed by Mr. and Mrs. Bird on the Ohio shore, while awaiting safe passage to Canada.

But this was 1864, after all, and it is Fred Stowe, the wounded son rescued from the perils of Gettysburg, who most insistently comes to mind. Hum is a stand-in for Fred, whose uncertain fate was constantly on Stowe's mind that summer. The bird, bleeding from its ruby throat, is characterized as a wounded "son." When "our chief medical authority"—presumably Calvin Stowe—reaches a diagnosis of "a probable hemorrhage from the lungs," the family christens the stricken bird "Hum, the son of Buz." As he recovers, it is Hum's martial qualities that Stowe insists on. As he swoops about the room, she discovers that "his bright, brilliant blood was not made out of a simple vegetarian diet." When mosquitoes and flies strayed into the apartment, Hum "would lay about him spitefully, wielding his bill like a sword." Like Fred, he was given to "different moods," depressed on gray days but perking up with the sun's return.

AND SO IT was that Harriet Beecher Stowe, at the height of the Civil War, found herself drawing a hummingbird. She considered herself an artist as well as a writer, especially during these summer vacations, and in "Hum, the son of Buz" it was as an artist that she portrayed herself. Like Martin Heade, who worked just down the coast from Rye in Newburyport, she was drawn to fleeting and evanescent subjects: the lightning flash of the hummingbird or a quickly wilting magnolia blossom. She waited for Hum to alight, and went to work. "When absorbed in reflection," she noted, "he sits with his bill straight up in the air, as I have drawn him."

Here is the scene Stowe captured in her sketchbook:

Hum had his established institutions in our room, the chief of which was a tumbler with a little sugar and water mixed in it, and a spoon laid across, out of which he helped himself whenever he felt in the mood—sitting on the edge of the tumbler, and dipping his long bill, and lapping with his little forked tongue like a kitten. When he found his spoon accidentally dry, he would stoop over and dip his bill in the water in the tumbler; which caused the prophecy on the part of some of his guardians that he would fall in some-day and be drowned. For which reason it was agreed to keep only an inch in depth of the fluid at the bottom of the tumbler. A wise precaution this proved; for the next morning I was awaked, not by the usual hum over my head, but by a sharp little flutter, and found Mr. Hum beating his wings in the tumbler—having actually tumbled in during his energetic efforts to get his morning coffee before I was awake.

Tumbling into a tumbler is a good little joke, while Stowe's habit of waking to the sound of a hummingbird's hum may owe something to a couplet of Alexander Pope, another connoisseur of small things: "Yet by some object ev'ry brain is stirr'd; / The dull may waken to a Humming-bird."[20]

The striking drawing that Stowe made of Hum that summer was used as the basis for an illustration for her children's story "Hum, the Son of Buz," which she published with other animal stories in *Queer Little People* (1867). As in the description in the story, her painted bird is perched on the rim of a drinking glass on which a fluted spoon is also balanced. The crystal cup, evidently about a third full of liquid, has inscribed on its side, in flowery script, the letters "Hum" along with the date, "1864." But the letters can also easily be read as "Rum."[21] The ambiguity was presumably intentional.

Harriet Beecher Stowe, ca. 1864 (Harriet Beecher Stowe Center, Hartford, Connecticut)

There is another visual pun in the drawing as well. A spoonful of sugar was the favorite treat of hummingbirds, but it was also often added to rum. These hints of alcohol are present in the drawing but minimized in the published story. The illustration that accompanied the story, an engraving based on Stowe's drawing, eliminated the inscribed "Hum" or "Rum" from the tumbler. The Beechers, a family scarred by alcoholism, nonetheless liked to joke about imbibing liquor, as when Stowe writes of the "stiff glass of sugar and water" that she prepared for Hum. Another story in *Queer Little People* is about a squirrel named "Whiskey." These hints of alcohol suggest that Fred Stowe's fate was in the back of Stowe's mind as she treated her injured hummingbird.

Was Stowe familiar with Emily Dickinson's charming poem about the "little tippler," published three years earlier in the May 4, 1861, issue of the *Springfield Daily Republican*? The speaker of the poem, reeling from inn to inn, is a hummingbird.

I taste a liquor never brewed,
From tankards scooped in pearl;
Not all the vats upon the Rhine
Yield such an alcohol!

Inebriate of air am I,
And debauchee of dew,
Reeling, through endless summer days,
From inns of molten blue.

When landlords turn the drunken bee
Out of the foxglove's door,
When butterflies renounce their drams,
I shall but drink the more!

Till seraphs swing their snowy hats,
And saints to windows run,

To see the little tippler
Leaning against the sun![22]

A second manuscript, used for the newspaper publication, has an alternate final line: "To see the little tippler/ From Manzanilla come!" Scholars have debated the meaning of Manzanilla. Does it refer to Manzanillo, a Cuban port associated with the export of rum, or a Spanish town for which a local wine is named?[23] My guess is that Dickinson had all of these in mind, but especially the connection to rum (or hum!). For Dickinson, the drunken hummingbird is a figure of ecstasy; for Stowe, of vulnerability.

Stowe's hummingbird sketch may be taken as an extension of the theme of domesticity. Her domestic essays were meant to show what the Northern army was fighting for: an orderly way of life centered on hearth and home. This was the ideal in *Uncle Tom's Cabin* as well, where Tom's orderly cabin is presented as the domestic dream of all freed slaves, and the disruption of slave families as the root of Southern evil. The hummingbird sketch depicts a domesticated bird, after all, a bird who has been taught table manners. Stowe sketched a sewing basket below the bird, an emblem of domestic life and her own civilizing presence. If the left-hand portion of the sketch may be taken to express a civilized way of life, the right-hand clump of rank vegetation, to which the handle of the spoon directs our eye, seems to allude to the wild, to which the bird has momentarily turned his back.

A return to the wild turned out, for Hum at least, to be impossible. "When our five weeks at the seaside were up, and it was time to go home, we had great questionings what was to be done with Hum. To get him home with us was our desire; but who ever heard of a humming-bird traveling by railroad?" Here, *Hum* and *home* almost seem like homonyms. Home in Hartford, though, "the equinoctial storm came on," and Hum was "lonesome, and gave way to depression."

The tumbler, as it is for the alcoholic, proved both refuge and release: "One chilly morning he managed again to fall into his tumbler, and wet himself through; and notwithstanding warm bathings and tender nursings, the poor little fellow seemed to get diphtheria, or something quite as bad for humming-birds." All is in vain, as it was for Little Eva in *Uncle Tom's Cabin*. He lies in a sunny parlor, "where ivy embowers all the walls and the sun lies all day." But toward evening, "he was put to sleep on a green twig laid on the piano. In that sleep the little head drooped—nodded—fell; and little Hum went where other bright dreams go—to the Land of the Hereafter."

5.

Fred Stowe's return to Hartford, after his convalescence in New York from his battle wounds at Gettysburg, was an uneasy mix of moral resolve and dashed hopes. In January 1864, in church with his mother, he made a shaky confession of Christian faith: "I am afraid sometimes that this is all false but I shall believe it real until I fail in my reform." By October, he was drinking again, and one evening walked out into the falling rain and vanished for several days, amid rumors that he had been spotted in gin mills nearby. His sisters were mortified, and Harriet improved the occasion by reminding them that their own flighty addiction to fashion was no better than his: "He is no weaker, no more unsuccessful against his besetting sin than you against yours—only the consequences to him are more fatal & dreadful."[24]

Something more strenuous than faith or social opprobrium was needed, and Harriet seized an invitation by some of Fred's army friends, in 1866, for him to join them on a cotton plantation in northern Florida along the St. Johns River. She provided the money for his stake and determined to serve as housekeeper for the gentlemen-farmers. The Florida venture appealed to Harriet Beecher Stowe for a number of reasons. Fred's well-being was the primary motive; she hoped to domesticate her wayward son as she had domesticated Hum. She also wished to escape the harsh northern winters, and her aging and hypochondriac husband would surely benefit from the warmer climate.

There were political imperatives as well. Stowe had taken a personal interest in the postwar American South, laying out her views in one of the *Chimney Corner* papers titled "A Family-Talk on Reconstruction." Slavery, she felt, had degraded labor. "We of the North," she wrote, "who know the dignity of labor, who know the value of free and equal institutions, who have enjoyed advantages for seeing their operation, ought, in true brotherliness, to exercise the power given us by the present position of the people of the Southern States, and put things thoroughly right for them."[25] Florida, with its small population and pleasant climate, its needy black workforce and its investment opportunities for Northerners, seemed ripe for Yankee colonization.

Harriet Beecher Stowe with her brother Charles as companion boarded a ship in New York on March 6, 1867, just four days after Congress had voted into law the first Act of Reconstruction, its ambitious plan to remake the South. They sailed first to Savannah, on very rough water, and then on smaller vessels through the inland waterway to Jacksonville. The city had been rebuilt during the three years since Colonel Higginson had left it in smoldering ruins. Hotels catering to a burgeoning clientele of tourists from the Northeast were under construction, slated for opening in 1868.[26] By 1870, the number of winter visitors had mushroomed to 14,000.[27]

Harriet was charmed by the view from Jacksonville of the mouth of the St. Johns River: "In all my foreign experience & travels I never saw such a scene. The fog was just up as we came in—the river broad as the Connecticut in its broadest parts. . . . The shores white and dazzling like driven snow & out of this dazzling white rise groves of palmetto pine."[28] She felt transformed by the passage south: "I feel as if I had wings," she wrote.[29] As she kept house for Fred and his partners, in a shanty transformed into a house with gables, she put into practice many of the domestic ideas she had floated in her *House and Home Papers*. She wrote triumphantly that she had "extended the dominion of law & order over [the front verandah]" and that "we no longer bolt the door by drawing a sack of sweet potatoes in front of it."[30]

Stowe stayed well into April, beyond her planned return on the first, convinced that she had found in semitropical Florida, the land of flowers, a second base of operations for her family and her writing. She began looking seriously for a piece of land for a winter home, determined to join what her friend Gail Hamilton called the "birds of passage flitting North & South on the slightest change of air."[31]

Stowe found what she was looking for in the quiet hamlet of Mandarin, thirty acres flush with wild orange groves on the east side of the river: "a wild uncultured country forest all around the sea on one side & the broad St. Johns five miles wide on the other."[32] On a bluff overlooking the river stood a quaint cottage and an extraordinary tree, like some fantasy dwelling in a fairy tale:

> I found a hut built close to a great live-oak twenty-five feet in girth, and with overarching boughs eighty feet up in the air, spreading like a firmament, and all swaying with mossy festoons. We began to live here, and gradually we improved the hut by lathe, plaster, and paper. Then we threw out a wide veranda all round, for in these regions the veranda is the living-room of the house. Ours had to be built around the trunk of the tree, so that our cottage has a peculiar and original air, and seems as if it were half tree, or something that had grown out of the tree.[33]

6.

Harriet Beecher Stowe's plans for growing oranges in Mandarin turned out much better than Fred's cotton venture. In July 1867, he returned unannounced to Hartford, again overwhelmed by drinking. This time, his parents had him committed to an institution in Binghamton, New York, where he went cold turkey from both alcohol and nicotine. That December, poor Fred begged his sisters not to feel ashamed of him for his "coarse life": "Do not let the feeling of shame bear too heavily on you at the thought of my being here," he wrote, "it is better far better that I should be here than out in the world disgracing the name you bear it is far more honorable to have it said that he is here than to have it said that he has gone to the bad."[34]

Calvin Stowe took his lost son on a trip to the Mediterranean the following summer, while Harriet worked on *Oldtown Folks*, a novel about two children, a brother and a sister, lost in the New England marshes. Whatever benefit the trip was meant to provide clearly failed. In early February 1871, still fighting his drinking problem, Fred wrote a poignant letter to his mother: "Did I only think of my own comfort I would kill myself and end it all, but I know that you and all the family would feel the disgrace such an end would bring upon you and the talk and scandal it would give rise to." He decided to go to sea instead.

During the summer of 1871, Captain Frederick Stowe boarded a ship in Florida bound for California and the Far East. According to his brother Charles, Fred was "possessed with the idea that a long sea voyage would do him more good than anything else."[35] His aunt Isabella Beecher Hooker helped Fred acquire his credentials for the merchant marine. Isabella's lawyer husband, John, had served as a young man in the China Trade. Fred's ship circled Cape Horn and sailed up the west coast of South America.

Fred went ashore in San Francisco. He was thirty-one years old, a former student at Harvard Medical School and a veteran of Bull Run and Gettysburg. He was the oldest surviving son of the most famous writer in the United States. He stepped off the ship and vanished into thin air. He was never heard from again.

7·

Can we follow Fred Stowe's journey any farther? Not in any real sense: the documentation ends with his departure from the ship. It is a cold case, stone-cold for more than a hundred years. But consider his mother, the novelist. Wouldn't she try to follow him in her imagination, as she had followed the slave-mother Eliza and her child across the ice-choked Ohio River?

Imagine Fred Stowe pausing, getting his bearings, his sea legs adjusting to dry land. The wind off San Francisco Bay is blowing on his bad ear, still throbbing eight years after the vigil on Cemetery Ridge. He wanders along the seedy waterfront, oyster bars and gin mills. He has a drink, and another. He asks a bedraggled stranger at the bar the direction to the town center. Market Square is that way. That way he goes, no clear plan in his clouded mind, no clearer than the stormy rounding of the Horn. He walks as others walk. He is in the crowd, of the crowd. He turns a corner. Gone.

But consider another scenario. Why did he go to California? To kill himself? It seems unlikely. He went to California to escape his shame. To escape his name. The first thing he does when he leaves the ship is to shed both. Incognito, under an assumed name, he ponders the possibilities. *Possessed with the idea of a long sea voyage.* He has tried the Atlantic, the Old World, making resolutions in Rome with his mother, staying sober on a Mediterranean cruise with his father. But the Pacific is something else altogether. Hawaii, Tahiti, Japan. Tattoos and cannibals, geisha with white-painted faces, and Melville's dark-eyed nymph, Fayaway.

Fred Stowe was not the only young man adrift in the wake of the Civil War. That very summer, another strayed son of a famous author, Charles Longfellow, got off a ship in San Francisco and wondered where to go next. He too carried a scar from the war. The bullet wound was visible on his back. On June 1, 1871, he telegraphed his father, Henry Wadsworth Longfellow: "Have suddenly decided to set sail for Japan today. Good-bye."[36]

And why not? The mysterious island country was newly opened. There was regular steamship service from San Francisco to Yokohama, begun in 1867. A young man without attachments could see something of the unknown parts of the globe, invent a new identity for himself, get himself tattooed.

Once in Yokohama, Charles got his tattoo: a giant carp ascending a waterfall covered the length of his back, obscuring the bullet wound in his shoulder.

Gone.

Chapter Three

BEECHER'S POCKETS

Are we the only man that sits down on eggs? Is not the whole world hunting nests, and laying up their treasures in pockets behind them, and sitting down on all their spoils, when it is too late?

                ✄ HENRY WARD BEECHER

I.

"My POCKETS HAVE been the occasion of great trouble to me," Reverend Henry Ward Beecher wrote in 1862, at the height of his worldwide fame and influence.[1] The spendthrift preacher with the boyish good looks and the long, flowing hair was only partly joking. Money leaked from Beecher's pockets like water from a sieve, for Beecher was a passionate collector of expensive trifles. "Every man that has curious things, old books, venerable old maps, etchings, engravings, or pictures, has heard about my pockets," he wrote. But if Beecher's pockets bulged with receipts and unpaid bills, they also concealed more intimate things. On the backs of letters folded in his pockets unread, he scribbled ideas for sermons, those mesmerizing effusions—marvels of confession, homely detail, and inspiration—that he delivered every Sunday to the crowds that swelled the Plymouth Church in Brooklyn.[2] Beecher in the pulpit was a natural force, a magnetic presence, and some of those crumpled missives were from his many secret admirers: "All those obliging little notes, those pleasant letters of sentiment which it is so agreeable to receive and so awkward to explain, if by any negligence I leave them in my pocket."

So awkward to explain to his wife, Beecher meant, for the literal-minded Eunice Bullard Beecher, emptying her careless husband's pockets as a matter of course, was not one to make allowances for pleasant letters of sentiment. The "affectionate catechism" that ensued, however, was nothing compared to what Beecher faced a decade later, when he found himself—like a real-life version of Hawthorne's wayward minister in *The Scarlet Letter*—at the heart of the biggest sex scandal in the history of American religion. At that troubling time, the contents of Beecher's pockets were scrutinized by lawyers and jurors as well, and published in the nation's newspapers for all to see. The question of what the handsome preacher had done, and what he had left undone, with regard to one of his female parishioners was debated endlessly, and indeed is still debated. But that was another time, almost another era, in the roller-coaster life of Reverend Henry Ward Beecher.

With his public swagger and Byronic charm, young Beecher—Beecher as we see him before the Civil War—was a sensualist and a connoisseur, unafraid to admit his whims and temptations since, he felt certain, there were limits to his appetites. "I am free of all vices," he wrote. "I do not gamble, drink, smoke, race, or bet. The worst that I know of myself is an addiction to bookstores, print-shops, and picture-dealers' haunts."

2.

On October 13, 1859, while lingering in Boston after giving one of his innumerable public lectures the previous day, Henry Ward Beecher wandered into a picture gallery. It was the kind of thing Beecher liked to do on his travels, a bit of quiet shopping by himself, among discreet dealers in art or rare books, as a respite from his grueling round of sermons and lectures. Amid the usual clutter of portraits and nostalgic genre scenes—children skating, farmers bringing in the hay—a dramatic seascape captured Beecher's attention. In the picture, threatening clouds loomed on the horizon; a great wave broke on the shore; miniature sandpipers scuttled across the exposed beach.

Intrigued, Beecher made inquiries. He learned that the painting was called *Storm Clouds on the Coast* and had been painted earlier that year by Martin Johnson Heade. Beecher agreed to pay Williams and Everett, Heade's Boston dealer, fifty dollars for the framed painting—as usual, he didn't have the necessary cash in his pocket—and arranged to have his new treasure sent to his house in Brooklyn. While Beecher and Heade later become friends, it is unlikely that Beecher had heard of Heade at

Martin Johnson Heade, Storm Clouds on the Coast *(Collection of the Farnsworth Art Museum, Museum Purchase, Chartes L. Fax Fund, 1965)*

the time.[3] He might have felt, as he donned his velvet-lapelled black overcoat and swashbuckling cape, that he had made something of a discovery.

Beecher was drawn to things that flickered and flashed, like the shimmering filigree of breaking waves in Heade's painting. For Beecher, these were emblems of freedom and release. He liked to tell people that he was intoxicated by art, that its effect on him resembled the effects of wine—the wine he claimed not to drink, at least not often, except for medicinal purposes. "To find myself absolutely intoxicated; to find my system so much affected that I could not control my nerves; to find myself trembling, and laughing, and weeping, and almost hysterical"—such was the power that Beecher felt among great works of art.[4] Color in particular moved him deeply, color and light.

Beecher, not surprisingly, had a special fondness for gemstones. He was known to the jewelers of New York and London, and carried a selection of uncut precious stones concealed in the recesses of an inner vest pocket.[5] In times of anxiety or excitement, Beecher would finger these treasures, which he called "color-opiates," and derive narcotic comfort from their varying textures and shifting tints. An early biographer described what he called the "drug effect" of gems on Beecher:

> When disturbed or nerve-tired, or when, after some marked effort in the pulpit or upon the platform, he found his brain aflame and every nerve keyed to the highest tension, he would sit down in his study, take out from his pocket or table-drawer an opal, garnet, hyacinth, or flashing diamond, hold it lovingly in his open hand, drinking in through his eyes the soft, rich rays of color. Almost as if by magic, the turgid veins on brow and temple grew less prominent, the deep flush upon his face softened gradually into its natural color, the muscular tension abated, the nerve-strain relaxed, and a soft and gentle peacefulness settled down upon him, like the comforting shadow on an angel's wing.[6]

Beecher also collected porcelain miniatures and Japanese pottery, Bohemian glass and Venetian glass—anything diminutive that flickered in the light. He had a collection of stuffed hummingbirds, those winged gems so beloved of his generation, and another of birds of paradise.[7]

3 ·

In 1859, Henry Ward Beecher was already, at the youthful age of forty-six, the most famous minister in the United States and one of the best-known Americans at home and abroad. He seemed in certain ways a representative American by background and temperament. Born in New England, Beecher and his equally famous sister, Harriet Beecher Stowe, had settled as young adults in Cincinnati on the Ohio River, on the border of the Civil War divide.

Young Beecher showed a romantic streak from the start. When he enrolled as a teenager at Mount Pleasant Classical Institution in Amherst, Massachusetts, in 1829, in preparation for attending Amherst College, he made his first true friend in a young Greek orphan named Constantine Fontellachi, who had been adopted by an Amherst family. Fontellachi's parents had been killed by the Turkish army on the island of Chios, in the same war in which Byron died. Henry fell in love with Constantine, "a living replica of Lord Byron," as Constantine led one of the student divisions at Mount Pleasant in military exercises. "He was the most beautiful thing I had ever seen," Beecher said. "He was like a young Greek God. When we boys used to go swimming together I would climb out on the bank to watch Constantine swim, he was so powerful, so beautiful."[8]

Beecher then attended Amherst College, a sober-minded institution founded in 1821 by Samuel Fowler Dickinson (Emily's grandfather) and Noah Webster (compiler of the dictionary) to beat back the liberal tendencies of Unitarian Harvard. Despite the Puritan restrictions of the place, Beecher enjoyed his years in Amherst, a pleasant village set amid woods on a rise above the Connecticut River. He shot a white owl for sport and had it stuffed and mounted. And it was during his Amherst years that Beecher met and courted Eunice Bullard, a rather stiff little trophy herself, as he came to realize, after she accompanied him back to his first post in Indianapolis.

Henry Ward Beecher perfected his preaching style in small towns and camp meetings in the Indiana outback, where the congregation was hungry for home truths vividly expressed, and impatient with abstraction and long-winded argument. He also experienced slavery firsthand, and conceived a bitter hatred for the brutal institution. Indiana was a major station on the Underground Railroad, and the Beechers were known to have assisted escaping slaves. In 1847, when he received a call to lead the congregation in Brooklyn, Beecher brought some of the energy and informality of the West, as well as passionate political convictions, to his popular performances at the Plymouth Church.

From his pulpit in the crowded church, Beecher preached a dynamic and forward-looking "Gospel of Love" (the "gospel of gush" to his enemies) to replace the rigid Calvinist creed of his childhood and his training for the ministry at Amherst College. For the Calvinist doctrines of predestination and infant damnation, Beecher substituted the love of nature and the tender love of Jesus Christ.

In a typical sermon, Beecher would suddenly turn to the congregation and pose an unsettling question: "Have you ever, as a part of your obedience to Christ, taken time to sit down and think what birds and flowers mean?"[9] To the surprised relief of many of his auditors and the chagrin of his rivals, he raised doubts about the existence of hell. An electric presence in the pulpit and the leading figure in the liberalization of the Congregational Church, Beecher conferred on his eager parishioners his own florid and luxurious tastes. Instead of the stark, dark pews of the western churches, Beecher filled his church with sunlight and music, palm fronds and cascading flowers. His organ was said to be the largest in any American church.

But if Beecher was the most popular preacher in America, he was also among the most hated. A staunch abolitionist and opponent of the Fugitive Slave Act adopted in 1850—which rendered slaves vulnerable to their masters even in free states—Beecher sheltered escaped slaves in his Brooklyn church and encouraged his parishioners to support the great cause. He held mock "slave auctions" from the pulpit of Plymouth Church in Brooklyn, in which wealthy parishioners were invited to purchase the freedom of escaped slaves on the "block."

The most notorious of these occasions involved a flaxen-haired girl of mixed race named "Pinky," nine years old when Beecher led her to the platform in 1860. As donations of cash and jewelry filled the collection plates, Beecher drew from the pile an exquisite ring with a single opal in its setting donated by the well-known poet and writer Rose Terry, one of his friends. With his flair for the dramatic gesture, Beecher placed it on Pinky's finger, saying, "Now remember that this is your freedom-ring."

The next morning, he took the girl to the studio of Eastman Johnson, a painter known for his poignant genre scenes. At Beecher's direction, Johnson painted the girl seated on a tiger skin and gazing lovingly at the jewel on her finger, the symbol of her freedom. The girl adopted the name "Rose Ward" in honor of her two benefactors.[10] This was the quintessence of the Beecher performance: the emotion, the cause, the girl, the gesture, the painting, and the jewel. The tiger skin introduced an exotic and faintly erotic mood.

During the drawn-out struggle to make the territory of Kansas a free state, Beecher passionately endorsed the New England settlers who migrated west to swell the voting ranks of "free-soilers." He thought the settlers had the right to defend themselves, and he raised money in Plymouth Church to purchase twenty-five Sharpe's rifles. He argued, reasonably enough, that rifles served better than Bibles in an argument with wolves. Since one shipment of rifles was actually labeled "Bibles" for disguise, the guns came to be called "Beecher's Bibles." For this witticism Beecher was reviled, and his life threatened, throughout the slaveholding South. He was warned in the press that his "ease and comfort will be anything but safe in this country in six months from this time."[11]

4·

On that quiet October afternoon in 1859, in the picture gallery in Boston, Henry Ward Beecher could look back on a heroic decade of abolitionist work, and forward to a very uncertain future. He was, as usual, in the thick of things. The previous day, the Plymouth Church had decided to invite a young candidate for president, Abraham Lincoln, whose campaign had received little support in the Northeast, to speak in New York. This arrangement too was on Beecher's mind as he passed from picture to picture in the gallery.[12] The country was in peril, and a matching uncertainty seems to well up in the threatening clouds in the painting he purchased that day.

Just shy of two feet by three feet, Martin Johnson Heade's *Storm Clouds on the Coast* depicts two sharply contrasting worlds of shore and sky, diagonally divided by a dark and roiling sea. A peaceful circle of blue opens amid the darkest clouds; a brackish tangle of rocks and seaweed interrupts the smooth expanse of the sand. (In another seascape of 1859, *Approaching Thunder Storm*, Heade made this yin-yang scheme of a dark circle in a light ground and a circle of light within outer dark even more dramatic.) In the distance to the right, a ship sails into the darkness. In the foreground on the left, six sandpipers go about their business, heedless of the storm about to break. A great wave looms above a boulder on the beach, about to crash against the still sunlit shore. Echoed in a distant rise of rocks, it recalls Hokusai's famous image of a cresting wave.

Beecher's sermons of the time were full of references to coming storms, and art historians have suggested that Beecher saw in Heade's seascape an allegory of the nation's perils. Two months after buying the painting, on December 4, 1859, Beecher preached a sermon in Plymouth Church called "The Storm and Its Lessons." As Sarah Cash writes in *Ominous Hush*, her analysis of Heade's paintings of thunderstorms, Beecher "likened the nation's ultimate salvation from the impending doom of war to the rejuvenating abilities of nature following its seemingly life-threatening moments, such as the coming, breaking, and passing of a thunderstorm."[13] One lesson of the storm, Beecher suggested, was the "rain-drops" of the recent armed raid at Harper's Ferry. John Brown had been executed two days before Beecher's storm sermon.

As the sense of crisis intensified, Beecher continued to brood over his Heade painting, finding new meanings in its mingled light and shadows. Six months before the outbreak of the Civil War, Beecher gave another sermon in which he appeared explicitly to describe his recent purchase, again relating it to the national danger:

> To some it may seem that the light in this picture is too high, and that the background is not dark enough. I do not wish you to think that the background is not dark; for it is. There is excitement. There is brewing mischief. The clouds lie lurid along the Southern horizon. The Caribbean sea that breeds tornadoes and whirlwinds, has heaped up treasures of storms portentous, that seem about to break. Let them break![14]

All wars inspire bombast and propaganda, and the Civil War, compounded by the intimacy of its combatants, was as bombastic as any. As Lincoln said in his second inaugural address, both sides "read the same Bible and pray to the same God, and each invokes His aid against the other." If Beecher's metaphor of national peril was not his alone—both Longfellow and Whittier wrote of the imperiled ship of state—his language was highly influential, especially among the New England congregations that looked to him for insight and comfort.

5.

When Henry Ward Beecher was invited back to his alma mater during the summer of 1862 to address the literary societies of the graduating class at

Amherst College, he knew that he was delivering a funeral oration as well. Frazar Stearns, a first lieutenant in the Massachusetts Infantry and son of the Amherst College president, William Stearns, had been killed on March 14 in the Union victory at New Bern, North Carolina.

Beecher, a graduate of the Amherst class of 1834, was the second commencement speaker on July 9, 1862; the first was Judge Otis P. Lord, class of 1832 and a prominent Whig politician in Massachusetts. The audience, as Josiah Holland wrote in his account in the *Springfield Republican,* was "on tiptoe" in the hope that Lord would say "something connected with the war." Lord "spoke most feelingly," according to Holland, of the death of Frazar Stearns. But the rest of Lord's talk was dry: "the radically conservative . . . view of affairs, was unexpected, and did not elicit any very warm response either in the minds or heels of the hearers." The tepid reaction must have been disappointing to Lord's close friend and legal colleague Edward Dickinson, the treasurer of the college, who held a reception for Lord at his house on Main Street later that day.

Then it was Beecher's turn and the great man did not disappoint. Beecher's speech, in Holland's view, was "the exact counterpart of the forenoon's performance in every particular." Where Judge Lord was "unmagnetic, unpopular; Beecher was eloquent, earnest and right, and carried away the sympathies of the audience with him by storm."[15] "By storm" was an appropriate phrase for the occasion since, as Holland noted, Beecher invoked "the questions of the hour which are passing through a storm and an earthquake: the storm in the North, and the earthquake in the South."

Beecher's talk that afternoon was both personal and poetic; he reminded his college audience of the possibility of a military draft. Frazar Stearns, as everyone there knew, had volunteered for the military. A troubled young man who had traveled as far as Bombay in search of health and some meaning in life, he had enlisted for the war as a kind of desperate solution to his lack of direction. Stearns had been a close friend of Austin Dickinson, the Amherst treasurer's son, who, in contrast to Stearns, had paid the requisite five hundred dollars for a substitute to avoid military service. "Austin is chilled—by Frazer's murder," Emily Dickinson reported in late March. "He says—his Brain keeps saying over 'Frazer is killed'—'Frazer is killed,' just as Father told it—to Him. Two or three words of lead—that dropped so deep, they keep weighing."[16]

Beecher brought a mysterious gift to the college that day. As an undistinguished student at Amherst College, he had had a poor record in his classes but he had excelled in debating clubs, especially in the Athenian Society. Athena's totem was the owl, and that afternoon in July Beecher placed a snowy owl on the podium as he spoke, and later presented the owl to the Athenian Society. Beecher explained that as a student at Amherst he had shot the owl and had it stuffed, and now he wished to return it to the college. His sister Harriet painted the snowy owl. And the college photographer, John Lovell, a close friend of Edward Dickinson, photographed the owl, which became a symbol of Beecher's tie to the school.[17]

6.

The Amherst College graduates listened intently to the dueling speakers, Beecher and Lord. So did the Amherst treasurer's eldest daughter, Emily Dickinson, who referred to her annual attendance at commencement as "smiling at the gravities." At thirty-one, Dickinson had strong literary aspirations of her own. A couple of months earlier, she had sent a handful of poems to a prominent figure in the Boston literary world, Thomas Wentworth Higginson, asking for his advice. Ever since the speakers were announced in the *Springfield Republican* on December 16, 1861, seven months in advance, Dickinson had particularly looked forward to the commencement proceedings.

She knew all the principals personally. Her father hosted Judge Otis Lord—destined to be a very close friend (and more) of Emily Dickinson's. She was also a friend of the editor Josiah Holland, and would have found his contrast of the two speakers of great interest. And Beecher too was a family friend. Edward Dickinson's sister, Lucretia, had married Asa Bullard. Bullard's sister, Eunice, had married Henry Ward Beecher. So Beecher and Dickinson were almost brothers-in-law, and had known each other since they were young and ambitious, when their fathers had served together at Lane Seminary in Ohio.

For Emily Dickinson on that July afternoon, Otis Lord and Henry Ward Beecher represented two different kinds of Amherst man. She commemorated the contrast in a poem, in which the two friends of her father, Judge Lord and the owl hunter, became one:

> *The Judge is like the Owl—*
> *I've heard my Father tell—*
> *And Owls do build in Oaks—*
> *So here's an Amber Sill—*
>
> *That slanted in my Path—*
> *When going to the Barn—*
> *And if it serve You for a House—*
> *Itself is not in vain—*
>
> *About the price—'tis small—*
> *I only ask a Tune*
> *At Midnight—Let the Owl select*
> *His favorite Refrain.*[18]

Dickinson imagines herself providing a suitable house for this owl-judge. All she asks in return is a song: "Let the owl select his favorite refrain." Perhaps the poem represents a wish: that the qualities of the sober judge and the charismatic preacher might be combined to make an ideal man.

Though the two men were roughly the same age, they seemed to look in opposite directions. Lord was old school in style and conviction, a committed Calvinist and Whig bent on prosaic moderation, the perfect temperament for a judge. Beecher by contrast seemed of a younger, more imaginative generation, moving his flock by lyrical outbursts. Their diverging speeches reinforced the impression. As Josiah Holland noted, Lord called for a return to the better values of the past while Beecher stressed the need for adjustment to new realities.

In their respective dealings with the Dickinsons of Amherst, Lord and Beecher played their opposing parts to perfection. One summer day, when Judge Lord was dining at the home of Emily Dickinson's brother, Austin, during the commencement season, the conversation had turned to New England hymns. Judge Lord asked if anyone at the table remembered a particularly grim hymn that began with the lines

> *My thoughts on awful subjects roll*
> *Damnation and the dead*.

Nobody did. Judge Lord laid down his fork and, as Austin's wife, Susan, recalled, "made himself a little more stiff and erect behind his old-fashioned silk stock than usual, if that were possible, and recited with an energy worthy of himself and his subject, the whole hymn. There was really a horrible grandeur about it."[19]

It was the kind of grandeur, all death and damnation, that Beecher had set his whole career against. Beecher stood for poetry and passion, love and hope. When he was invited, with his colleague, friend, and fellow Amherst graduate, Reverend Richard Salter Storrs Jr., to the same house, Beecher made a very different impression. When he entered the parlor, as Susan Dickinson reported, he "made for a large vase of red lilies in the fireplace, stooping over them as if to caress them in his admiration." What followed was pure Beecher, as the red lilies took over the evening:

> Their beauty seemed to charm all the company, quite making the subject matter of conversation for the first part of the dinner. Someone spoke of the Syrian lilies in the illustration of our Lord, then of Julia Ward Howe's "Battle Hymn," "Christ was born among the lilies," then of the rare beauty and picturesqueness of this whole family of plants. The talk was very informal, but brilliant.
>
> As we strolled back to the parlor afterward, the gentlemen began to smoke, and Beecher grew very sober and tender in his mood, and fell to talking of our emotional natures, their responsiveness to slight external causes, and associations quite indefinable. For instance, he said, "When I was a boy in Litchfield I used to sit in the door of my home, listening to the wind in the branches over my head, looking up at the sky. I could hear the faint hum of the spinning wheel in the garret, and a tender sadness seemed to gather about me and melt my nature 'till I cried like a grieved child. What was it?"
>
> And we all sat hushed and softened by the great man.

All except Judge Lord, that is, for, as Susan Dickinson noted, Judge Lord "never seem[ed] to coalesce with these men, although he was often here with them." His individuality, she added, was "so bristling, his conviction that he alone was the embodiment of the law, as given on Sinai, so entire, his suspicion of all but himself so deeply founded in the rock bed of old conservative Whig tenacities, not to say obstinacies, that he was an anxious element to his hostess in a group of progressive and mellow although staunch men and women."

THESE, THEN, WERE the two men, the dour judge and the flowery preacher, whom Emily Dickinson listened to on that July day in 1862. But that afternoon, it was Beecher who spoke most deeply to her. Dickinson was particularly struck by Beecher's phrase about "an earthquake in the South."

She worked it into one of her poems, which characteristically raises doubts about whether Jesus hears our human pleas:

> At least—to pray—is left—is left—
> Oh Jesus—in the Air—
> I know not which thy chamber is—
> I'm knocking—everywhere—
>
> Thou settest Earthquake in the South—
> And Maelstrom, in the Sea—
> Say, Jesus Christ of Nazareth—
> Hast thou no Arm for Me?[20]

The image of a row of anonymous rooms, a sort of heavenly hotel, in which Jesus lives unnoticed is particularly striking. As a poem about the Civil War and the coming Southern earthquake, it is as oblique as Heade's storm painting or Beecher's evocation of "the storm and its meanings."

7.

Emily Dickinson's sense of recognition as she listened to Beecher inspired her to make her own distinctive contribution to the preservation of the Union. During late February and March of 1864, three poems by Emily Dickinson appeared anonymously in a Brooklyn-based newspaper called the *Drum Beat*, edited by Beecher's friend and collaborator Reverend Richard Salter Storrs, Beecher's dinner partner at the home of Austin and Susan Dickinson. The short-lived *Drum Beat* was conceived for the purpose of raising money for medical supplies and care for the Union Army, and Dickinson's poems, as Karen Dandurand has argued, "must be seen as her contribution to the Union cause."[21]

None of the three poems—"Blazing in gold, and quenching in purple" (titled "Sunset" in the *Drum Beat*), "Flowers—well, if anybody" ("Flowers"), and "These are the days when birds come back" ("October")— is in any obvious way a war poem. The sun, compared to a leopard in the first poem, does lay "her spotted face to die" on the horizon. And the famous poem "These are the days when birds come back," with its gorgeous evocation of Indian summer, does make implicit reference to the winter about to descend: "Oh, fraud that cannot cheat the bee!/ Almost thy plausibility/ Induces my belief."[22]

But it is the third poem, the little-known meditation on flowers, that seems most in tune with Beecher's temperament. Here is how the poem appeared in the March 2 issue of the *Drum Beat:*

> *Flowers—well, if anybody*
> *Can the ecstasy define,*
> *Half a transport, half a trouble,*
> *With which floods so contra flow,*
> *I will give him all the Daisies,*
> *Which upon the hill-side blow!*
>
> *Too much pathos in their faces,*
> *For a simple breast like mine!*
> *Butterflies from San Domingo,*
> *Cruising round the purple line,*
> *Have a system of esthetics*
> *Far superior to mine!*[23]

The poem makes a fanciful connection between flowers and floods, as though the word *flower* comes from the verb "to flow." Dickinson suggests that to define the ecstasy and pain ("Half a transport, half a trouble") of flowers is as difficult as to find the Fountain of Youth, which Ponce de León searched for in Florida, the "florid" land of flowers. Only the true connoisseurs of flowers, the "Butterflies from San Domingo,/ Cruising round the purple line," can really understand the "system of esthetics" of flowers. San Domingo, tropical land of slavery and rum as well as of flowers and butterflies, had a mixed appeal: "half a transport, half a trouble." It is a perfect phrase for Emily Dickinson's own imaginative realm, as well as for the next vivid period of her life.

Chapter Four

TRISTES TROPIQUES

What childishness is it that while there's a breath of life
in our bodies, we are determined to rush
to see the sun the other way around?
The tiniest green hummingbird in the world?

                                    ELIZABETH BISHOP

I.

ON SEPTEMBER 2, 1863, at the height of the Civil War, Martin Johnson Heade traveled to Brazil in search of hummingbirds. Heade took a passionate interest in the uncertain progress of the war. And yet, two months after the dramatic Union victory at Gettysburg, Heade—healthy and able-bodied at forty-four, a crack shot with rifle or pistol, and a staunch anti-slavery man—boarded the steamer *Golden City* in New York bound for Rio de Janeiro. Before his departure, Heade had publicized his trip among the Boston newspapers. On August 12, amid news of Robert E. Lee's retreat toward Richmond, the *Boston Transcript* reported that Heade, "the artist so well known for his landscapes . . . is about to visit Brazil, to paint those winged jewels, the hummingbirds, in all their variety of life as found beneath the tropics." Heade told the reporter of his ambition "to prepare in London or Paris a large and elegant Album on these wonderful little creatures, got up in the highest style of art," thus fulfilling "the dream of his boyhood."[1]

Heade first painted a hummingbird in 1862, the year before he traveled to Brazil, but his obsession began much earlier. "From early boyhood," he wrote, "I have been almost a monomaniac on hummingbirds."[2] Heade described his fixation as a sort of virus against which, in his dazed passivity, he could offer no resistance: "A few years after my appearance in this breathing world, I was attacked by the all-absorbing hummingbird craze and it has never left me since."[3] Heade found that he was not alone in succumbing to the craze, and he intended to build a big career around his superior knowledge of hummingbirds. No one could be an expert on their habits and habitats without traveling to South America, where the vast majority of species made their home.

It is doubtful that Heade traveled to Brazil to avoid the war. Like his friend Henry Ward Beecher, who traveled to London the same year and made the case for abolition among the British working class, Heade may well have considered himself a sort of roving envoy for the Union cause. During his six months in Brazil, he spoke of the war to anyone who would listen, including the Emperor Dom Pedro II. Besides, a passion for hummingbirds was hardly unknown among antislavery activists such as Beecher and Higginson, for whom the birds often served as emblems of freedom.

The *Golden City* arrived in the harbor of Rio de Janeiro on the evening of September 20, completing the passage, Heade noted in his travel journal, "in less than 19 days." The journal, written in a careful and legible hand, reads more like an extended letter for a general audience than a private horde of impressions. Heade evidently hoped that it might be published, perhaps in conjunction with his elegant album of hummingbirds, which he planned to call "Gems of Brazil." Previous American travelers had compared the beautiful harbor at Rio de Janeiro to the Bay of Naples. Others, including the Swiss-born Louis Agassiz, likened it to Lake Geneva near the Castle of Chillon, celebrated in a famous poem by Byron.

Heade made it clear from the opening pages of his journal that he was looking for another Italy. His journal begins on a grand tour note:

One is forcibly reminded, on entering the harbor of Rio Janeiro at night, of the view from the Pincian hill at Rome during an illumination of St. Peter's . . . There is an almost unbroken line of lights along the water, and an occasional thickly studded hill appears in the distance like an illuminated dome. In fact, the harbor is wonderfully beautiful by day or night.[4]

The comparison to Italy, where Heade had traveled in 1848, runs throughout his journal, as he tries to persuade his reader (and himself) that Rio offers sights and experiences analogous to Rome.

As he ventured out from his modest hotel in town, he was immediately disillusioned. Amid the squalor of Rio during his first days there, he felt "a crushing disappointment on mingling in the unsavory streets with the miserable race that peoples them." The brute fact of slavery, still legal in Brazil, struck Heade at every turn. "The whole city literally swarms with the raggedest and vilest looking set of slaves." As for more prosperous blacks, he decided that Brazil was "a very paradise for negroes—they can be as fancy as they please with impunity." As though to prove that his disgust was more patriotic than racist, Heade befriended an American slave, on shore leave from a Southern ship, who shared his scorn for the native population. "I asked one American negro whether this was not just the country for his color—'Oh, no,' says he. 'I'm very anxious to get back again: There's no society here: I have to associate with people that I wouldn't look at in the United States.'"

People, however, were not Heade's main quarry in Brazil. The whole point of his pilgrimage was to follow hummingbirds to their source, and to experience them in the wild. He knew that the English naturalist John Gould, the world's authority on hummingbirds and the leading artist in portraying them, had never been to South America. In sharp contrast to Gould, Heade aspired to be the Audubon of hummingbirds, the intrepid hunter-adventurer who would brave the wilds to learn the secrets of his prey. He brought his gun to Brazil but rarely used it; the hunting, he reported, was disappointing. But he doesn't seem to have made much effort in this regard, preferring to let others do the hunting for him. A few species could be found in the neighboring jungle, but Rio was as much a trading post for the lucrative bird skins as a base for hunting excursions. Indians brought their treasures from afar: hummingbirds to decorate ladies' hats in London and Paris, Boston and Newport. And each day Heade went to the market to see the day's catch.

2.

Heade's intimate experience of the natural world started early. He was born on August 11, 1819, the oldest of nine children, in the tiny hamlet of Lumberville, Pennsylvania, amid the Quaker farms and villages of rural Bucks County. His father, Joseph Cowell Heed (like Melville, Heade added a final "e" to his name, along with an "a," to make it look more aristocratic), was a farmer who supplemented his income by making guns and operating a sawmill. Heade's childhood was the river-centered world of Mark Twain, a friend and patron in later life. He attended the Eight Square School in Lumberville, named for its striking octagonal design, but his real life was outdoors. Heade wrote that as a child, from age five to fifteen, he "ran loose around the Pennsylvania hills along the banks of the Delaware River."

Heade particularly liked the disheveled farms of the neighborhood, "nearly every fence and old stone wall being hedged with bushes and briers, that harbored myriads of quail, while partridges could be flushed by the score in every thicket."[5] In later years, as railroads and canals encroached on this idyllic landscape and "took every vestige of its beauty away forever," Heade remembered "the glorious shooting of those days

[and] the finest fishing that a modest man would wish for." All his long life Heade remained the kind of conservationist who wants to preserve enough birds to shoot at.

Heade's mother, Sarah, died in 1837, and his father married a woman whose family ran one of the Bucks County newspapers. Around the same time, Heade began a two-year apprenticeship with the Quaker painter and preacher Edward Hicks, whose younger cousin, the painter Thomas Hicks, was also employed in the operation. Edward Hicks painted signs and coaches with a flair not often associated with Quaker simplicity, but he is best known for his series of paintings titled "The Peaceable Kingdom." These unschooled and visionary paintings of the harmonious world of nature take their inspiration from chapter 11 of Isaiah, and especially the prophecy contained in the familiar sixth verse:

> The wolf also shall dwell with the lamb, and the leopard shall lie down
> with the kid; and the calf and the young lion and the fatling together; and
> a little child shall lead them.

Sometimes, Hicks painted a miniature William Penn signing a treaty with American Indians in the distant background, another scene of conflict averted. He surrounded these stylized scenes of harmony in nature with borders on which he printed, as on a sign, the biblical prophecy.[6]

As a preacher for the Society of Friends (the preferred designation of the Quakers), Edward Hicks was closely allied with his cousin Elias Hicks, the Long Island mystic and leader of a schismatic faction within the Quaker community. The increasingly bitter division reached a crisis in 1827, when Elias Hicks was evicted or "written out" of the Philadelphia Friends Meeting. The Hicksite faction, as it was called, held that Quakerism as practiced in urban Philadelphia had lost its anchorage in the bedrock trust in the "inner light." The Hicksite Quakers, most of whom were small-time farmers without servants, were firmly committed to the immediate emancipation of the slaves, while the "orthodox" Quakers in Philadelphia, with significant financial ties to the South, favored a more gradual approach to abolition. The mystical and activist strain in Quakerism appealed to the young Walt Whitman, two months Heade's senior. Growing up in Brooklyn in a Quaker family, Whitman heard Elias Hicks preach and was deeply moved. He felt a "noiseless secret ecstasy" in Hicks's magnetic presence, and likened Hicks's improvised sermons to "the lightning flash in a storm at night."[7]

While Heade's mature paintings have a mystical aura, and may well have drawn inspiration from the mood in the Hicks household, Heade himself was not a Quaker, and enjoyed carrying his gun among his peaceable neighbors. In a reminiscence presumably drawn from his years with Hicks, Heade wryly recalled an amusing misunderstanding:

> When I was a boy I was at the house of an old Pennsylvania Quaker, and even then the shooting fever was strong, and I had my gun with me, which stood, when not in use, in one corner of the sitting room.
>
> One day the good old lady came gently up to me, and pointing toward that corner said: "If thee don't take that thing away I'll cut the spout off."[8]

Heade adopted the persona of the skeptical observer on the fringes of society, unafraid to "spout off" with opinions deemed unacceptable to "gentle" folk.

As a young man, Heade was drawn to both painting and writing; with a bit more encouragement and talent he might have become a professional poet. In 1839, when Heade turned twenty, the great Quaker poet John Greenleaf Whittier lived in the Lumberville area, working closely with William Lloyd Garrison and crusading for the abolition of slavery. A tall and lanky bachelor blessed with Byronic good looks, "Greenleaf," as he was known to his intimates, was a magnetic presence. Heade and his friends "were seriously affected by Whittier's short stay here," a local historian reported. "They all began to write poetry."[9] A portrait of Heade painted by Thomas Hicks around this time shows a well-fed and idealistic young man, with a large white dome of a forehead and already receding hair—the yearning young poet with eyebrows slightly lifted and soft eyes tilted upward.

At this early stage in his career, Heade drew inspiration from Hicks and Whittier, the most significant Quaker painter of his time and the most significant Quaker poet. Under his pen name, "Didymus" (the "Doubting Thomas" of the New Testament), Heade adopted the traditional poetic forms and romantic phrasing of Whittier's early poetry. He published a few poems in the Brooklyn *Daily Advertiser* in 1845, in one of which, "My Bonnie Brunette," he described a woman

> *With a delicate cheek, and a sweet, cherry lip*
> *Where a bee might in luxury linger and sip.*

In 1848, Heade made the obligatory young artist's pilgrimage to Italy, arriving just in time to experience the nationalist uprising in Rome. He painted picturesque newsboys hawking the news of the Roman Republic, and paintings inspired by Shelley. "Heade was a highly political person," Theodore Stebbins notes, "whose views blended social conservatism, economic populism, and a defiant individualism—libertarianism, in today's terms."[10] Returning to the United States, he continued his travels, settling briefly in St. Louis and Chicago before returning to the East Coast. In 1852, he published two poems on the death of Henry Clay, the Kentucky senator and antislavery founder of the Whig party who was at the time a hero of both Whittier and Heade. One of the poems begins: "A glorious orb has fallen! But fallen like the sun/ Who sinks to rest in splendor when his daily task is done."

What Heade learned from his other Quaker mentor, Edward Hicks, is less obvious than his debt to Whittier. A "folk" aspect lingers in some of his early portraits and seascapes, especially in his depiction of clawlike breaking waves and ghostly ships on the horizon. The art historian Barbara Novak notes "a certain quirkiness in his work, a very late trace of the gothic imagination."[11] Like Hicks, Heade tended to paint his pictures in series. But there is nothing conventional about the paintings Heade began producing during the late 1850s: his inlet coves darkened by impending thunderstorms; his peaceful marshes with their serpentine waterways and groomed haystacks;

and then, beginning during the Civil War, his intensely rendered hummingbirds.

3 .

Heade's love affair with salt marshes began in 1862, the year he first visited
Newburyport, Massachusetts, and painted his first hummingbird. He came
to Newburyport as the guest of Reverend James Cooley Fletcher, a liberal
Congregational minister, originally from Indiana, whom he met, apparently, through Fletcher's close friend and neighbor Whittier.[12] Fletcher, who
divided his time between his picturesque stone house on the Merrimack
River and Brazil, introduced Heade to the two landscapes—coastal marshland and tropical rainforest—that most deeply affected his art.

Fletcher was part of an extraordinary cultural network of writers and
artists radiating from the abolitionist stronghold of Newburyport. Whittier
and Garrison were central figures with national reputations. Then there was
Thomas Wentworth Higginson, along with his protégées Harriet Prescott
Spofford and, more distantly, Emily Dickinson. Slightly later, the writer
Celia Thaxter and the painter Childe Hassam adopted the region.[13] Fletcher's
stone house, which Spofford bought after the Civil War and named
"Hawkeswood," became a gathering place for pilgrims from all over. "He
who desires to see a meadow in perfection, full of emerald and golden tints
and claret shadows, withdrawing into distance till lost in the sparkle of the
sea, must seek it here," Spofford wrote, "where Heade found material for his
dainty marsh and meadow views."[14]

What Heade found in the salt marshes near Newburyport was a peaceable kingdom of his own. Though tiny cows and farmers are visible in the
distant background of most of these paintings, Heade's real subject is the
shifting light on the empty meadows and tidal rivulets. No one among his
contemporaries painted anything like these pictures almost without subjects.

One would have to go to Thoreau, who claimed to "derive more of my subsistence from the swamps which surround my native town than from the cultivated gardens in the village," or to Whitman, who titled a section of his 1860 *Leaves of Grass* "Calamus," a stiff grass from the swampy meadows, to find a kindred pleasure in these seemingly desolate places.[15]

With a visual intensity that rivals Monet, though with a precision far from the painterly expressiveness of Impressionism, Heade returned again and again to his simple repertory of forms: meadow, haystack, river, horizon, cloud, and light. Eventually he painted more than a hundred of such scenes, almost always in the same severely horizontal format, twice as long as wide, to emphasize the lateral extent of the marshes. An excellent example is *Summer Showers* in the Brooklyn Museum, probably painted during the 1860s, when Heade's impression of Newburyport was still fresh. Everything about the picture suggests the fleeting and evanescent effects of summer weather. The fringe of thunderclouds that hangs like a dark curtain from the upper edge of the painting will shed its rain and move on, leaving the marshland to the bright summer light that floods the background. This outer scene

Heade, Summer Showers *(Brooklyn Museum of Art)*

seems to correspond to a private, interior landscape of shifting moods and feelings.

Having introduced Heade to these meditative meadows in 1862, Reverend Fletcher opened Heade's perspective to Brazil as well. Fletcher, who had first served as a missionary in Brazil and then headed the American delegation there, was a leading authority on Brazil and had published a popular guidebook to the country. Fletcher knew of Heade's passion for hummingbirds, and could assure him that Brazil was just the place to follow them to their haunts. In his book *Brazil and the Brazilians*, Fletcher reported: "Everywhere throughout Brazil this little winged gem, in many varieties, abounds, while in North America, from Mexico to the fifty-seventh degree of latitude, it is said that there is but one species of the hummingbird." He added, as though writing to an audience unfamiliar with hummingbirds, "The males are among the most belligerent of creatures,—rarely meeting without having terrible combats."[16] These observations were accompanied by engravings of a long-tailed hummingbird and a hummingbird nest.

An intrepid traveler, Fletcher had made an expedition up the Amazon to collect specimens for the Harvard naturalist Louis Agassiz. Agassiz asked Heade in turn whether he might bring back some hummingbird eggs from Brazil. At the time Heade came to know him, Fletcher continued to push for better ties between Brazil and the United States, and apparently felt that Heade's project of painting Brazilian hummingbirds would aid in the mutual understanding of the two countries. Fletcher supplied Heade with letters of introduction to the emperor and other high-ranking officials.

4 ·

On October 18, barely a month into his stay, Heade was returning to Rio de Janeiro by ferry from church services nearby. Suddenly, someone on the boat shouted, "Hello! Here's Fletcher." To Heade's delighted surprise, Reverend Fletcher himself had made an unannounced visit to Brazil, with plans to stay only a week. Fletcher now assumed the burden of persuading Heade that Brazil, despite initial appearances, was a civilized place. "Fletcher has been taking great pains to eradicate the unfavorable impressions I've received of the Brasilians," Heade noted in his journal on October 23, " . . . and I must admit that there are noble specimens of humanity even in this country." He was particularly impressed with Francesco Baston, whom he called the "Henry Clay of Brasil," an allusion to Baston's commitment to innovation in travel and industry, reminiscent of Whig policy in the United States. "He is the leading advocate for steam communication with America— north." Heade added that Baston "had seen a couple of my pictures, and immediately wrote a glowing notice of them."

Despite the brevity of his sojourn in Rio, Fletcher made a point of personally introducing Heade to the Emperor Pedro II. Heade was lucky in the timing of his visit. After winning its independence from Portugal in 1822, amid the chaos of the Napoleonic wars, the fledgling nation-state had faced an uncertain future. With its plantation economy based on African and Indian slavery, its far-flung colonial communities fanned out along the coast, and its largely unexplored expanses of rainforest and river, the country posed extraordinary challenges to a young ruler. Grandson of the king of Portugal, Pedro II was fourteen when he assumed the throne. But under the leadership of this progressive and energetic emperor, the young nation of Brazil had, by the winter of 1863, experienced a decade of prosperity and peace.

By temperament, Pedro II was well suited to the task. An avid reader and amateur scholar, with a passion for science, poetry, and art, Dom Pedro was never happier than when he was surrounded by his books. He followed developments in French technical journals, seeking to apply them to his country. He was an amateur photographer in the early days of the daguerreotype, and an eager astronomer. He passionately admired the poets and thinkers of New England, and had translated poems by Longfellow and Whittier into Portuguese. Dom Pedro liked opera as well; a bit of a playboy himself, he regretted missing a performance of Mozart's *Don Giovanni* in Paris in 1866.[17]

During the decade before Heade's arrival, Pedro II unleashed his considerable energies in a sustained effort to modernize his young nation. He had initiated the construction of railroads, had made a start in harnessing electrical power, and was pursuing, with Fletcher's help, the possibility of regular steamboat service to New York. Two projects in particular made the moment of Heade's arrival ripe for Pedro II's curiosity. The first was a comprehensive scientific survey of the Brazilian interior. A team of researchers—a geologist, an ethnographer, and so on—was detailed to the outback in 1856. Such scientific expeditions were common during the nineteenth century; Pedro's in particular was designed "both to assert Brazil's legitimacy as part of the civilized world and to make known in scientific and cultural terms a region of the country about which the regime at Rio de Janeiro was largely ignorant."[18] When the results of the disorganized commission, which explored the remote northern province of Ceará from 1859 to 1861, were dismissed in the press as "the butterfly commission," Pedro II was eager for foreign expertise. He embraced Louis Agassiz's journey up the Amazon in 1865 (with the young William James onboard).[19] Heade's promise to collect and portray all the hummingbirds of Brazil appealed to the emperor's scientific, artistic, and nationalistic instincts.

The other issue on Pedro II's mind in late 1863 was slavery, an institution that he regarded as a regrettable vestige of Brazil's colonial past and an impediment to its progressive future. Personally opposed to slavery, he hoped that the advent of foreign immigrant labor would hasten its abolition. Brazilian officials avidly followed the progress of the American Civil War. They knew that with the Emancipation Proclamation and the Union victories at Vicksburg and Gettysburg, Brazil would likely emerge as the only independent country in the Western hemisphere to countenance legalized slavery.

On January 14, 1864, during Heade's residence in Brazil, Pedro II wrote to the head of his cabinet that "Events in the American Union require us to think about the future of slavery in Brazil"; the emperor proposed a measure to free the children of slaves and thus bring about a gradual but certain abolition of slavery.[20] Whittier greeted the news with a poem in *The Atlantic Monthly* titled "Freedom in Brazil," addressing Pedro II as "thou, great-hearted ruler," and including these ringing words:

> *Crowned doubly by man's blessing and God's grace,*
> > *Thy future is secure;*
> *Who frees a people makes his statue's place*
> > *In Time's Valhalla sure.*[21]

Whittier's celebration proved premature, however, as conservative landowners vigorously opposed any change in policy. Slavery was not abolished in Brazil until 1888, and abolition cost Pedro II his rule.

AT THE TIME of his surprise arrival in October, Fletcher wrote to Pedro II asking if he might bring his friend Heade to meet him. An invitation from the emperor quickly followed. "Being of rather an obliging disposition, I concluded to go," Heade wrote in his journal. "So I got myself white kidded and clerically cravatted, and we were at the door of the shanty half an hour before the time." The emperor was a large man, six feet four, with a full beard and alert, intelligent eyes; his sedentary life and sweet tooth accounted for his generous paunch.[22] He liked to receive visitors in his library, three rooms in the royal palace (the "shanty" of Heade's journal entry) crammed to capacity with books, maps, photographs, engravings, and journals.

Heade brought two gifts for the emperor, presumably at Fletcher's prompting: a handsome copy of Longfellow's poetry and a photograph of F.O.C. Darley's *Charge into Fredericksburg*. But the most important things Heade brought for the emperor's perusal were a few of his own paintings. Pedro II "expressed great delight," according to Heade, "on seeing two of my unfinished 'oiseau mouches'"—French for "fly-birds" or "humming-birds."[23]

On January 10, when Heade had finished a dozen of his hummingbird paintings, Heade and the emperor met again. This time they had what Heade called "a very agreeable and satisfactory interview." The emperor pledged his support to Heade's projected album of Brazilian hummingbirds, to be published "under his royal patronage." The emperor "smiled *so* sweetly," according to Heade, "that its insinuating influence is 'still so gently o'er me stealing.'" The quotation from Bellini's *La Sonnambula* suggests that the two men shared an interest in opera as well as hummingbirds. The emperor brought his two daughters to attend the annual exhibition of the Academy of Fine Arts in Rio on February 14, Valentine's Day, where Heade showed several of his paintings, including dramatic harbor views of Rio. One of these, now at the National Gallery in Washington, is remarkable for its lack of exotic touches. Its bare level beach and level sea, with small waves breaking over rocks, could be almost anywhere. No palms or banana trees rise in the background, but just an unfurling of smoke from a distant chimney.

By that time, Heade, like most of Brazilian elite society, had shifted his major base of operations to the winter capital of Petrópolis, in the mountains north of Rio. This little town had been founded in emulation of European cities, with an imperial palace surrounded by buildings dedicated to the arts and sciences. German immigrants from the Rhineland were encouraged to settle in the area, giving it a European flavor. From December to April, when yellow fever was a danger in Rio, the emperor and his family spent the southern summer in Petrópolis.

James Watson Webb, an American journalist and official at the United States Mission in Brazil, and his young wife had befriended Heade two days after his arrival, and invited him to visit their estate in Petrópolis. General Webb was one of those talented scoundrels whose escapades so delighted Mark Twain. A spokesman for the conservative wing of the Whig party, which he claimed to have named, he had battled against the more liberal faction of Samuel Bowles (editor of the *Springfield Republican* and a close friend of Emily Dickinson) and Edward Dickinson. As a reward for his efforts, Webb had been named minister to Brazil in June 1861, after refusing to be "exiled" to Turkey on a low salary. Accustomed to the political and financial hurly-burly of his native New York City, where he had edited two newspapers and vigorously backed the interests of William Seward, Lincoln's secretary of state, Webb went to Brazil in the fall of 1861, with a view to making the Amazon a central piece of American foreign policy, and enriching himself along the way.

This he planned to do in three ways. First, he wished to engage Confederate warships in Brazilian harbors, and contest at every turn official Brazilian neutrality in the Civil War. Second, he proposed to "open" the Amazon to American navigation and commercial development. And third, he suggested a solution to the problem of freed slaves: colonize the "empty" Amazon with them. Webb spent much of 1862 urging on a reluctant Brazil and Washington his "dream to settle . . . four million American Negroes in the Amazon."[24] His attempt, in conjunction with Fletcher, to establish a steamship line connecting New York and Brazil was met with more encouragement until it was discovered that Webb proposed to put his own son in charge of it. As Lincoln wrote: "The expectation of the minister to make himself the beneficiary of the project was entirely indefensible."[25]

But it was the much younger Mrs. Webb, who urged Heade to join her in "botanizing" forays in the mountains, with whom Heade spent more intimate moments. At first, consumed with his hummingbirds, he declined. "Although it might be a very nice sort of thing for an old bachelor to ramble through the woods with the pretty, young wife of an old minister, I have to say 'business first, etc.'" Eventually, having made some progress in his painting, Heade accepted Laura Webb's invitation. Her diary records several visits, but Heade himself drew a curtain in his journal on the precise nature of their activities.[26]

As his social life blossomed, Heade found other pleasures as well. The delicious white figs reminded him of Italy and he swam in the harbor every day, finding Rio "as cool as Newport in the summer." The surf, he noted, "rolling lazily up the sand makes a refreshing sort of music for us that I had not brought within my calculations of a tropic life." He collected butterflies and flowers. "There is probably no country," he wrote, "where a person interested in ornithology, entomology, botany, mineralogy or beautiful scenery could find so much to keep him entertained."

Heade had enjoyed the Carnival in Rome, and looked forward to its counterpart in Rio, when the poor descended from the settlements above the city to dance and play music in the narrow streets. But for Heade, Brazil again fell short of Italy. Its Carnival, he sniffed, would disgust "every decent and civilized person." The raw sexuality of the festivities disturbed him. "In Rome it is conducted decently," he noted, "and some brain is displayed in costumes, etc. But here their low, beastly nature is exhibited . . . I saw exhibitions that would have sent them before the grand jury of any respectable country, but no notice whatever was taken here."

Carnival was to have filled a lively chapter of his travel journal, as the Roman Carnival had enchanted Goethe and so many other visitors to Rome. As his hopes for a publishable travel account faded amid what he called "this earthly 'hades,'" Heade's journal slowly devolved into a fragmentary repository of notes and stray impressions, making the texture of his days elusive. "The Journal is a farce," he concluded; having once "formed a resolution never to attempt keeping another journal," he regretted having strayed from his resolve. About the only thing he found to admire in Brazil was the café au lait, "being so unlike the common vegetable concoction called coffee in our own country."

5.

The paintings of hummingbirds that resulted from Heade's Brazilian campaign were essentially portraits, and formal portraits at that. It is as though these colorful birds entered a studio in their Sunday best and asked to be painted as respectable loving couples. Their courtship is staid; they survey their nests like proud homeowners, sharing the pleasures of parenthood. (Like Thomas Wentworth Higginson, Heade refused to believe that male hummingbirds—those miniature fighters and Don Juans—have nothing to do with protecting the nest or feeding the young.[27]) These hummingbirds are stuffed shirts—they were, in fact, stuffed birds—and exhibit the pre–Civil War proprieties that Heade wished upon the Brazilian populace. The "Gems of Brazil" are not, by any measure, Heade's greatest paintings of hummingbirds; those would have to wait another half dozen years, as the experience of the tropics gestated in his memory.

Heade, Amethyst Woodstar *(anonymous collection)*

Americans liked to believe that Brazil was a sort of Garden of Eden, where the origins of life were on display. Frederic Church's great canvases of the "Heart of the Andes," with their tangled vegetation illuminated by sublime sunlight, confirmed the equation. But Heade's Eden of 1864 is orderly and well behaved. The concept of nature on display in "Gems of Brazil" was not the chaos of creation but rather the multiplicity of fixed species. Each species was carefully cataloged, male and female as God created them, perched or hovering protectively over their nests, with nestled eggs or hungry little birds completing the domestic scene. Distinguishing marks such as ear tufts or unfurled tail feathers are highlighted for easy recognition. The best of these paintings have a flat, friezelike decorative decorum; the ornithological information about the birds is presented efficiently and pleasingly. For most of these paintings, Heade borrowed a formula familiar from Audubon and classical Chinese bird-and-flower painting, in which one bird is displayed in profile while the other is presented frontally with the head turned.[28]

In *Amethyst Woodstar,* Heade depicted the species he considered "the most fairy-like in form" of all hummingbirds, among a looping pattern of heart-shaped leaves and tendrils, like a trellis on which the couple has come to roost and flirt, while a pair of baby birds look on from the safety of their nest below.[29] Such works are essentially updated versions of Edward Hicks's "Peaceable Kingdom," the lessons learned applied to a more accurate and naturalistic frieze of God's creatures at peace.

If in one respect Heade failed in his aspirations to follow Audubon's lead, in others he was faithful to his purpose. He passed up the opportunity to travel up the Amazon in search of hummingbirds, or venture into the rainforest toward Ecuador and Peru, where so many of the world's hummingbirds live. What Heade did manage to do, however, was to imagine hummingbirds in their relation to other forms of life. Just as Audubon had rejected the traditional eighteenth-century mode of identifying and representing birds, with each bird laid out in stiff profile to show its distinguishing marks, Heade aimed for a more naturalistic placement of birds in their environment.[30] In this approach to birds, which anticipates our later commitment to environmental and ecological interests, Audubon and Heade were preceded by the naturalist and explorer William Bartram.

6.

It is a striking fact, and difficult to dismiss as pure coincidence, that three of the greatest bird painters in the history of American art—William Bartram, John James Audubon, and Martin Heade—came of age in Quaker settlements on the outskirts of Philadelphia. Of these, only Bartram was a Quaker; Audubon and Heade, by contrast, were avid sportsmen who were happiest when shooting birds in woodlands or wetlands. And yet, all three artists adopted some of the reverential and visionary attitude of the Quakers toward the natural world. That attitude played out differently among these three extremely distinctive and even eccentric painters.

While he carried a gun into the wilderness regions of Florida and the Carolinas during the Colonial conflicts of the 1770s, Bartram was a pacifist who extolled the virtues of the rattlesnake and deplored the senseless murder of these majestic animals. As a young man, Bartram had joined his father on a journey into northeastern Florida, on the banks of the St. Johns River—the same region that Thomas Wentworth Higginson, Harriet Beecher Stowe, and Martin Johnson Heade would come to know so well.

The Bartrams were among a party sent to draw up a treaty between the Colonial government and the Creek Nation. Surprised in the woods by a six-foot rattlesnake, William Bartram killed it on impulse, and the American governor of the province served it up for dinner. Bartram found he could not swallow it and regretted having killed the snake. "He certainly had it in his power to kill me almost instantly," he reflected, "and I make no doubt but that he was conscious of it. I promised myself that I would never again be accessory to the death of a rattle snake, which promise I have invariably kept to."[31] One sees in these proceedings the same combination of themes that later preoccupied Hicks: the peace treaties between potentially dangerous Indians and white settlers on the one hand and peaceable relations with potentially dangerous animals on the other.

Bartram's many paintings of snakes, alone or among other animals, have a reverential mood. In one remarkable and visionary painting, Bartram portrays a whole interlocking system of peculiar plants and animals. Behind an arrowhead fern, a snake's jaws ingest a hapless frog. Two snails, a large lotus seedpod, and a couple of bricks occupy the foreground. Surveying the proceedings from above are an airborne dragonfly and, perched in the uppermost branch of a flowering shrub, a ruby-throated hummingbird.[32]

There is a paradox in Bartram's paintings that helps explain their beguiling mystery. Each plant and animal is rendered with an almost taxonomical attention to detail, the result of both Bartram's own intense pleasure in correct identification and his contract with English botanists to collect new species for their greenhouses and gardens. At the same time, however, Bartram arranged his curious finds in patterns of his own devising: an orchid unfurling over an Indian pipe; another ruby-throated hummingbird sipping a flax blossom, his tail feathers just out of reach of the claws of a Chesapeake stone crab.

The naturalistic accuracy, the sense of design, and the wit of Bartram's paintings resemble little else in American or European art, and seem instead to recall the effects of certain Chinese paintings, which Bartram encountered in the Quaker merchants' homes in Philadelphia. Bartram mentions such works amid his Florida travels, not in relation to a snake but to a bird that resembles a snake:

> There is in this river [the St. Johns] and in the waters all over Florida, a very curious and handsome species of birds; the people call them Snake Birds; I think I have seen paintings of them on the Chinese screens and other India pictures: they seem to be a species of cormorant or loon . . . but far more beautiful and delicately formed than any other species that I have seen . . . the tail is very long, of a deep black, and tipped with a silvery white, and when spread, represents an unfurled fan. They delight

to sit in little peaceable communities, on the dry limbs of trees, hanging over the still waters, with their wings and tails expanded, I suppose to cool and air themselves, when at the same time they behold their images in the watery mirror.[33]

Bartram, who died in 1823, was still alive when Heade was born, and among the best-known naturalists in the region. Thomas Jefferson had asked Bartram to accompany Lewis and Clark on their explorations of the Louisiana Territory, but Bartram in 1804 was more interested in his pet crow and his garden than in resuming the arduous travels of his youth. Aside from any question of direct influence, however, one finds a shared sensibility in such passages from Bartram: the delight in ornithological variation and design; the notion that animals exist in "little peaceable communities"; the amused analogy to human vanity, as the birds behold their images in the watery mirror; the awareness of Chinese bird-and-flower paintings and such Asian flourishes as the unfurled fan. Heade's Brazilian hummingbirds have some of this eighteenth-century flavor. Despite their charm, they haven't yet moved into the mood and texture of Heade's own time.

There is, finally, something sad, something triste, about Heade's first encounter with the tropics. One feels that his commitment to propriety has been a barrier to any self-transformation. The chaotic sexuality and swirl of the Carnival and the rainforest are closed to him; the palisades above Rio, with their patterns of settlement that Claude Lévi-Strauss likened to "fingers bent in a tight, ill-fitting glove," separated him from the teeming jungle beyond. The great fact of sex, which Darwin's work would slowly bring home to respectable Americans, could still be held at bay in 1864, amid the narrow streets of Rio. Heade dutifully collected his bird specimens and staged his decorous domestic fantasies; he flirted with Laura Webb and botanized on the hillsides. But the real life of the forest—expressed in the gigantic orchids that he glimpsed on horseback rides outside of Petrópolis—remained peripheral to his activities and commitments. Only once, in a painting of a blue morpho butterfly with glorious wings outstretched along lichen-clad vines and blossoms, did something of the overwhelming force of the tropics enter Heade's art at this time.

7.

Heade left Rio de Janeiro on April 8, 1864, bound for London and feeling buoyant. He had found nearly sixty subscribers among the Brazilian elite for his folio of "Gems of Brazil," and secured the emperor's patronage. But his year in London proved difficult. He arrived with little money and soon had less; he pawned his watch, his gun, and many of the pictures he had brought with him. He got no help from Vose, one of his American dealers, and became so angry that he wrote what he called a "savage letter," which he later regretted. As he told his Providence friend John Bartlett: "Henry Ward Beecher says a man never loses his temper without making a fool of himself, & I certainly did it."[34] To make matters worse, Heade's collaborations with British printers were disappointing, and failed to capture the colors and backgrounds of the originals. And the English, who were familiar with Gould's recently published folio of hummingbirds, were less eager to sign up for Heade's projected album than the Brazilians had been. Schooled by Gould's fantastic elaborations, the English expected something airier and more fanciful than Heade's sturdy domestic couples.

As the "Gems" languished, Heade slowly located collectors interested in his work. He eventually made enough money on sales to rent what he called "one of the finest studios in London," which "a literary maiden—a correspondent of Hawthorne's," had found for him.[35] The insider sound of that remark is characteristic of Heade, who liked to think of himself as operating in inner circles of power and prestige. In Brazil, he had secured an audience with the emperor; in England he pursued various dukes and duchesses, dropping their names at every opportunity.

In London as in Brazil, Heade sometimes gave the impression that he regarded himself as some kind of agent for the Union cause. He continued to follow the Civil War news avidly. He arranged a meeting with Charles Francis Adams, the capable United States minister, perhaps by dropping Webb's name. Adams spent the war years trying to fend off British sympathy for the South, and potentially fatal British recognition of the Confederacy. Like other Northerners, Heade worried about General Sherman's progress through Georgia: "I have the greatest fears for Sherman yet." Then, with Atlanta in sight, he wrote with relief, "The end of the rebellion is at hand."[36] He worried about Lincoln's prospects for reelection, and expressed concern about how the union might be reestablished after the war.

Heade turned forty-six in 1865. With the end of the war, he made his way back across the Atlantic to resume an uncertain career in New York, with his usual detours and restless forays. In retrospect, Heade's sojourn in London seems like another false start for a painter whose career sometimes seems composed mainly of false starts and repetition. And yet, he had identified two subjects that would continue, in various guises, to occupy him for the rest of his life: salt marshes and hummingbirds.

By 1865, Heade's nomadic patterns of travel were well established. He was drawn to the extremes of civilization. At home in fashionable surroundings in New York and elsewhere, Heade continued to make excursions to the less settled regions of the world. He wasn't finished with the tropics, not by a long shot. He liked guns; he liked women; and he liked drawing rooms. Some of his greatest paintings and most intense personal relationships were yet to come.

Part Two

AT
THE HOTEL
BYRON

Chapter Five

THE PRISONER OF CHILLON

Such enjoyment as I got of the castle was mainly my distant daily view of it from the garden of the Hotel Byron—
a little many-pinnacled white promontory, shining against
the blue lake. When I went, Baedeker in hand, to "do" the
place, I found a huge concourse of visitors awaiting the
reflux of an earlier wave. "Let us at least wait till there
is no one else," I said to my companion. She smiled in
compassion of my naïveté, *"There is never no one else,"*
she answered.

❦ HENRY JAMES

I.

IN MID-JULY 1853, on the banks of Lake Geneva, Harriet Beecher
Stowe was sitting at her window in the Hotel Byron, writing a letter
to friends and family back home in New England. There was much
to tell. A few weeks earlier, as she launched her triumphant tour of Europe
in celebration of the publication of *Uncle Tom's Cabin,* she had met Lady
Byron, the poet's frail and diminutive widow, at a lunch party in Oxford,
and the two had shared a few moments of "deeply interesting conversation."

To Stowe's delight, Lady Byron had taken an interest in a young couple escaped from slavery in America, William and Ellen Crafts, who had begun a new life in England.[1]

No one she met on her travels had made more of a lasting impression on Stowe than the ethereal Lady Byron: "No words addressed to me in any conversation hitherto have made their way to my inner soul with such force." The fragile Lady Byron seemed already on the threshold of heaven, in marked contrast to her notorious husband, presumably consigned to the other place. Stowe was still under the spell as she looked out the window at the placid lake and its castle—the Castle of Chillon—made famous by Byron for the horrors perpetrated within its stone walls.

At the time of Stowe's first meeting with Lady Byron, the Byron marriage had been a source of fascination for many years on both sides of the Atlantic. George Gordon, the sixth Lord Byron and heir of the dilapidated Newstead Abbey, had come of age, as had Stowe herself, in a strict Calvinist family. He attended Harrow and Trinity College, Cambridge, where he began to write verse. Already famous at twenty-four, following the publication of the opening two sections of his melancholy travel poem *Childe Harold's Pilgrimage*, Lord Byron had married Annabella Milbanke four years later, in January, 1815. Despite Byron's reputation as a profligate, it seemed a promising marriage: Annabella was well born, wealthy, and a woman of considerable learning, especially gifted in mathematics. Their daughter, Augusta Ada, was born on December 10, by coincidence Emily Dickinson's birthday as well.

A month after Ada's birth, Lady Byron abruptly left her husband. The rickety marriage had lasted exactly one year. That April, affronted by ugly rumors about his reputed treatment of his wife and barred from polite society, Lord Byron left England, never to return. He fled to Geneva, where he joined the poet Shelley. In 1816, Byron published the third canto of *Childe Harold* as well as "The Prisoner of Chillon," his poem about a political prisoner who comes to prefer captivity to freedom. In 1817, his illegitimate daughter Allegra was born, to Claire Clairmont, and he published his dramatic poem of incestuous love, *Manfred*. In 1818, he moved in with another mistress, Teresa Guiccioli. In 1823, while working on his great satirical poem *Don Juan*, Byron sailed for Greece to take part in the war of liberation. A poet-turned-man-of action, Lord Byron died at Missolonghi on April 19, 1824. He was thirty-six.

2 .

Harriet Beecher Stowe was thirteen when she learned of Byron's death. "I remember taking my basket for strawberries that afternoon," she wrote, "and going over to a strawberry field on Chestnut Hill," a wooded upland near her house in Litchfield, Connecticut, dotted with daisies, violets, and the "pink shell blossoms of trailing arbutus." Stowe found herself "too dispirited to do anything; so I laid down among the daisies, and looked up into the blue sky, and thought of that great eternity into which Byron had entered, and wondered how it might be with his soul."[2] Like other girls growing up in the waning years of Puritan New England, Stowe had been warned against Byron's wicked works. Such admonitions only increased the allure. She was "astonished and electrified" when she read Byron's *The Corsair* as a child, puzzling over lines such as "One I never loved enough to hate."

When news of Lord Byron's death in Greece reached New England during the spring of 1824, Reverend Lyman Beecher preached a funeral sermon for the great and wicked poet. Stowe remembered her father saying, "with a sorrowful countenance, as if announcing the death of someone very interesting to him, 'My dear, Byron is dead—*gone*.'" The formidable preacher was silent for a moment, and then added, with a sigh, "Oh, I'm sorry that Byron is dead. I did hope he would live to do something for Christ. What a harp he might have swept!" The last of the great Puritan ministers, Lyman Beecher admired men of force and passion like Byron—men of "executive genius," as his daughter put it. He had a lifelong affection for Napoleon, whom he called "a glorious fellow," and when he was asked to compare Napoleon to the kings he had supplanted, he replied that it was "better that a wise and able bad man should reign than a stupid and weak bad man."[3]

Beecher was confident that if he could only have spoken with Byron, "it might have got him out of his troubles." For his sermon, he chose as his text: "The name of the just is as brightness, but the memory of the wicked shall rot." He sketched Byron's career and botched marriage, passed judgment on his poems, and concluded that some of his work would last forever but that the "impurities" lodged in other writings would "sink them in oblivion." He closed, as his daughter remembered, "with a most eloquent lamentation over the wasted life and misused powers of the great poet."[4]

The "Byronic fever," as Stowe called it, was at its height among the young people of New England during the 1820s; no historical figure was more fascinating to Lyman Beecher's children than Lord Byron. When Stowe came to write *Uncle Tom's Cabin*, she modeled her character Augustine St. Clare after Byron. St. Clare is Uncle Tom's kindly master in New Orleans, an unbeliever who gropes toward the light after two devastating losses. First, he loses the woman he loves through the deceit of her father; and second, in one of the most famous scenes in nineteenth-century literature, he witnesses the death of his beloved daughter, Little Eva. In Stowe's view, St. Clare is the aspiring soul, honest and forceful despite his skepticism about the existence of God. "The gift to appreciate and the sense to feel the finer shades and relations of moral things, often seems an attribute of those whose whole life shows a careless disregard of them," Stowe wrote, sounding very much like her father. "Hence Moore, Byron, Goethe, often speak words more wisely descriptive of the true religious sentiment, than another man, whose whole life is governed by it."[5] St. Clare's decision to set Tom free is nullified, however, when St. Clare intervenes in a bar fight and is killed, sealing Tom's tragic fate, as he is sold to the sadistic Simon Legree.

For a generation of young Americans, Lord Byron embodied a contradictory set of emotions. He represented, with his passions and his flair, an escape from the prison of Puritan repression. At the same time, he seemed, at least to believing Christians, to have purchased this freedom with the loss of his eternal soul. For the Beechers and their circle of intimates, Byron was a potent symbol of the confusions of the 1870s. Chief among these, in the wake of Darwin's findings and the weakening of religious institutions, was a new understanding of sexuality and carnal love.

Among the many uncertainties of the post-Civil War era was this ineluctable "fact of sex," as Thomas Wentworth Higginson called it, and the instability of erotic attachments. Marriage, that bedrock institution in an age of arranged marriages, seemed a shakier foundation when marriage was supposed to be based on love. The older generation of New England parents agreed that Lord Byron was a troubling beacon—"mad, bad, and dangerous to know," as one of his lovers, Lady Caroline Lamb, characterized him. Still, two generations of New Englanders—including Harriet Beecher Stowe and Emily Dickinson—charted their emotional course according to his impassioned allure.

3.

"Castle Chillon, with its old conical towers, is silently pictured in the still waters," Stowe wrote in her letter that summer of 1853. No other words were necessary for her readers back home. She was in Byron country. In his dramatic monologue "The Prisoner of Chillon," Lord Byron assumed the voice of François Bonnivard, the sixteenth-century hero of Swiss independence, imprisoned for six years, from 1530 to 1536, in the castle dungeon by the evil French occupier the Duke of Savoy.

The most poignant of all Byron's monologues, "The Prisoner of Chillon" was a particular favorite of young American readers. Engravings based on Delacroix's painting of the languishing prisoner decorated many

New England houses. Readers knew Byron's opening lines by heart, and with a chance remark or turn of phrase, they could evoke a shared interior landscape.

> *There are seven pillars of gothic mold,*
> *In Chillon's dungeons deep and old,*
> *There are seven columns, massy and grey,*
> *Dim with a dull imprisoned ray.*

In the poem, Bonnivard's two brothers die in captivity while he himself lives on. He is sustained by the song of a bird perched on the prison bars: "A light broke in upon my brain,—/ It was the carol of a bird." If hope, as Emily Dickinson said, is "the thing with feathers," Bonnivard never gives up hope: "I know not why/ I could not die."

And then comes the great and memorable surprise of the poem: when the Duke of Savoy is defeated on the battlefield and the partisans of Geneva arrive in triumph to liberate Bonnivard, he hesitates unaccountably, and is reluctant to leave the familiar dungeon:

> *These heavy walls to me had grown*
> *A hermitage—and all my own!*

He almost resents his liberators: "And half I felt as they were come/ To tear me from a second home." He has made other friends, other attachments:

> *With spiders I had friendship made,*
> *And watch'd them in their sullen trade,*
> *Had seen the mice by moonlight play,*
> *And why should I feel less than they?*
> *We were all inmates of one place,*
> *And I, the monarch of each race,*
> *Had power to kill—yet, strange to tell!*
> *In quiet we had learn'd to dwell,*

Nor slew I of my subjects one,
What Sovereign hath so little done?
My very chains and I grew friends.

Like so many other visitors at Lake Geneva, Harriet Beecher Stowe longed to see the site of the great Bonnivard's sufferings. She and her entourage boarded a boat, with two men at the oars, passing

leisurely along the shores, under the cool, drooping branches of trees, to the castle, which is scarce a stone's throw from the hotel. We rowed along, close under the walls, to the ancient moat and drawbridge. There I picked a bunch of blue bells, "les clochettes," which were hanging their aerial pendants from every crevice—some blue, some white.[6]

A Swiss guide who had taught herself English led them through the dungeon with its seven pillars, on one of which Stowe found Byron's name. She brooded over Bonnivard's imprisonment: "Six years is so easily said; but to *live* them, alone, helpless, a man burning with all the fires of manhood, chained to that pillar of stone, and those three unvarying steps! Two thousand one hundred and ninety days rose and set the sun, while seedtime and harvest, winter and summer, and the whole living world went on over his grave."

Pilgrims and guide proceeded to the torture chamber with its pulleys and ovens and a great stone.

On that stone, our guide told us, two thousand Jews, men, women, and children, had been put to death. There was also, high up, a strong beam across, where criminals were hung; and a door now walled up, by which they were thrown into the lake. I shivered. "'Twas cruel," she said; "'twas almost as cruel as your slavery in America."[7]

The comparison was particularly gratifying for the author of *Uncle Tom's Cabin*.

4·

"The Iliad of the blacks"—that was how the crusading French novelist George Sand described Stowe's epic tale of slavery. Twenty years after the publication of *Uncle Tom's Cabin*, in which she challenged Americans to do something about the horrific crime of slavery, Harriet Beecher Stowe challenged the British to do something about the horrific crimes of Lord Byron. In "The True Story of Lady Byron's Life" (1869), Stowe circled like a predatory bird around what she delicately called Byron's "improper intimacy" with his half-sister, Augusta Leigh.[8] In retrospect, it is easy to see why Lady Byron recruited Stowe for her own long-deferred defense. The little woman who had started a war in defense of "the lowly" could be counted on to launch a kindred campaign for poor, oppressed Lady Byron. But Stowe's reasons for accepting the challenge—aside from her instinctive defense of a woman wronged—remain puzzling to this day, and some of her motives were almost certainly obscure to herself.

Stowe had met Lady Byron in passing in 1853, when she stayed at the Hotel Byron and visited the Castle of Chillon. On her return to England during the fall of 1856, when she secured copyright for her second novel, *Dred,* Stowe impulsively sought Lady Byron's advice after a stinging review of the novel appeared in the *Edinburgh Review.* "O do not be susceptible to these 'darts,' my dear friend," Lady Byron replied. "No one can tell you better than I that there is an invisible shield which turns them away."[9] It was on this ground of shared victimhood that the two diminutive and world-famous women met several times, and it was during these intimate sessions that Lady Byron revealed to Stowe the scandalous truth of Lord Byron's crimes, far exceeding his American reputation as a freethinker, a seducer, and a rake.

While no hard facts regarding the causes of the so-called "separation" of 1816 had come to light, Byron's flight from England and his many love affairs on the Continent had contributed to his legend as a sort of Satanic hero. Among the many malfeasances ascribed to him—any one of which might have sufficed as grounds for marital dissolution—were that he had sodomized Lady Byron; that he had had sex with Greek boys; that he drank to excess or took drugs; and that he had beaten Lady Byron or otherwise insulted her. To these charges, as Stowe listened intently, Lady Byron added another: that Lord Byron; before his marriage, had entered into a sexual relationship with his own half-sister, Augusta Leigh; that the relationship had continued during the early months of his marriage; and that a daughter, Medora, had been born to this incestuous affair.

A counterlegend, developed by Lord Byron's friends and supporters after his death, had meanwhile gained currency: that Lady Byron's coldness, her mathematical "precision," and her moralistic disdain had driven Lord Byron from the family hearth and then from England. A cheap edition of Byron's poems was about to be launched in Great Britain around the time of Stowe's visit, and the likelihood that Lady Byron would again be maligned in the prefatory matter was what ostensibly prompted her appeal to Stowe. Should she, Lady Byron now asked, break her long silence and go public with her explosive charges? By her own account, Stowe hesitated:

> The writer [i.e., Stowe herself] was so impressed and excited by the whole scene and recital that she begged for two or three days to deliberate, before forming any opinion. She took the memorandum with her, returned to London and gave a day or two to the consideration of the subject. The decision which she made was chiefly influenced by her reverence and affection for Lady Byron. She seemed so frail, she had suffered so much, she stood at such a height above the comprehension of the coarse and common world, that the author had a feeling that it would almost be like violating a shrine, to ask her to come forth from the sanctuary of a silence where she had so long abode and plead her cause.[10]

Why, then, did Harriet Beecher Stowe advise Lady Byron to preserve her silence in 1856, and then break it herself in 1869? One reason was that Lady Byron had died in 1860, and that no one, according to Stowe, had come forward to defend "the most remarkable woman that England has produced in this century." A second reason—the reason that Stowe most insisted upon—was that the Countess Guiccioli, one of Byron's lovers, had recently published her own memoir of Lord Byron, which was selling well in America, and included slighting remarks about Lady Byron, as a "narrow-minded, cold-hearted precisian, without sufficient intellect to comprehend [Byron's] genius or heart to feel for his temptations." And finally, Stowe had her own reasons for feeling victimized in 1869, as her newly published novel of old New England life, *Oldtown Folks,* was being ridiculed by a largely male press.[11]

Stowe's article, "The True Story of Lady Byron's Life," certainly caught the attention of William Dean Howells, the young editor temporarily in charge of *The Atlantic Monthly* while his boss, James Fields, traveled in Europe. Howells, temperamentally averse to Romantic excess, thought the article might help put an end to the Byron craze, which lingered on in America. Meanwhile, Stowe herself was so anxious about the public reaction to her revelations that she suffered a physical collapse and retired to her daughter Georgiana's home in Stockbridge, Massachusetts, to brace herself for the publication of the article.

"THE TRUE STORY of Lady Byron's Life," which appeared in the September 1869 issue of *The Atlantic Monthly,* is hardly the hysterical screed that it is sometimes purported to be. The article is evenhanded, almost legalistic in its assessment of the facts of the case. Stowe speaks as Lady Byron's advocate, a forceful voice interceding for the "silent woman." She also speaks for all those women, including herself, who had maintained a hope for Lord Byron's salvation: "During all these years, when he was setting at defiance every principle of morality and decorum, the interest of the female mind all over Europe in the conversion of this brilliant prodigal son was unceasing, and reflects the greatest credit upon the faith of the sex."

But mainly Stowe speaks for the prosecution, basing her case first on the evidence provided by Byron's poetry and second on the revelations confided to her by Lady Byron. She delayed her main accusation until nearly halfway through the article, so that it arrived with the force of a depth charge: "From the height at which he might have been happy as the husband of a noble woman, he fell into the depths of a secret adulterous intrigue with a blood relation, so near in consanguinity that discovery must have been utter ruin and expulsion from civilized society."

Was the charge true? It is now generally assumed that it was. Was Stowe the first to make it? Not exactly, since Lady Byron hadn't been quite as silent as she claimed, though Stowe was certainly the first to publish it far and wide—from the rooftops, so to speak. Did Stowe's argument carry the day? Hardly. Questions were raised, predictably, about the veracity, and even sanity, of Lady Byron, who could hardly be considered a disinterested party. The charge of incest among an urban aristocracy struck many as incredible on its face; James Russell Lowell sniffed that such things might happen "in lonely farmhouses" but not in civilized society.[12] Stowe's shaky evidence rested primarily on Lady Byron's assertions, and on stray passages from poems—hardly the sort of thing to stand up in court. Even Henry Ward Beecher gently suggested that his sister might have provided more documentation for her case. And this she proceeded to do, as she hurriedly expanded her essay into the book-length polemic *Lady Byron Vindicated*.

Harriet Beecher Stowe's disclosure of Byron's crime was meant to expose a scandal, but it created one as well—for the staid *Atlantic Monthly*. The publication of Stowe's essay almost ruined the magazine. Shocked readers, put off by unsavory details, canceled their subscriptions by the thousands. The defense launched by women's rights advocates hardly helped the matter, since arguments about the so-called enslavement of women were not likely to convince the *Atlantic* readership. There were problems with this interpretation in any case, since Byron had forced himself on neither his sister nor his wife.[13] Almost alone amid this tempest, Howells rejoiced. He was convinced that Stowe had struck a blow for realism, puncturing the glamour of the Byron legend.[14]

If Stowe's fascination with the Byron case remains puzzling, this is in part because her motivations were deeply personal, and familial. Her sense of identification with Lady Byron is clear enough, but certain peculiar details in her article render the identification even closer. Among these is her characterization of Lady Byron's relationship with her husband as that of mother and son—or, to be more precise, mother and "prodigal son." Faced with Byron's incest, "there arose within her, stronger, purer, and brighter, that immortal kind of love . . . which holds the one wanderer of more account than the ninety and nine that went astray." According to Stowe, Lady Byron continued to love her wayward husband "with that love resembling a mother's." And, toward the end of Stowe's article, she mentioned how Lady Byron had comforted a friend who had lost a son: "Dear friend, remember, as long as our loved ones are in *God's* world, they are in *ours.*" It is difficult not to detect in these charged passages, which fit oddly into any analysis of the Byron marriage, the shadow of Stowe's own experience with a "prodigal son," namely, her lost son, Fred.[15]

5.

"How is your little Byron?" Emily Dickinson asked her close friend Elizabeth Holland, wife of the editor and novelist Josiah Holland, in a brief and brilliant letter of 1860. The Hollands' infant son Theodore, born the previous December, had undergone surgery to correct a congenital problem in the tendons of one of his feet. Dickinson was reminded of Lord Byron's clubfoot, treated by a quack when Byron was a child.

> How is your little Byron? Hope he gains his foot without losing his genius. Have heard it ably argued that the poet's genius lay in his foot— as the bee's prong and his song are concomitant.[16]

As usual, Dickinson's imagination is moving on several tracks here. Byron's genius, she suggests, was linked to his deformed foot. She seems to imply a more general theory of creativity—like Edmund Wilson's interpretation of the myth of Philoctetes, in which the Greek warrior's diseased foot is balanced by his legendary skill as an archer. And then there is the matter of poetic "feet": a poet's genius lies in how he marshals such building blocks of verse.

But what are we to make of that last extraordinary leap: "as the bee's prong and his song are concomitant"? Is Dickinson thinking of Byron's "prong," his legendary capacity for making love to women even as he wrote poems like *Don Juan*? The joke illuminates a whole vista of Dickinson's poetry, in which humming bees and hummingbirds make love to yielding flowers. "Blossoms belong to the bee," she wrote to Mrs. Holland, "if needs be by *habeas corpus*." In one poem, she writes that "The Flower must not blame the Bee—/ that seeketh his felicity/ too often at her door," and concludes with a Lake Geneva setting: "But teach the Footman from Vevay—/ Mistress is 'not at home'—to say—/ To people—any more!"[17]

Lord Byron, who stayed in Vevey when he visited the Castle of Chillon in 1816, seems to be the invoked "Lord," hummingbird or bee, in another erotic fantasy:

> *I tend my flowers for thee—*
> *Bright Absentee!*
> *My Fuschzia's Coral Seams*
> *Rip—while the Sower—dreams—*
>
> *Geraniums—tint—and spot—*
> *Low Daisies—dot—*
> *My Cactus—splits her Beard*
> *To show her throat—*[18]

Dickinson was never more explicit in her sexual imagery than here.

6.

Elizabeth Holland wasn't just Emily Dickinson's friend and confidante, however. She also served as Dickinson's confidential mail carrier, shuttling Dickinson's messages to her own Byronic heartthrob.[19] Five years earlier, during the spring of 1855, Emily Dickinson had met her first Lord Byron. Dickinson at twenty-five was making the only extended journey of her life. Her sociable childhood in Amherst was drawing to a close. Her friends were getting married, and she herself had had her share of admirers. Her father, Edward Dickinson, was completing his single term in the United States Congress, and decided that his two unmarried daughters might benefit from a view of the larger world.

They checked into the Willard Hotel—Emily Dickinson's only experience of a grand hotel—in Washington on February 10, 1855. Dickinson found the small city overpowering: "all is jostle, here—scramble and confusion," she wrote.[20] Pleading ill health, she found refuge in the self-enclosed world of the hotel, so distant from Amherst and yet preserving, in its formal introductions in the hotel lobby and strolling conversations down the corridors, the decorum of a small town. Among the hotel guests, Representative Thomas Dawes Eliot, also of the Massachusetts delegation, was most appealing to the Dickinson sisters. "Mr. New Bedford Eliot," as they called him, granduncle of the poet T. S. Eliot, was their "girlish ideal" of the perfect man, according to Lavinia.[21]

As antislavery Whigs, Eliot and Dickinson were embroiled in a battle within their broad compromise party. They were trying to pressure the Whig Party to adopt an abolitionist plank, with the threat that they and other Northern Whigs were prepared to bolt the party and form an alliance with the so-called "Free Soilers," who were fighting to keep the Nebraska and Kansas territories free of slavery.[22] The national Whig convention of 1855 was held in Philadelphia, Emily Dickinson's next destination. Horace Greeley, the antislavery editor of the *Tribune*, sent Dickinson's friend Samuel

Bowles to monitor the situation. Bowles was hoping to see the Northerners bolt to join the Republican Party, founded the previous year, and "unite the North in an all-powerful and effective party against the aggressiveness of slavery."[23] On the conservative side of the debate was Greeley's rival, the flamboyant editor James Watson Webb of the New York *Courier and Enquirer,* who had adamantly opposed black suffrage in New York and later served as Lincoln's minister to Brazil.

If Emily Dickinson was aware of these controversies, she made no mention of them, nor did she seem to notice that Washington was a city, the first in her experience, that was run in large part by slave labor. She noticed, instead, that the maple trees were in bloom, already in late February, and that the grass was green in the sunny places. There was some obligatory sightseeing for the Dickinson sisters, a trip to "sweet" Mount Vernon, but the three weeks in Washington made little impression on Emily Dickinson. She admired General Washington's tomb, "no less wise or sad for that marble story," but "the pomp—the court—the etiquette" of the city named in his honor repelled her.[24]

A STOPOVER IN Philadelphia on the return journey to Amherst was more momentous. She was taken by friends to the Arch Street Presbyterian Church to hear Reverend Charles Wadsworth, one of the charismatic pulpit performers of his time. Only Henry Ward Beecher had a comparable reputation.[25] The two preachers had interests in common, such as a fascination with gemstones; in a sermon titled "My Jewels," Wadsworth compared the spiritual life to the process of crystallization.

But where Beecher was sweetness and light, preaching the Gospel of Love, Wadsworth at forty-one seemed like Hawthorne's minister clad in a black veil. There was something exotic about his appearance and manner. An article that appeared in the *Springfield Republican* in 1850, the year he began preaching in Philadelphia, reported that Wadsworth's "dark eyes, hair, and complexion have decidedly a Jewish cast."[26] Unlike Beecher, who fraternized with his flock and made endless social and ministerial calls,

Wadsworth preserved a distance from his congregation, "letting himself be known only through his preaching."[27]

Something in Wadsworth's brooding manner appealed to Dickinson. She sought a meeting with him; he played the Byronic role to perfection. Years later she described their encounter: "Once when he seemed almost overpowered by a spasm of gloom, I said 'You are troubled.' Shivering as he spoke, 'My Life is full of dark secrets,' he said. He never spoke of himself, and encroachment I know would have slain him."[28] The allure for Dickinson was in the secrets themselves, the hint of a dark past too horrible to be disclosed. Wadsworth assiduously cultivated the impression. When his alma mater, the Princeton Theological Seminary, asked for news, he replied enigmatically that he had lived "extempore" and "was born *without a memory*."

What precisely were Wadsworth's dark secrets? He was born in 1814 near the Beecher fiefdom of Litchfield, Connecticut. His family connections seemed prosperous at the outset; he referred to his father, a miller, as "Lord of the Manor." But in 1830, the year of Dickinson's birth, Wadsworth's father died insolvent and the family's fortunes were derailed: no lordship for sixteen-year-old Charles. His education was bumpy; like Byron, he was expelled from college—Hamilton, in upstate New York—and completed his education at nearby Union.

Wadsworth dealt with life's bitterness by writing poetry; he was indeed a poetic prodigy, publishing his gloomy poems in various newspapers and journals. Eschewing his own name, which resembled "Wordsworth," he chose the pen name "Sedley," a combination perhaps of "Shelley" and "sadly." His influences were "orthodox Calvinism, eighteenth-century 'graveyard' meditation, and . . . Lord Byron," as Alfred Habegger notes. "Like the latter's Childe Harold, Sedley seems weighed down by a gloomy and premature initiation into life's sorrows. He is evidently in exile from New England and oppressed by memories of a vanished Eden."[29]

Wadsworth then performed the feat that all Byron's New England admirers wished their idol had achieved: he found his way back, "upward out of unbelief," to his Calvinist faith.[30] He renounced what he called "the infirmities of the poetic impulse" and celebrated instead, in sermon after sermon, the healthier claims of the practical world. Around 1852, he embraced the lyricism of modern life, adopting the Whig vision of railroads and canals that also inspired Congressman Edward Dickinson of Amherst. Sounding like some Italian futurist of the early twentieth century, Wadsworth proclaimed that the steam engine was a "mightier epic than the Paradise Lost" and that the telegraph was "a lovelier and loftier creation of true poetry than Spenser's Fairy Queen or Shakespeare's Tempest."[31]

This is the "Man of sorrow," in Emily Dickinson's phrase, who remained a kind of touchstone for her—Byronic, ironic, and sad. This is the man Dickinson called "my Philadelphia," "my Clergyman," "my dearest earthly friend."

Soon after her return from Philadelphia, the Dickinson family moved back into the brick mansion on Main Street they called the Homestead. This was the house in which Emily Dickinson was born and in which she would die. Her grandfather, Samuel Fowler Dickinson, had built it in 1813 before bankruptcy forced him to sell it; her father had rented part of it when she was young; now, in the fall of 1855, the family repossessed it as a visible sign of Edward Dickinson's prosperity.

The move around the corner in Amherst consisted of barely three blocks, but to Emily Dickinson it felt like three hundred miles. She invoked the transits of planets, when Venus, for example, passes across the face of the sun. "I supposed we were going to make a 'transit,' as heavenly bodies did," she wrote Mrs. Holland in January 1856.[32] She invoked the Free-Soilers, emigrating to the disputed territories to keep Kansas free. "It is a kind of *gone-to-Kansas* feeling, and if I sat in a long wagon, with my family tied behind, I should suppose without doubt I was a party of emigrants!" She concluded with a brilliant summation of her feelings: "They say that 'home is where the heart is.' I think it is where the *house* is, and the adjacent buildings."

In March 1860, when he was in mourning for his mother and in an even blacker mood than usual, Reverend Charles Wadsworth paid a visit to Emily Dickinson in the Homestead in Amherst. Then, in April 1862, this apostle

of progress accepted a call from the Calvary Presbyterian Society in San
Francisco, greatly increasing the distance that separated Emily Dickinson
from her mysterious man of sorrow.

7.

Perhaps it was the news of Wadsworth's impending departure that sent
Emily Dickinson's spirits spiraling downward during the early 1860s. Or
perhaps it was some sudden descent into mental illness, after which she
found herself unable to feel at ease with other people, or to leave the comfortable confines of her father's house. Maybe the national crisis of the Civil
War, and the Amherst war dead, shook her faith in civilization, and intensified her own fears that death was final and eternal life a myth. Maybe it was
some lethal combination of all these ingredients. Whatever the cause of the
crisis, she responded by writing poems, hundreds of them, and turning again
and again for solace to "The Prisoner of Chillon." Byron's poem became the
Rosetta stone of her own tortured destiny.

Dickinson felt herself in some kind of captivity: "A Prison gets to be a friend,"
she wrote in one poem, alluding unmistakably to Chillon. "The Liberty we knew,"
she wrote, is "Avoided—like a Dream."[33] In one of her clearest statements about
the purpose of poetry, she imagined herself immured in a prison of "prose" from
which the only release was writing poems.

> *I dwell in Possibility—*
> *A fairer House than Prose—*
> *More numerous of Windows—*
> *Superior—for doors—*[34]

Here, "prose" is conceived as a house with few doors or windows. ("Doom
is the house without the door," she wrote in another poem.[35]) We are meant

to hear behind the word *prose*, like a verbal shadow, the alliterative word *prison*, just as *possibility* in the poem is a synonym for *poetry*.

The same feelings structured another poem of 1862:

> *They shut me up in Prose—*
> *As when a little Girl*
> *They put me in the Closet—*
> *Because they liked me "still"—*
>
> *Still! Could themselves have peeped—*
> *And seen my Brain—go round—*
> *They might as wise have lodged a Bird*
> *For Treason—in the Pound—*[36]

Writing to her Norcross cousins in 1861 about the heroism of women writers, Dickinson mentioned the suffocating childhood of the French novelist George Sand, "who must make no noise in her grandmother's bedroom." In Dickinson's experience, poetry was the key that unlocked the unbearable prison of prose, but it was an inner freedom, akin to that of the prisoner of Chillon. Birdsong and birds in flight were always emblems of freedom for Dickinson as they had been for Byron's prisoner.

In her own favorite poem from her first creative surge, "Safe in their Alabaster Chambers," Dickinson imagined the "meek members of the Resurrection" sleeping in their prisonlike tombs:

> *Light laughs the breeze*
> *In her Castle above them,*
> *Babbles the Bee in a Stolid Ear,*
> *Pipe the Sweet Birds in ignorant cadence,—*
> *Ah, what sagacity perished here!*[37]

The whole stanza is steeped in Byron and Chillon: the castle above the dungeon, the babbling bee, the bird outside, and the wise captive.

8.

"'Chillon' is not funny," Dickinson wrote in one of the three passionate and anguished love letters addressed but not sent, from around the spring of 1858 to the summer of 1861, to an unidentified "Master." By then, the three unavailable men she had selected to guide her fate—Wadsworth the minister, Bowles the editor, Thomas Wentworth Higginson the writer-soldier—had fused in her mind into a single lover. She addressed all three as "master," invoking Chillon in a letter to Bowles, requesting that Higginson serve as her "master," and treating Wadsworth as her spiritual guide. She imagined herself as a flower who signed her letters "Daisy"; he was the Byronic "bee" whose prong was his song:

> Daisy—who never flinched thro' that awful parting—but held her life so tight he should not see the wound . . . Shut her in prison—Sir—only pledge that you will forgive—sometime . . . Wonder stings me more than the Bee.[38]

In these fantasies of domination, Dickinson pictured herself as the passive flower about to be ravished by the masterly bee.

And then, abruptly, she changed the metaphor. The prisoner of Chillon, without the power to die, became instead a loaded gun. Like him, she had led an indoor life, "in corners," before her master and owner claimed her and released her into the "sovereign woods."

> *My life had stood—a Loaded Gun—*
> *In Corners—till a Day*
> *The Owner passed—identified—*
> *And carried Me away—*

And now We roam in Sovereign Woods—
And now We hunt the Doe—
And every time I speak for Him
The Mountains straight reply—

Like many of Dickinson's poems, "My life had stood" ends with a riddle about her "owner":

Though I than He—may longer live
He longer must—than I—
For I have but the power to kill,
Without—the power to die—[39]

It is the same riddle faced by the prisoner of Chillon, who first said, "I know not why/ I could not die" and then, on being offered his freedom:

And I, the monarch of each race,
Had power to kill—yet strange to tell!
In quiet we had learn'd to dwell,
Nor slew I of my subjects one,
What Sovereign hath so little done?

For the next twenty years of her life, Emily Dickinson confronted her own existential riddle. Like the prisoner of Chillon, she felt cut off from her contemporaries, except from those rare spirits, like Reverend Wadsworth, who lived behind a kindred veil, or sturdier temperaments, like Judge Lord, who seemed to promise anchorage in an uncertain world. And yet, there were rich rewards for her confinement. She felt a dangerous power inside her, a great unleashing of the imagination that filled her with mingled pride and dread. Dickinson experienced a special intimacy with birds and flowers; she developed an almost hallucinatory awareness of the power of individual

words; and she discerned, behind the curtain of custom, the palpable nearness of the great facts of life and death.

9 ·

"Daisy" and "Chillon"—how odd that these two charged names from
Emily Dickinson's secretly coded life should reappear in Henry James's
novella *Daisy Miller*, published in 1878. James's impetuous heroine, the
first of his wealthy but unsophisticated American girls in search of love
and adventure in the Old World, has arrived in Switzerland, determined
to have some fun before the winter's decorous sojourn in Rome. Daisy
Miller remarks that Europe, in her experience, is "nothing but hotels," and
James is careful at the outset to evoke the artificial hotel world of foreign
tourists:

> At the little town of Vevey, in Switzerland, there is a particularly
> comfortable hotel. There are, indeed, many hotels; for the entertain-
> ment of tourists is the business of the place, which, as many travelers
> will remember, is seated upon the edge of a remarkably blue lake—a
> lake that it behoves every tourist to visit. The shore of the lake pre-
> sents an unbroken array of establishments of this order, of every cat-
> egory, from the "grand hotel" of the newest fashion, with a
> chalk-white front, a hundred balconies, and a dozen flags flying from
> its roof, to the little Swiss *pension* of an elder day, with its name in-
> scribed in German-looking lettering upon a pink or yellow wall, and
> an awkward summer-house in the angle of the garden. One of the
> hotels at Vevey, however, is famous, even classical, being distin-
> guished from many of its upstart neighbours by an air both of luxury
> and of maturity.

James lightly disguises his famous hotel, though any reader would know he meant the Hotel Byron, blessed with "a view of the snowy crest of the Dent du Midi and the picturesque towers of the Castle of Chillon."

In her comfortable hotel, Daisy Miller has struck up an acquaintance with another American, who bears the ominous name (at least for daisies) of Winterbourne. Winterbourne lives in Geneva, the "little metropolis of Calvinism," as James calls it, and "the dark old city at the other end of the lake." Daisy tells Winterbourne of her intense desire to see the Castle of Chillon: "I want to go there dreadfully," she tells him. "Of course I mean to go there. I wouldn't go away from here without having seen that old castle."

Much of the first half of the story concerns the preparation, completion, and aftermath of Daisy's visit to the Castle of Chillon, guided by the grave Winterbourne who, according to Daisy, looked as if he were taking her "to a funeral."

> In the castle, after they had landed, the subjective element decidedly prevailed. Daisy tripped about the vaulted chambers, rustled her skirts in the corkscrew staircases, flirted back with a pretty little cry and a shudder from the edge of the *oubliettes,* and turned a singularly well-shaped ear to everything that Winterbourne told her about the place.

Daisy shows little interest in the story of Bonnivard, dutifully recounted to her by Winterbourne. "The history of Bonnivard had evidently, as they say, gone into one ear and out of the other." Byron goes entirely unmentioned—James counts on the reader's familiarity with both the legend and the poem.

Only when the setting shifts to Italy does Byron enter the scene. Winterbourne follows Daisy to Rome, where rumors of her flirtations with disreputable Italian suitors are already making the rounds of the American expatriate society. Winterbourne is torn: as an American, he is drawn to Daisy's democratic flouting of the rules, but as a European, from the

Calvinist city of Geneva, he just as instinctively hews to civilized strictures. Daisy thinks he is a coward, and she is probably right.

Just as she longed to visit Chillon, she now finds a way to fulfill her long-held dream of experiencing the Colosseum by moonlight. It is a dream drawn from Byron's poetry. Winterbourne searches for the doomed Daisy, finding her at midnight in the moonlit Colosseum, where she will contract the fever that will kill her. As he enters the arena, he "began to murmur Byron's famous lines out of Manfred." Here too Henry James counts on us to know the lines:

> *I stood within the Colosseum's wall,*
> *'Midst the chief relics of almighty Rome;*
> *The trees which grew along the broken arches*
> *Waved dark in the blue midnight, and the stars*
> *Shone through the rents of ruin; from afar*
> *The watchdog bayed beyond the Tiber; and*
> *More near from out the Caesars' palace came*
> *The owl's long cry, and, interruptedly,*
> *Of distant sentinels the fitful song*
> *Begun and died upon the gentle wind.*

Winterbourne, murmuring Manfred's meditation on human mortality in the face of the ruined colossus, sees his Daisy among the stones. "'And thou didst shine, thou rolling moon, upon / All this, and cast a wide and tender light.'"

There can be no question of direct influence from Dickinson's "Daisy" and Chillon to Henry James. Dickinson's secret letters and mostly unpublished poems are from the 1860s and Henry James's story dates from 1878; there is no evidence that he knew of her or her work at that time. James was aware of Dickinson during the 1890s, when his sister, Alice, wrote to him of her enthusiasm for Dickinson's poetry and her delight at the English critics' disdain for it.

But James's explicit working out of the Daisy-Winterbourne-Chillon nexus nonetheless helps us to understand what Emily Dickinson was getting at with her flowers, her birds, and her prisons. There is a seasonal myth, an underlying suggestion of ritual, in all these narratives. Stowe too had been struck by wildflowers growing from the walls of Chillon, and when she first heard of Byron's death, she lay down in a field of daisies. What Byron's poetry promised—for Stowe, Dickinson, and Henry James—was escape from the wintry prison-house of custom and Calvinism, and access instead to nature and to feeling. Byron broke the rules; Daisy Miller broke the rules; Harriet Beecher Stowe and Emily Dickinson, in their way, sought to break the rules as well.

10.

William Dean Howells had hoped that the publication of Harriet Beecher Stowe's exposé of Byron's incest would put a stake through the Byron craze in America, making way for the realism favored by Howells. But it was another writer in Howells's stable who did a better job of making Byron's Romanticism look ridiculous. By the late 1870s, a visit to Chillon had become such a necessary part of every tourist's itinerary that it was ripe for satire. Mark Twain, as usual, was up to the task. "I had always had a deep and reverent compassion for the sufferings of the 'prisoner of Chillon,' whose story Byron had told in such moving verse;" he wrote in *A Tramp Abroad*, "so I took the steamer and made pilgrimage to the dungeons of the Castle of Chillon, to see the place where poor Bonnivard endured his dreary captivity three hundred years ago."

Compared to the cramped hotel rooms he himself had endured in Europe, Mark Twain thought Bonnivard had nothing to complain of. "His dungeon was a nice, cool, roomy place, and I cannot see why he should have been dissatisfied with it." It was a "pretty dungeon," surely. And Mark Twain proceeded to enumerate its charms as though he were advertising a hotel:

> It has romantic window-slits that let in generous bars of light, and it has tall, noble columns, carved apparently from the living rock; and what is more, they are written all over with thousands of names; some of them— like Byron's and Victor Hugo's—of the first celebrity. Why didn't he amuse himself reading these names? Then there are the couriers and tourists—swarms of them every day—what was to hinder him from having a good time with them? I think Bonnivard's sufferings have been overrated.[40]

Chapter Six

BIRDS OF PASSAGE

... Or Arctic Creatures, dimly stirred—
By Tropic Hint—some Travelled Bird
Imported to the Wood—

❧ EMILY DICKINSON[1]

I.

ON A COLD January day in 1867, Mark Twain checked into the
Metropolitan Hotel, a six-story brownstone at the corner of
Broadway and Prince in lower Manhattan. Travel-stained and ex-
hausted, Twain was a low-profile guest. An obscure newspaper reporter
from California, he was unmarried, a heavy drinker, and a wit. His jokingly
informative reports from the Sandwich Islands, deep in the Pacific Ocean,
had earned him a modest readership in the San Francisco newspapers. He
had tried many jobs and failed at most of them. Like one of his own adventurous rascals, he had come east, by a roundabout way, to try to make his
increasingly elusive fortune as a travel writer.

A nomad by temperament and necessity, Twain at thirty-one had already
traversed a good portion of the United States and wished to go farther. Born into
a slaveholding family in the prairie town of Florida, Missouri, in 1835, he had

grown up in Hannibal on the banks of the Mississippi River. His father was a self-educated lawyer who had an indifferent career as a small-town judge and failed as a farmer, a storekeeper, a hotel keeper, and an investor in real estate. He died in 1847, leaving the family destitute. His widow, Jane Clemens, though only forty-three, retreated into a world of "omens and dreams," according to Twain's biographer, "and grew deeply absorbed in the color red."[2]

Twain's formal education ended at age twelve; like Benjamin Franklin, he found his first significant work setting type in a printing firm. He published his first sketch, in 1851, in his older brother Orion's local newspaper. Twain practiced his trade with mixed success in St. Louis, New York, Philadelphia, and Cincinnati. By the time he reached Cincinnati, he already had his eyes on the tropics. Twain had read William Herndon's vivid book *Exploration of the Valley of the Amazon* (1854), and was determined to travel to Brazil himself:

> I made up my mind that I could go to the head waters of the Amazon and collect coca and trade in it and make a fortune. I left for New Orleans in the steamer "Paul Jones" with this great idea filling my mind. When I got to New Orleans I inquired about ships leaving for Pará and discovered that there weren't any, and learned that there probably wouldn't be any during the century. It had not occurred to me to inquire about these particulars before leaving Cincinnati, so there I was. I couldn't get to the Amazon.[3]

It would be another five years before Reverend Fletcher and General Webb prepared the way for steamboat connections between the two countries.

Disappointed, Twain returned to Hannibal in 1857 to train as a pilot in steamboats on the Mississippi River—a career interrupted by the outbreak of the Civil War in the spring of 1861. In his memorable "Private History of a Campaign That Failed," Twain minimized his two weeks in the trenches with the Missouri militia: "You have heard from a great many people who did something in the war; is it not fair and right that you listen a little moment to one who started out to do something in it, but didn't?"[4]

After his brief military service on the Confederate side, and seeing a way to distance himself from the war, Twain shifted allegiances when his brother

Orion—who had supported Lincoln's candidacy—was awarded a patronage job as secretary to the Nevada Territory. The brothers arrived in Carson City, armed with a six-pound unabridged dictionary and little else, in August 1861, where Twain was more successful writing humorous sketches for newspapers in Nevada and California than he was prospecting for silver—a pattern set for the rest of his life.

It was as a correspondent for the Sacramento *Union* that Twain made his five-month journey to the Sandwich Islands (later renamed Hawaii) in 1866, detailed in *Roughing It*. Relieved to find that the missionaries had not been completely successful in Christianizing the natives, Twain described "the lascivious *hula hula*" and spied on "parties of dusky maidens bathing in the streams or in the sea without any clothing on and exhibiting no very intemperate zeal in the matter of hiding their nakedness."[5]

It had taken him a month of precarious travel to get from San Francisco to New York, and he was only getting started. The *Alta California* newspaper had signed him up for an epic voyage, promising its readers, on December 15, 1866, that Twain was embarking on nothing less than "a journey over the world." The intrepid traveler planned to cross the Atlantic to view the world's fair in Paris. Then he would proceed "through Italy, the Mediterranean, India, China, Japan, and back to San Francisco by the China Mail Steamship line." The editors had faith in their fledgling reporter: "We feel confident his letters to the ALTA . . . will give him a worldwide reputation."[6] Meanwhile, the capacious and richly furnished hotel, with room for six hundred guests and particularly popular with travelers from California, was a perfect place for restoring Twain's waning spirits.

2.

The passage south from San Francisco through a terrible storm had been bad enough. Some of the passengers had resorted to prayer while others, more practical, prepared the lifeboats. The ship limped into port at San Juan del Sur, in Nicaragua, only to learn of a cholera outbreak onshore. When the impatient passengers disembarked after a day's delay, the "bright green hills," according to Twain, "never looked so welcome, so enchanting."[7]

Off the beaten track of American tourists, narrow Nicaragua mainly served, in those pre–Panama Canal days, as a convenient and reasonably comfortable overland passage for travelers making their way between California and the Atlantic coast. San Juan, Twain discovered, consisted of "a few tumble-down frame shanties—they call them hotels—nestling among green verdure and overshadowed by picturesque little hills." Despite the lack of tourist amenities, however, commercialization had already left its mark. As the passengers mounted rented mules and squeezed into carriages for the twelve-mile journey overland, on a "hard, level, beautiful road" leading to the Lake of Nicaragua, they noticed something looming in the distance, "a guideboard perhaps, or a cross, or a modest gravestone of some ill-fated stranger. But it was none of these. When we drew near it turned out to be a sign nailed to a tree, and it said, 'Try Ward's shirts!'"[8] More alluring to Twain were the women by the roadside, with their "liquid, languishing eyes" and their "glossy, luxuriant hair." He was struck by their "voluptuous forms, and such precious little drapery about them."[9]

Twain was equally stunned by the beauty of the landscape, especially the perfect pyramidal mountains rising abruptly from the lake. Dutifully noting Nicaraguan natural resources such as opals and the insect-derived red dye known as cochineal, Twain joked that an American company had bought an extinct volcano as well; "they think they can make it go again."[10]

The travelers made their way by boat across the lake and past the dilapidated Fort San Carlos, a relic of imperial exploits, and entered the San Juan River. Twain was fascinated by the tangle of vegetation: "trees with large red blossoms; great feathery tree ferns and giant cactuses; clumps of tall bamboo; all manner of trees and bushes . . . webbed together with vines; occasionally a vista that opened, stretched its carpet of fresh green grass far within the jungle, then slowly closed again."[11]

As the river narrowed, aspects of the scene took on a hallucinatory dimension, as though the ship had entered a kaleidoscope. An abandoned steamer, wreathed with vines and bright garlands, had metamorphosed into an emerald island. As manmade things reverted to nature, natural forms mimicked the most intricate architecture.

> And everywhere in these vine-robed terraces were charming fairy harbors fringed with swinging garlands; and weird grottoes, whose twilight depth the eye might not pierce; and tunnels that wound their mysterious course none knew whither; and there were graceful temples—columns— towers—pyramids—mounds—domes—walls—all the shapes and forms and figures known to architecture, wrought in the pliant, leafy vines, and thrown together in reckless, enchanting confusion.[12]

And then there were the birds, incredible birds, unnamed and unknown. Amid "waterfalls of glittering leaves" one could see and hear "birds warbling—gorgeous plumed birds on the wing—Paradise itself."[13] Twain marveled as "birds with gaudy feathers and villainous hooked bills stood stupidly on overhanging boughs, and startled one suddenly out of his long cherished, dimly-defined notion that that sort of bird only lived in menageries."

Great parrots flew by, cleaving the air. Twain turned to see "a prodigiously tall bird that had a beak like a powder horn, and curved its neck into an S, and stuck its long legs straight out behind like a steering oar when it flew."[14]

IT WAS RAINING in Greytown on New Year's Day, 1867, when Mark Twain, like a bird of passage himself, boarded the steamboat *San Francisco* for the Caribbean voyage from the east coast of Nicaragua north to New York. The trip turned out to be even more of a nightmare than the shaky first leg of the journey. On January 2, two cases of cholera were reported onboard, and the ship, like a third victim, broke down that night when the first of the passengers died. Twain himself felt sick and feared the worst, scrawling barely decipherable notes in his journal. "Folded his hands after his stormy life," he wrote, "& slept in serenest repose under the peaceful sighing of the summer wind among the grasses over his grave."

By January 5, as the cases mounted, the ship seemed to Twain "a floating hospital." A baby died and then Reverend St. Michael Fackler, an Episcopal clergyman, succumbed as well. The following day, the ship arrived in Key West and many of the sick left the ship. "This Key West *looks*," Twain wrote in his notebook, "like a mere open roadstead, but they call it one of the best *harbors* in the world . . . a very pretty tropical looking town, with plenty of shade trees." Twelve passengers in all died on the journey. The weather turned frigid as the ship lumbered northward and a cold rain fell. A week later, a ghost of its former self, the ship came in view of the flickering lights in New York Harbor.[15]

3.

The years immediately following the end of the Civil War were a boom time for American travel, and Mark Twain, at the outset of his career, was well positioned to record its splendors as well as its miseries. Improvements in transportation had made the traditional journey to Europe cheaper and faster; what had been a destination reserved for the elite became so popular that travelers complained about the glut of American tourists in Paris and Rome.

A self-enclosed world of conveyances and hotels, often outfitted with tour guides, artists-in-residence, and other sophisticated entertainments, made tourist attractions increasingly reliable and safe. Writers and artists confirmed the value of the familiar attractions in a seemingly endless stream of travel narratives and picturesque images of a quaint and overexposed Europe.

But what had once seemed an adventure became, in the process, increasingly predictable, a checklist of familiar sights, from Notre Dame to the Colosseum, to be "done." For those with the means and temperament, more strenuous journeys beckoned, as steamboat lines were established to remote points on the globe in Latin America, the Middle East, and Asia. The challenge for more adventurous writers and artists was to discern something fresh and enlivening in out-of-the-way locales not yet codified and commercialized for tourist consumption.

The tropics were a particularly seductive destination, exuding a promise of relaxed moral codes and vivid, untrammeled landscapes. And so it was that two restless, rootless wanderers—one in flight from New York, the other in flight to it—happened to cross paths in the forests of Nicaragua in 1866. Mark Twain was a writer with an extraordinary visual imagination. Martin Johnson Heade was a visionary painter who wrote on the side. For both Twain and Heade, the passage through the tropics marked a critical moment of self-recognition. Each recognized in the other's work a kindred quest.

4.

Martin Johnson Heade had left London in late 1865, pleased with the victory of Abraham Lincoln's great Army of the Republic, but disappointed that his own ambitious campaign for a luxury album of Brazilian hummingbirds had met with so little enthusiasm among potential English patrons. Back in the United States, Heade resumed his nomadic ways, looking for a possible resting place—or nesting place—in Providence, Trenton, or New York. Nothing seemed quite right, however; and so, like a moth to moonlight, Heade set off again for the tropics, spending much of the summer of 1866 in Nicaragua.

This time Heade's goal was less specific than his journey to Brazil in search of hummingbirds. He had read a book on Nicaragua by a travel writer who had praised "the matchless tints of the skies, the living emerald of the forests, and the light-giving azure of the waters," where "the birds are rainbow-hued."[16] He told his Providence friend John Bartlett that he went to Nicaragua "to get material for a good-sized picture," presumably the kind of tropical grandeur of mountains and waterfalls that Frederic Church had found so lucrative.[17]

Heade's Nicaraguan journey was the opposite of Twain's, from Greytown into the narrow interior, where he lingered on the lake. He did produce a carefully painted view of Omotepe, one of the two extinct volcanoes rising dramatically from the lake. When Heade told Bartlett that he had "found only one thing to make such a picture," he was presumably referring to the volcano.

But such conventional grandeur wasn't really Heade's strength. He was a miniaturist at heart, a collector of small things. Even the volcano picture, he told Bartlett, "I shall not make very large." His desultory Nicaraguan sketchbooks zero in on smaller things: a derelict fort, the same one Mark Twain had noticed, notched into a hillside at the mouth of the San Juan River; a hut, "red red red," as he noted on the drawing; tree moss, "very long and beautiful—light yellow grey."[18]

In such notations, Heade was groping his way toward what really interested him in the tropics: the rank and sprawling vegetation overtaking any human presence. He couldn't get enough of the great green walls surrounding islands in the lake and river; the flamboyant tree ferns with their seemingly fragile trunks; the ubiquitous orchids and passionflowers.

The orchids above all. The orchids and the birds.

In the paintings Heade began after his Nicaraguan sojourn, the old Sunday school decorum of the Brazilian hummingbirds is banished forever. In the amazing painting of 1870 known as *Tropical Landscape with Ten Hummingbirds*, Heade summoned up a tropical dreamscape of lake and mountains in the background, with a frieze of hummingbirds of different species and different locales cavorting promiscuously among passionflowers and moss.

A hothouse sensuality pervades Heade's intense renderings of nesting hummingbirds and oversized orchids, as well as a hint of potential violence. As Sanford Schwartz has written of these pictures:

> They're about a kind of partnership between the orchid plants, which have a startlingly aggressive presence, and the birds, which seem oblivious of the nearby flowers yet are much smaller than them and appear truly diminutive for the first time in Heade's work. The paintings seem to present a threat that isn't being sufficiently acknowledged—which makes the images even more suspenseful . . . Heade's seemingly omnivorous orchids, rearing up on muscular stems and accompanied by unfriendly rubbery pods, certainly convey at least a visual threat.[19]

At the same time, a new awareness of death and decay creeps in. Rotting branches stuccoed with lichen intertwine with mottled and molding seedpods. The mood is a paradoxical combination of scientific precision and rank Gothicism, as though we have stumbled into Rappaccini's garden in Hawthorne's tale.

5.

On the morning of February 3, 1867, Mark Twain, a scant three weeks after his arrival in Manhattan from sultry Nicaragua, took the Brooklyn Ferry across the ice-choked East River to hear Henry Ward Beecher preach at the Plymouth Church. Moses Sperry Beach, owner and editor of the New York *Sun* and a member of the congregation, had urged him to do so. And besides, Twain had brought with him from California letters of introduction to the great man.

"The thermometer was at 180 degrees below zero," Twain wrote, but the red-brick church was filled to capacity with parishioners and curious visitors. All the pews were taken, and Mark Twain squeezed a little stool grudgingly given him by an usher into a space "about large enough to accommodate a spittoon," and waited for the spectacle.[20]

Beecher in the pulpit was something to see. He had a large, well-formed head with hooded eyes and long, flowing hair; he looked like someone who enjoyed being alive. Twain found him "a remarkably handsome man when he is in the full tide of sermonizing, and his face is lit up with animation," though he added that Beecher was "homely as a singed cat when he isn't doing anything." Surrounded by the burgeoning flowers and foliage he favored, as though he were outside under the trees, Beecher was always in motion—walking, gesturing, talking, his magnetic voice modulating from natural speech to sudden flights of passion and poetry. Beecher's mobility, drawn from camp meetings in Indiana and Ohio, was not lost on Twain:

> Whenever he forsook his notes and went marching up and down his stage, sawing his arms in the air, hurling sarcasms this way and that, discharging rockets of poetry and exploding mines of eloquence, halting now and then to stamp his foot three times in succession to emphasize a point, I could have started the audience with a single clap of the hands and brought down the house.[21]

Twain was drawn to this fellow westerner. His mother had insisted that he attend church as a child in Hannibal, Missouri—another border region—where, during the 1840s, he listened to the fire-and-brimstone tenets of backwoods Presbyterianism. He had considered becoming a minister himself, and throughout his life, even toward the end, when he became a staunch unbeliever, he enjoyed the company of liberal Protestant ministers—the "fast nags of the cloth," as he called them. "Preachers are always pleasant company when they are off duty," he wrote.[22]

Perched on his stool in the crowded church, Twain recognized in Beecher's calculatedly relaxed art some of the strengths of his own public presence. Beecher, he wrote, got up and preached one of the liveliest and most sensible sermons I ever listened to. He has a rich, resonant voice, and a distinct enunciation, and makes himself heard all over the church without very apparent effort. His discourse sparkled with felicitous similes and metaphors (it is his strong suit to use the language of the worldly), and might be called a striking mosaic work, wherein poetry, pathos, humor, satire, and eloquent declamation were happily blended upon a ground work of earnest exposition of the great truths involved in his text.[23]

6.

Loitering in New York that winter and spring, in search of promising material for newspaper articles, Twain got wind of an ambitious plan emanating from Plymouth Church. His friend Moses Beach was probably his informant. Subscribers were sought for an epic journey to Europe and the Holy Land aboard a steamer called *The Quaker City*. It was to be the first luxury cruise, and the combination of religion and commerce appealed to Mark Twain's satirical imagination. "It was to be a picnic on a gigantic scale," as he wrote in *The Innocents Abroad*.

> The participants in it, instead of freighting an ungainly steam ferry-boat with youth and beauty and pies and doughnuts, and paddling up some obscure creek to disembark upon a grassy lawn and wear themselves out with a long summer day's laborious frolicking under the impression that it was fun, were to sail away in a great steamship with flags flying and cannon pealing, and take a royal holiday beyond the broad ocean, in many a strange clime and in many a land renowned in history![24]

Besides, Beecher himself was on the passenger list. The cruise, Twain decided, was his lucky break, and at least a partial fulfillment of his projected voyage around the world. He managed to secure the ample fare from the San Francisco *Alta* and waited impatiently for departure.

Accompanied by a music critic from the *Tribune* named Edward House, Twain arrived a bit tipsy at the booking agent's office on Wall Street one morning in late February. House introduced him as "the Reverend Mark Twain," a Baptist missionary just back from the Sandwich Islands. Going along with the gag, Twain asked if the rumor was true that Beecher would be onboard, and expressed concern that a preacher of another denomination might not be welcome. "I am only a Baptist, you see, but I'd like to have a show," he said.

"You don't look like a Baptist minister," the booking agent replied, adding, "you don't smell like one either."[25] Twain returned the next day, contrite and sober, and signed on. But Beecher, along with another celebrity passenger, General William Tecumseh Sherman, canceled at the last minute, much to Twain's disappointment.

7.

When the departure of the *Quaker City* was delayed, Twain, probably at Beecher's suggestion, spent considerable time in the picture galleries of Brooklyn and Manhattan. In late May, Twain attended an exhibition at the National Academy of Design. There he found the enchanted vision he had tried so hard to paint in words in Nicaragua. The painting, *Lagoon in Nicaragua*, was by Martin Johnson Heade, a painter whom Beecher admired.

In a letter published in the *Alta*, Twain described Heade's view of Nicaragua:

> There was a dreamy tropical scene—a wooded island in the center
> of a glassy lake bordered by an impenetrable jungle of trees all woven
> together with vines and hung with drooping garlands of flowers—the

still lake pictured all over with the reflected beauty of the shores—two lonely birds winging their way to the further side, where grassy lawns, and mossy rocks, and a wilderness of tinted foliage, were sleeping in a purple mist. I thought it was beautiful.[26]

Twain found that Heade's evocation of what he called the "charming confusion" of the Nicaraguan landscape, with its "fairy harbors fringed with swinging garlands," matched his own.[27] Each detail—the garlands of flowers, the tinted foliage, the lonely birds—had already appeared in Twain's dispatches to the *Alta*. The roving writer and the roving artist, crossing the Lake of Nicaragua within weeks of each other, had zeroed in on the same vision. Twain worried for a moment whether "one of the birds' hind legs was out of line."[28]

Like a steering oar when it flew.

We know what Heade's *Lagoon in Nicaragua* looked like because Mark Twain saw it and described it so well. The painting itself has vanished from sight, Twain's words its only trace.

8.

A few days later, Mark Twain visited the Tenth Street Studio Building in Manhattan, where Heade was ensconced in his friend Frederic Church's workplace. We can assume that they met on this occasion. Heade's studio would have been difficult to miss. He had decked out the walls to look "like a recess in the woods . . . arched and festooned by long palm-branches." Among the foliage, "multitudes of butterflies from South America glitter like blue, scarlet, or green gems . . . and eagles' heads and stuffed cockatoos make it a fit surrounding to paintings of tropical luxuriance."[29]

Twain's admiration for Heade's work endured. Many years later, around 1882, he purchased another of Heade's tropical scenes, a large Florida landscape, for his dining room in Hartford. The painting, visible in a photograph of Twain's house, has vanished as well.[30]

It was Heade's delicacy that appealed to Mark Twain, the same delicacy of touch that one finds in the best descriptions of the river in *Adventures of Huckleberry Finn*. This was the book in which Twain learned to harness his great themes of mobility and flight to create an indelible portrait of America on the move. The nearly mystical account of the shimmering sunrise over the Mississippi that opens the nineteenth chapter seems to borrow some of its tonal shifts and evanescence from Heade:

> Not a sound, anywheres—perfectly still—just like the whole world was asleep, only sometimes the bull-frogs a-cluttering, maybe. The first thing to see, looking away over the water, was a kind of dull line—that was the woods on t'other side—you couldn't make nothing else out; then a pale place in the sky; then more paleness, spreading around; then the river softened up, away off, and warn't black any more, but gray; you could see little dark spots drifting along, ever so far away—trading scows, and such things; and long black streaks—rafts; sometimes you could hear a sweep screaking; or jumbled up voices, it was so still, and sounds come so far; and by-and-by you could see a streak on the water which you know by the look of the streak that there's a snag there in a swift current which breaks on it and makes that streak look that way; and you see the mist curl up off the water, and the east reddens up, and the river, and you make out a log cabin in the edge of the woods, away on the bank on t'other side of the river . . .[31]

9.

On June 10, the *Quaker City* finally departed New York. As Mark Twain took note of the peculiar mix of Plymouth Church faithful and globetrotting wastrels onboard, he realized that he had material for something grander and more complex than the usual travel narrative. The tedium of the voyage, compounded by hymn singing and restrictions on alcohol consumption, itself became a subject for satire. "Such was our life aboard the ship," he wrote, "solemnity, decorum, dinner, dominoes, prayer, slander."

For Twain, the allure of the voyage was at the opposite extreme from the unfamiliar attractions of Nicaragua, rendered so vividly in Heade's painting. It was the very familiarity of the European sights, drilled into the pilgrims by a thousand reproductions and travel posters, that made the journey ripe for ridicule. "We recognized the brown old Gothic pile in a moment," he wrote of Notre Dame; "it was like the pictures." Of Versailles: "I used to think the pictures exaggerated these distances and these dimensions beyond all reason . . . I know now that the pictures never came up to the subject in any respect, and that no painter could represent Versailles on canvas as beautiful as it is in reality." And as for the dungeons where Dumas's heroes "passed their confinement," Twain remarked that "the place had a far greater interest for us than it could have had if we had known beyond all question who the Iron Mask was, and what his history had been, and why this most unusual punishment had been meted out to him. Mystery! That was the charm."[32]

By the time the *Quaker City* returned to New York in the late fall, Twain had ample material for *The Innocents Abroad*, his first major book. He received publishing advice from an unexpected source.

Soon after his return, Twain was invited to dinner at Henry Ward Beecher's house in Brooklyn. Yet again, Moses Beach, who had taken the *Quaker City* voyage with his daughter, was the go-between. Another guest at the Sunday dinner was Harriet Beecher Stowe. The dinner was "tip-top," Mark Twain told his mother, "but nothing to drink but cider." He told Beecher that "no dinner could be perfect without champagne, or at least some kind of Burgundy." Beecher confided that "privately he was a good deal of the same opinion, but it wouldn't do to say it out loud." Such sentiments greatly appealed to Twain; "Henry Ward is a brick," he exclaimed.

When Twain was bogged down a few weeks later in negotiations with a

Hartford publisher, Beecher took him aside. "Now here—you are one of the talented men of the age—nobody is going to deny that—but in matters of business, I don't suppose you know more than enough to come in when it rains. I'll tell you what to do, and how to do it."[33]

It is difficult to overstate the importance of Henry Ward Beecher's influence on the course of Mark Twain's mature life.[34] During the following years, Mark Twain almost became a Beecher by adoption. A fellow passenger on the *Quaker City* cruise was a dissolute seventeen-year-old named Charles Jervis Langdon. Charlie showed Twain a photograph of his pretty sister, Olivia, back home in Elmira, New York. Twain liked the looks of the girl. The Langdons were on intimate terms with Thomas Beecher, Henry's half-brother and the leading minister in Elmira. Beecher later presided at Mark Twain's marriage with Olivia. When Twain and Olivia, during the early 1870s, built their dream house in Hartford, Connecticut, they lived next door to Harriet Beecher Stowe and near her half-sister Isabella Beecher Hooker.

I O.

"A man who manufactures stupid lies and palms them off on the public with intent to deceive, is a sort of nuisance," Martin Johnson Heade wrote. "But there are such things as interesting liars. Mark Twain, for instance, whose munchausenisms are always filled with wit and fun."[35] (The Baron von Munchausen was the subject of exaggerated tales.) But not everyone was amused by Mark Twain's interesting lies. If Brooklyn and Hartford favored Mark Twain's destiny, Amherst—Beecher's beloved Amherst—most decidedly did not. In a peculiar twist of fate, Mark Twain's marriage and early career were almost derailed by two of Emily Dickinson's closest and most admired friends.

One was Reverend Charles Wadsworth, the Byronic preacher who had made such an impression on Emily Dickinson during her stopover in Philadelphia. In April 1862, Wadsworth had accepted a call from the Calvary Presbyterian Society in San Francisco. Mark Twain heard Wadsworth preach in San Francisco in 1866, and was impressed with his subtle wit:

> Dr. Wadsworth never fails to preach an able sermon; but every now and then, with an admirable assumption of not being aware of it, he will get off a first-rate joke and then frown severely at anyone who is surprised into smiling at it. . . . Several people there on Sunday suddenly laughed and as suddenly stopped again, when he gravely gave the Sunday school books a blast and spoke of "the good little boys in them who always went to Heaven, and the bad little boys who infallible got drowned on Sunday," and then swept a savage frown around the house and blighted every smile in the congregation.[36]

Twain remained an admirer, and one of the letters of introduction he carried to New York was apparently from Wadsworth. Then, on a visit to California after the *Quaker City* voyage, Twain attended a meeting of a literary society in Wadsworth's church, in April 1868; the following month, Wadsworth complimented his *Quaker City* letters to the *Alta*.[37]

A connection with Wadsworth was particularly useful to Twain at the time. He needed a veneer of respectability. He desperately wanted to marry Olivia Langdon, but her father, Jervis Langdon, had heard disturbing rumors about Twain and wanted reassurance.[38] Twain thought he knew Wadsworth well enough to secure from him a character reference. Wadsworth complied. But it proved a miscalculation on Twain's part. Wadsworth confidently predicted that the prospective bridegroom would fill a drunkard's grave.[39] "I would rather bury a daughter of mine than have her marry such a fellow."[40] Somehow Mark Twain's commitment to Olivia Langdon, aided by his signed temperance pledge, survived these dire predictions, and the wedding went forward.

The following year, Mark Twain sought employment at the Hartford *Courant*. The editor, Joseph Hawley, sought the advice of Samuel Bowles, editor of the nearby *Springfield Republican*, and another of Emily Dickinson's closest friends. Bowles had met Mark Twain during a journey to the West, and was no more impressed than Wadsworth had been. "What he'd seen," Ron Powers notes, "prompted him to secretly steer Hawley away" from Twain. Of Bowles's covert backstabbing, Mark Twain told his wife, Olivia, "I . . . find myself calling him in my secret heart a born & bred *cur*, every time."[41]

YET ANOTHER OF Dickinson's closest friends, Thomas Wentworth Higginson, never had much use for Mark Twain either. When he met him for the first time at a dinner for the British novelist Wilkie Collins, Higginson found Twain "something of a buffoon, though with earnestness underneath; and when afterwards at his own house in Hartford, I heard him say grace at table, it was like asking a blessing over Ethiopian minstrels." The notion that there was something exotic, even alien, about Twain was widespread among Boston Brahmins. James Russell Lowell suspected that Twain was Jewish; Higginson's remark suggests that he thought Twain might be black. "He had no wine at his table," Higginson noted approvingly, "and that seemed to make the grace a genuine thing."[42] For his part, Twain was shrewd enough not to waste good liquor on a prig like Higginson.

When Twain lectured in Amherst, on February 27, 1872, the response was predictable. "Mark Twain's lecture, as we anticipated, drew a large audience last evening, about 800 being present," the Amherst *Record* reported. "As a lecturer we are of the opinion that he is a first-class failure."[43]

11.

Harriet Beecher Stowe visited Amherst a few weeks after Twain and got a better reception. At a time when her reputation was still tarnished by the

Lady Byron article, Stowe was preparing to embark on a lecture tour, and distracted herself by taking up oil painting. Tropical flowers were her specialty. "These flowers keep me painting in a sort of madness," she wrote George Eliot from Mandarin in May 1872. "I have just finished a picture of white lilies that grow in the moist land by the watercourses. I am longing to begin on blue iris."[44] For inspiration she had on her wall a print of Frederic Church's painting *A Morning in the Tropics*. "I am painting a *Magnolia grandiflora*," she wrote in April, capturing the three stages of bud, partial opening, and full flowering.[45] She painted passionflowers against a black ground, a dark eroticism exuding from the three-pronged leaves. "Hawthorne," she wrote, "ought to have lived in an orange grove in Florida."[46]

And then, in a big format of two feet by three feet, she painted a snowy owl like a great ghost bird, perched on a gothic branch against a tropical sunset.

Stowe spent the summer of 1872 in Amherst, a few blocks from the Dickinson Homestead, helping her daughter Georgiana, the "drooping bird" of the family. The *Record* for March 13 reported: "Mrs. Harriet Beecher Stowe will spend the summer in Amherst . . . Her daughter, as some of our readers may not know, is the wife of Rev. H. F. Allen, the new Episcopal rector."[47] Georgiana, addicted to morphine and slipping into a deeper dependency on the drug, kept up a brave front. Her husband, Henry Allen, was minister of Grace Church on the lovely, tree-lined Amherst Common, which had recently been redesigned by Frederick Law Olmsted, designer of Central Park in New York and a friend of Austin Dickinson.

Literary visitors were frequent in Amherst, and the Dickinsons usually served as their hosts. Emerson and Wendell Phillips had lectured in Amherst before the war, and stayed at the Evergreens, the stylish house of Emily Dickinson's sister-in-law, Susan Dickinson. The Dickinson and Beecher families were united by ties of marriage and friendship; Susan Dickinson and Harriet Beecher Stowe met on several occasions. Emily Dickinson probably made Stowe's acquaintance as well.

The morning after a visit at Reverend Allen's house, Susan Dickinson took Stowe driving through the Amherst countryside.

I invited her to drive a day or two afterward, and as I knew she was taciturn at times, I took no pains to draw her out, allowing her the freedom of her larger nature undisturbed. The glory of the October morning was too much for her—she clapped her hands in her joy over the yellow maples, begging me to stop now and then that we might sit longer in the golden glory.

They visited a graveyard, and another ghost bird appeared.

I never pass the little cemetery at South Amherst without recalling her interest in the clean, cared-for look of it, quite insisting that the dove finishing one of the marble slabs at the top was a real feather bird; and she would only be convinced to the contrary when I strolled through the grass and put my hand upon it.[48]

12.

"This is a lovely place," Thomas Wentworth Higginson wrote to his wife on August 16, 1870. He had checked into the Amherst House Hotel the night before, and found that Amherst was "unspeakably quiet in the summer afternoon." He walked down Main Street from his hotel to meet "my hitherto unseen correspondent."[49]

In 1867, some of Higginson's old Boston friends had founded the Radical Club, which met each month to discuss papers on literary and philosophical topics by its members. Higginson, still recuperating in Newport from his Civil War trauma, began to make the short trip north for these occasions, delivering a couple of lectures on Buddhism, his latest enthusiasm, a religious philosophy that promised to grant meaning to his own floating and ephemeral existence.[50]

In late 1868, the *Springfield Republican* ran an editorial, presumably by

Samuel Bowles, nominating Higginson for the vacant presidency of Harvard College; the job went to Charles Eliot instead. In 1869 Higginson preached, for the first time in ten years. He chose immortality as his theme; the talk was published in the Radical, the literary journal of the club.

Emily Dickinson alluded to the article when she wrote that June, "A Letter always feels to me like immortality because it is the mind alone without corporeal friend."[51] She had refused all Higginson's entreaties to visit him. But she renewed her invitation to have him visit her. "Could it please your convenience to come so far as Amherst I should be very glad, but I do not cross my Father's ground to any House or town."

Flowers are the dominant theme of Higginson's encounter with Dickinson, as he later recorded it for The Atlantic: "It was at her father's house, one of those large, square, brick mansions so familiar in our older New England towns, surrounded by trees and blossoming shrubs without, and within exquisitely neat, cool, spacious, and fragrant with flowers."[52] Higginson wrote to his wife while the impression of Dickinson's dramatic entrance on the scene was still fresh in his mind:

> A step like a pattering child's in entry & in glided a little plain woman with two smooth bands of reddish hair & a face . . . with no good feature—in a very plain & exquisitely clean white pique & a blue worsted shawl. She came to me with two day lilies which she put in a sort of childlike way into my hand & said "These are my introduction" in a soft frightened breathless childlike voice— & added under her breath Forgive me if I am frightened; I never see strangers & hardly know what I say— but she talked soon & thenceforward continuously— & deferentially— sometimes stopping to ask me to talk instead of her—but readily recommencing.[53]

Higginson's hour with Dickinson reveals the chasm that separated their temperaments. Her remarks charmed and shocked him by turns. When he asked her whether she missed having employment and visitors she answered, "I never thought of conceiving that I could ever have the slightest approach to such a want in all future time," then added, "I feel that I have not expressed myself strongly enough." As though in explanation for how she spent her time, she asked Higginson, to his dismay: "How do most people live without any thoughts? There are many people in the world (you must have noticed them in the street). How do they live? How do they get strength to put on their clothes in the morning?" She seemed to think that Higginson might answer her questions. "Is it oblivion or absorption when things pass from our minds?"

Higginson floated through life, buoyed by the sunnier, more cheerful things. He identified himself with the water lily, that "floats in lonely dignity," and the hovering hummingbird. Dickinson, by contrast, plunged to the essence. His floating world, a Buddhist world perhaps, was not for her. "I never was with anyone who drained my nerve power so much," he wrote his wife. "Without touching her, she drew from me. I am glad not to live near her. She often thought me *tired* . . . " He suspected "an excess of tension," and "something abnormal" in her.[54]

Higginson would have been glad, as he wrote in *The Atlantic*, to bring his relations with her "down to the level of simple truth and every-day comradeship, but it was not altogether easy. She was much too enigmatical a being for me to solve in an hour's interview.

"I could only sit still and watch, as one does in the woods," Higginson concluded. "I must name my bird without a gun, as recommended by Emerson."

13.

Colonel Higginson was back in Newport, at the home of the historian George Bancroft, when Pedro II, emperor of Brazil, made a surprise visit. Higginson was prepared to tell the emperor about many things—Harvard, the Civil War, the rise of American women writers—but what impressed

Dom Pedro was that Higginson was a close friend of the poet John Greenleaf Whittier. After the meeting, Higginson remembered well "the desire that he expressed to see Whittier, and the comparative indifference with which he received our conversation on all other subjects."[55]

Dom Pedro had translated, into his native Portuguese, Whittier's "Cry of a Lost Soul," about a mysterious Brazilian bird whose anguished song resembles a soul consigned to hell. The point of the poem is that as long as nature endures, the soul of man is never utterly lost:

> *But in the traveller's heart a secret sense*
> *Of nature plastic to benign intents,*
> *And an eternal good in Providence,*
>
> *Lifts to the starry calm of heaven his eyes;*
> *And lo! rebuking all earth's ominous cries,*
> *The Cross of pardon lights the tropic skies!*

In gratitude for the poem, Dom Pedro sent the Quaker poet a brace of stuffed and mounted specimens of the bird that had inspired the poem.[56] Now he was eager to meet the poet as well.

During the spring of 1876, Dom Pedro had decided that the time was right to visit the United States. A gracious host to so many American visitors to Brazil, including the scientist Agassiz and the hummingbird painter Heade, Dom Pedro wished to see the country he so admired. He wanted to see the poets and paintings, the factories and prisons, the rivers and railroads. He wanted to see everything. His strategy was simple: first, spend as much time as possible at the Centennial International Exhibition in Philadelphia, the great world's fair that honored the hundredth birthday of the republic by showcasing advances in technology; and second, travel as much as possible during the three months allotted for the visit.

Dom Pedro and his entourage traveled nine thousand miles in all, crisscrossing the country from New York to California by rail and from St. Louis to New Orleans by river. Along the way, he managed to visit every astronomical observatory—his particular passion—as well as art galleries, prisons, factories, and notable people. The treatment of criminals and the insane, Dom Pedro noted with satisfaction, was more humane in Brazil than in the cramped and manacled cells of the United States. He was particularly eager to pay his respects to the poets and novelists of New England: Whittier, Longfellow, and Harriet Beecher Stowe.

Dom Pedro was only the second foreign head of state (after the king of Hawaii) to visit the United States, and popular interest was keen. A reporter for the *New York Herald* accompanied the imperial entourage, which also included the empress and the emperor's private instructor in Sanskrit. The reporter noted with approval the emperor's witticisms (when he learned how many revolutions per minute the Corliss engine made, he said, "That beats our South American republics on revolutions") and his pride that Brazil's waterfalls dwarfed the Niagara. He also reported that Dom Pedro was a staunch Darwinian: "The theory of Darwin is undeniable," the emperor stated. Darwin, for his part, returned the favor: "The Emperor has done so much for science that every scientific man is bound to show him the utmost respect."[57]

Boston was Dom Pedro's favorite American city; he felt most at home among the intellectuals and writers and reformers. Mrs. Agassiz hosted a dinner at the Radical Club in Boston, having consulted beforehand with the emperor about the list of guests. He was disappointed to learn that Harriet Beecher Stowe, whom he was eager to meet, was in her Florida retreat in Mandarin. But Whittier was there, and Dom Pedro tried to bestow on his idol the Brazilian bear hug of greeting. The shy Quaker poet fended him off with a warm handshake and the two spent an intimate half hour in each other's company. Whittier confided in the emperor his fervent hope that Brazil would complete the work of emancipating its slaves. A festive dinner hosted by Longfellow followed. Longfellow described the modest emperor as a "modern Haroun-al-Raschid wandering about to see the world as a simple traveler, not as a king. He is a hearty, genial, noble person, very liberal in his views."

A glimpse of the northern skies through a modern telescope was second in the emperor's mind only to a glimpse of Whittier. The emperor's party reached Washington on May 7 and checked into the Arlington Hotel. That very evening, before meeting President Grant or any other American officials, the emperor was received at the Naval Observatory by Professor Simon Newcomb, the leading American astronomer.[58]

Later, at Vassar College, the emperor surprised the great astronomer Maria Mitchell—one of Higginson's summer companions at Newport—with his sophisticated questions about her instruments. He asked whether Alvin Clark had made the glass of the equatorial and "seemed much more interested in the observatory than I could possibly expect," she wrote. "I asked him to go on top of the roof [of the observatory], and he said that he had no time; yet he stayed long enough to go up several times."[59]

Chapter Seven

COVERT FLOWERS, HIDDEN NESTS

There is a flower that Bees prefer—
And Butterflies—desire—
To gain the Purple Democrat
The Humming Bird—aspire—

🦋 EMILY DICKINSON[1]

I.

HENRY WARD BEECHER was back in Boston, idling away an afternoon in his favorite haunts. The picture galleries as always were a drug and a distraction for him. Now, in 1867, they were full of still lifes, of the kind Beecher's sisters Catherine and Harriet were recommending in their latest manifesto of domestic taste, *The American Woman's Home*. Beecher, like a bumblebee, loved flowers; he celebrated them in his sermons and filled his church with them. Here on the gallery walls were roses and lilies, in vases and crystal bowls. The picture dealers resembled conservatories, gardens, woodland paths. Beecher's head was awash with images; he was thrilled, intoxicated.

His eye fell on a picture called *The Trailing Arbutus*.[2] He realized immediately that this was what he had come for.

He bought it and carried it back to Brooklyn, as a gift for one of his parishioners. Her name was Elizabeth Tilton. And here, in this painting of a lowly spring wildflower that blooms in the melting snow—"Pink—small—and punctual," as Emily Dickinson described it—is a clue to the biggest romantic scandal of the nineteenth century in America.[3] At the heart of the question of what Henry Ward Beecher did or did not do with Elizabeth Tilton was a strange and tantalizing tale of birds and flowers—a New England tale played out for the nation's amusement and horror.

2.

Beecher's Plymouth Church was a congregation of transplants, homesick New Englanders marooned in Brooklyn and determined to hold on to their favorite cults and rituals, and their own distinctive offshoot of New England Congregationalism. They called their church "Plymouth" after the original settlement of the Pilgrims on the Massachusetts coast. It was the Quaker poet and abolitionist John Greenleaf Whittier who had spread the attractive legend that the Pilgrims, after their dreadful first winter on Plymouth Rock, had espied the first flower of spring—the first flower they had seen in the New World. They called it the mayflower, after the ship that had brought them. Never mind that the designation referred to another flower in England; henceforth, in New England, the mayflower and trailing arbutus were one and the same.

Whittier's poem "The Mayflowers" opened with a startling metaphor, as the ship became a flower in winter:

Sad Mayflower! Watched by winter stars,
And nursed by winter gales,

With petals of the sleeted spars,
  And leaves of frozen sails?

What had she in those dreary hours,
  Within her ice-rimmed bay,
In common with the wild-wood flowers,
  The first sweet smiles of May?

Yet, "God be praised!" the Pilgrim said,
  Who saw the blossoms peer
Above the brown leaves, dry and dead,
  "Behold our Mayflower here!"

For Whittier, the mayflower was a covenant between God and the Pilgrims; these "sacred flowers of faith and hope" were a sign, like the rainbow, of a special providence for the hardy settlers who would bring life from the rocky soil and frozen sod of New England, thus celebrating "Our Freedom's struggling cause":

Behind the sea-wall's rugged length
Unchanged, your leaves unfold,
Like love behind the manly strength
Of the brave hearts of old.

For Whittier and later acolytes of the arbutus cult—Henry Ward Beecher, Harriet Beecher Stowe, Thomas Wentworth Higginson, Martin Johnson Heade, and Emily Dickinson—the special allure of the flower was both its earliness and the way it seemed to coexist with winter and other signs of mortality. Trailing arbutus grew close to the ground, and often lay concealed beneath snowdrifts, its splotched and brown-speckled leaves in striking contrast to its pretty clusters of pink petals. The flower seemed to

Heade, Trailing Arbutus *(Mr. and Mrs. Stuart P. Feld, New York)*

partake of both winter and spring, of death and life: "And through the dead leaves of hope shall spring / Afresh the flowers of God!"[4]

Whittier's poem was on the lips of many men and women who took to the New England woods in April to be the first to find the hidden flower that was, as Dickinson wrote, "Covert in April" but "Candid—in May."[5] Forays into the woods in search of trailing arbutus were a mating ritual in New England as well as a religious and patriotic quest. Dickinson marked each spring with a report of the first sighting of arbutus, and identified herself so closely with the shy and "covert" flower that she signed a poem—a riddle in verse form—"Arbutus," one of only nine poems she signed.

Martin Johnson Heade's exquisite painting of 1860, *Trailing Arbutus*, is as much a portrait as a memorial of a quest achieved and trophy brought home. The single acorn on the table beside the great horizontal spray of blossoms and mottled leaves looks like a stand-in for Heade himself, admiring the profusion of early spring. Heade had a special feeling for trailing arbutus, which he painted again around 1869 in his Whittier-inspired picture *Flowers of Hope*.[6] It was just such a picture that caught Henry Ward Beecher's eye in the picture gallery in Boston.

3.

No one was more closely identified with the arbutus cult than Henry Ward Beecher. In a popular essay of 1862, he described a foray into the hills above Elmira, New York, where he was visiting his half-brother Thomas, and where Mark Twain later spent his summers. Beecher personified the flower in a particularly seductive way:

> Its little viny stem creeps close to the ground, humble, faithful, and showing how the purest white may lay its cheek on the very dirt, without soil or taint.

> The odor of the arbutus is exquisite, and as delicate as the plant is modest. Some flowers seem determined to make an impression on you. They stare at you. They dazzle your eyes. If you smell them, they over-fill your sense with their fragrance. They leave nothing for your gentle-ness and generosity, but do everything themselves.

Not so the gentle arbutus:

> But this sweet nestler of the spring hills is so secluded, half covered with russet leaves, that you would not suspect its graces, did you not stoop to uncover the vine, to lift it up, and then you espy its secluded beauty. If you smell it, at first it seems hardly to have an odor. But there steals out of it at length the finest, rarest scent, that rather excites desire than satis-fies your sense. It is coy, without designing to be so, and its reserve plays upon the imagination far more than could a more positive way.[7]

It is no wonder that Beecher's mail in April was full of boxes of arbutus and soil sent from women all over America. But there was a particular woman among his admirers whom Beecher associated with the "sweet nestler of the spring hills."

4 ·

During the late 1860s, when his fame was at its height—fueled by the legend that on his visit to England in 1863 he had single-handedly swayed British public opinion in favor of the Union side—Beecher had rashly taken on a challenge that even he, with his gift for language and sentiment, was finding all but insuperable. He had agreed to write a novel. His sister Harriet had excelled at the art, with no great show of effort, so why shouldn't he? Beecher signed a contract, for a considerable sum, only to discover that he had no gift for fixing characters or shaping a narrative. He needed help, someone who had more confidence in his prowess than he did. And he found it in Elizabeth Tilton, the wife of his best friend.

Theodore Tilton was like a son to Beecher. He had grown up in the expensive pews of Plymouth Church; he had worshipped there and married there. He knew Beecher's improvised sermons better than Beecher himself did, having transcribed them, first by shorthand and then for the printer. When their work at the church was done, Beecher and Tilton would take the ferry to Manhattan, and spend hours together at the picture galleries and bookstalls. Tall and thin, with shoulder-length hair and soulful eyes, Tilton looked like a Romantic poet and aspired to be one. He wrote tepid verse for children early on; later in life he wrote tepid verse for adults. But Tilton's literary energy, such as it was, went into radical causes. As writer and editor for newspapers hatched and funded by the Plymouth Church, especially the influential *Independent*, Tilton enthusiastically embraced the causes of his mentor, abolition and temperance, while going much further than Beecher in taking up the cause of women's rights. Beecher was all for women's dignity and respect, but his views on women's place more closely chimed with the views of his famous sisters, Harriet and Catherine (and his wife, Eunice), regarding the "American woman's home." Tilton by contrast believed that women should have the right to vote and the right to divorce. He was a close friend of Elizabeth Cady Stanton and Susan B. Anthony; his intimacy with them brought about his downfall.

The birdlike Elizabeth Tilton, reclusive and shy, "a strangely earnest little brunette" according to her teachers, seemed in some ways an unlikely match for the outgoing Tilton.[8] As Tilton toured the country espousing his catalog of causes to enthusiastic audiences, Elizabeth stayed at home alone to care for their five children in the cozy house on Livingston Street. She adored her preacher, Reverend Beecher, and when he came to visit—making his rounds—they spent a good deal of time together. Theodore Tilton, feeling guilty about his own incessant travel and proud of his idol's pleasure in his wife's company, encouraged these visits. "There is one little woman down at my house who loves you more than you have an idea of," Tilton told Beecher. After his trip to England in 1863, when he preached the cause of abolition to audiences of workingmen, Beecher brought Elizabeth Tilton a brooch of Brazilian topaz.[9]

Beecher labored over his novel, tearing up pages and repeatedly beginning over. Like Coleridge, he found solutions in his dreams: "I have *dreamed* two plots," he wrote a friend. "But forgot them as soon as I *waked*!" Finally he managed to coax a few chapters into existence. Nonetheless, he confessed, "I was about in despair, and I needed somebody or other that would not be critical, and that would praise it, to give me the courage to go on with it." Eunice Beecher was nothing if not critical, an unlikely muse in every way, so Beecher went to Elizabeth Tilton— Theodore was again away—and read his manuscript pages aloud to her. "She was good enough to speak very enthusiastically of them," he reported, "and was particularly delighted with that scene in which the heroine was born, when the old doctor had gone out into the fields and gathered a crown of trailing arbutus."[10]

THE SCENE IN the fifth chapter of *Norwood* seems like something from a dream. Dr. Reuben Wentworth, a good man in a village modeled on Amherst, Massachusetts, wishes to celebrate the birth of his daughter. It is early spring, thunder cracks the sky, and the doctor goes out in search of the earliest trailing arbutus: "Flowers live. All things are coming forth. Her time is come. But she must have her crown." The hired man draws a blank when the doctor asks him where to look for trailing arbutus, but understands when he mentions mayflowers.

> Clearing away the leaves he revealed the sweetest flower that opens to the northern sky. It is content, though lying upon the very ground. It braves the coldest winters. All the summers can not elaborate a perfume so sweet as that which seems to have been born of the very winter. It is like the breath of love. The pure white and pink blossoms, in sweet clusters, lie hidden under leaves, or grass, and often under untimely snows. Blessings on thee! Thou art the fairest, most modest and sweetest-breathed of all our flowers!

Beecher completes this paean to fertility. The next morning, "while the air was soft and balmy, and roots were swelling, and buds opening, and blossoms coming forth, and birds singing love-songs in all the trees, was born ROSE WENTWORTH."[11]

Of course, it wasn't difficult for Elizabeth Tilton to imagine herself, under the grateful preacher-novelist's eyes, as resembling the capitalized heroine—fair, modest, and sweet-breathed. And when, shortly after, Beecher presented her with the picture of trailing arbutus he had bought for her in Boston, she could only feel confirmed in her suspicions and her hopes. Elizabeth Tilton proudly showed the picture to Susan B. Anthony and to other visitors at Livingston Street.[12]

In August 1868, the Tiltons' infant son, Paul, suddenly fell ill and died, and now it was Elizabeth's turn to seek support from her pastor. The mutual need—Beecher for encouragement for his novel, Elizabeth for comfort in her mourning—drew them even more closely together. On October 10, 1868, a date that was to be cited again and again in the trials that followed, Elizabeth Tilton wrote a single entry in her private diary: "A Day Memorable."

Precisely what made the day memorable was to be debated among the parties and in the press for many years to come. On the steamy night of July 3, 1870, Elizabeth Tilton told her husband, Theodore, that it was on that fateful day of October 10, 1868, that she had first committed adultery with her pastor, Reverend Henry Ward Beecher, and that the affair had continued for a year and a half until that spring. Elizabeth told her husband that Beecher, drawing on a metaphor from *Norwood*—the novel for which she, Elizabeth, had served as muse—had urged her to regard concealing their secret as "nest-hiding."[13] In the novel, Mrs. Wentworth conceives of her love for her husband as a divine thing, to be hidden from mere mortals:

> It would seem as if, while her whole life centered upon his love, she would hide the precious secret by flinging over it vines and flowers, by mirth and raillery, as a bird hides its nest under tufts of grass, and behind leaves and vines, as a fence against prying eyes.[14]

Beecher implied that for such "higher natures" special laws of the heart apply. "The world is good for a nest, but it is bad for a flying place," Beecher wrote in a sermon of 1872. "It is a good place to be hatched in, but it is a sad place to practice one's wings in. If a man has power to fly, he does not want to be confined to a nest. The glory and power of the eagle is never known while he lives on his cliff—not till he has abandoned that and sought his new home."[15] Beecher, who imagined himself an eagle, was at his most Nietzschean, or his most Byronic, in such passages.

Beecher asked Elizabeth Tilton to hide the sacred nest, but whose nest was being hidden remained unclear, for at least three domestic arrangements were in peril: those of the Tiltons, the Beechers, and the improvised love nest of Henry Ward Beecher and Elizabeth Tilton.

And then there was the larger nest of Plymouth Church.

5·

The strategy from the outset was concealment. Frank Moulton, who became known in the press as the "mutual friend," brought the parties together. A freethinking friend of Theodore Tilton's, Moulton was agnostic in matters of religion, and agnostic too in matters of the heart. Though his wife attended Plymouth Church, he himself did not, thus preserving (in Tilton's view) an impartial distance on the famous preacher. Moulton had met Beecher when Beecher was having his portrait painted, at Tilton's behest and expense, by Thomas Hicks, the fashionable painter who probably introduced his friend Martin Johnson Heade to Beecher.[16]

Like a skilled marriage counselor, Moulton coaxed confessions and forgiveness from each side. He pocketed the confessions and placed them in a locked safe. It became clear from the outset that all parties were willing to sacrifice Elizabeth Tilton; she was either a straying wife (Tilton's view) or a fantasist (Beecher's claim). The marriage to be saved was not the Tilton marriage but rather the more intimate and volatile relationship between Tilton and Beecher.

Things may have stayed this way, the little nest concealed, had not a larger domestic intrusion occurred, in the extraordinary person of Victoria Woodhull. "The Woodhull," as she came to be known in disapproving newspapers, was one of those larger-than-life characters spawned by the haphazard and informal arrangements of a still Wild West on an unassuming Eastern establishment. Her father, Reuben Claflin, was a gambler, a horse dealer, and a counterfeiter who had drifted west from Massachusetts, married a housemaid named Roxanna along the way, and fathered ten children in the upstart town of Homer, Ohio, where they lived, as Robert Shaplen remarks, "in squalor and chaos in an unpainted, largely bedless frame shack on a hillside."[17] Victoria, the seventh child, was a revivalist preacher by age eleven and a spiritualist thereafter. At fifteen she married a drunken quack named Canning Woodhull, "Dr. Woodhull" to his hoodwinked clients. Victoria tried many professions—she worked as a cigar girl in California and an actress before teaming up with her sister Tennessee (who wrote her name "Tennie C.") as a touring spiritualist act. On a stop in St. Louis she met and fell in love with a luxuriously bearded Civil War veteran called Colonel James Blood; with five bullet wounds in his body, he too, it turned out, was a spiritualist. Conveniently, Blood believed in the new creed of "free love," and Dr. Woodhull, soothing whatever jealousy he may have felt with drink, went along with the new arrangement.

Victoria Woodhull's true public career began in 1868, when her favorite spirit, Demosthenes, appeared in a vision and summoned her to New York. During the next few years, working closely with Tennie C., she became one of the most visible and controversial women in the country. She had a talent for being the first in many things. When Cornelius Vanderbilt fell under Tennie's spell, he set up the two sisters in a brokerage firm in early 1870; they were the first female brokers on Wall Street. In *Woodhull and Claflin's Weekly*, the newspaper Vanderbilt funded, the sisters were the first to publish the English translation of Marx and Engels's *Communist Manifesto*. And when Benjamin Butler of Massachusetts wanted a woman—the first woman to testify before Congress—to plead the cause of women's suffrage, Victoria Woodhull was happy to oblige. (General Butler, an unseemly schemer, was an unlikely defender of women's rights; as the officer in charge of the Union occupation of New Orleans, annoyed with insults hurled at his men, he had issued the notorious "woman's order," requiring his soldiers to treat any unaccompanied woman found on the streets of the city as a common prostitute.)

And then, to cap an already spectacular career, in May 1872 Woodhull accepted the nomination of the newly formed Equal Rights Party to run for the presidency of the United States; her running mate was Frederick Douglass.

Woodhull, not surprisingly, had many enemies—she was, in her way, as polarizing a figure as John Brown. It did not help her prospects for the presidency that Frederick Douglass had not attended the convention and refused to campaign for the new party. It did not help her prospects for leadership of the women's rights movement that she supported organized labor and continued to preach—and practice—a form of "free love" inimical to her more conservative supporters. Elizabeth Cady Stanton and Susan B. Anthony soon distanced themselves from Woodhull. Cornelius Vanderbilt withdrew his support for Woodhull's newspaper.

But the most vocal of Woodhull's opponents were two sisters of Henry

Ward Beecher: Catherine Beecher and Harriet Beecher Stowe. Stowe had published a series of letters attacking Woodhull's views and had caricatured her in her satirical novel *My Wife and I*. In 1872, Woodhull decided to fight back. She had what she considered a trump card. Theodore Tilton, wallowing in self-pity and indignation, had confided the secret of his wife's infidelity to Elizabeth Stanton, who in turn conveyed it to Woodhull. And now Woodhull decided to cash it in. She wrote a letter to Beecher, demanding an interview:

> Two of your sisters have gone out of their way to assail my character and purposes, both by the means of the public press, and by numerous private letters written to various persons with whom they seek to injure me, and thus to defeat the political ends at which I aim.
>
> You doubtless know that it is within my power to strike back, and in ways more disastrous than anything that can come to me; but I do not desire to do this. I simply desire justice from those from whom I have a right to expect it. I speak guardedly, but I think you will understand me.[18]

Beecher called her bluff. At a convention of spiritualists in Boston, during the fall of 1872, Woodhull leveled her charge against Beecher. The conservative Boston press refused to print the story. She repeated the charge to reporters in New York. Again, nothing.

And so, on November 2, 1872, Victoria Woodhull printed a final issue of her *Weekly*, spelling out her accusation that Beecher was a hypocrite for practicing "free love" while refusing to preach it. "I am impelled by no hostility whatever to Mr. Beecher, nor by any personal pique toward him or any other person," she wrote. She claimed to admire the great man for acting on his "immense physical potency" and "the indomitable urgency of his great nature." Beecher's intimacy with a "noble and cultured woman" like Mrs. Tilton should hardly be viewed as "a bad thing as the world thinks, or thinks it thinks, or professes to think that it thinks," but rather as "one of the grandest and noblest of the endowments of this truly great and representative man." In short, Beecher was to be commended for acting on his healthy desires; he was to be condemned only for trying to conceal them. "The fault with which I charge him," Woodhull concluded, "is not infidelity to the old ideas, but unfaithfulness to the new."

Anthony Comstock, the self-appointed scourge of all things scurrilous, requested a copy of the paper by mail, then had Woodhull arrested for sending immoral materials through the U.S. mail. Victoria Woodhull, the Equal Rights Party candidate for president, spent Election Day in jail.

6.

The details of the highly publicized adultery trials that followed—first the official investigation by the Plymouth Church, in 1873, into its preacher's possible wrongdoing, and then the civil proceeding the following year brought by Theodore Tilton against his former friend—have been told innumerable times, and need not be repeated here. The nation was transfixed by the testimony of Tilton, Beecher, their servants, and their friends. There were new, salacious accusations—for example, that Elizabeth Tilton had aborted a "love child" in 1869, and that Beecher was its father.

Everyone agreed that the lawyers were magnificent; William Evarts, Beecher's chief attorney, was particularly impressive. Beecher's supporters filled the courtroom with flowers—bouquets of lilies, roses, and camellias—mute witnesses to his innocence. None of the testimony was particularly flattering for Beecher, however, whose own performance as a witness was fumbling at best. His best defense was that he seemed to remember nothing, not even—so he claimed on the witness stand—his own novel.

Beecher was asked if he had given Mrs. Tilton a picture called *The Trailing Arbutus*. Beecher remembered that he had done so. Did he do so after reading *Norwood* to her? This too Beecher conceded. Did he recall that in *Norwood* he had called the blossom of trailing arbutus "the breath of love"? Beecher said he remembered no such thing.[19]

The question of precisely what Beecher had meant by "nest-hiding" came up during the civil trial, for Mrs. Tilton had written a letter to Beecher in 1871 calling it one of her "weapons," along with the higher love she felt for her pastor. Beecher claimed he was unfamiliar with the phrase. On cross-examination, he continued his denials:

> Q: Do you remember, in writing that book [*Norwood*], of borrowing from the habit of the bird in hiding its nest a figure to illustrate the way that love might be concealed, if it were necessary? A: I do not, Sir.
>
> Q: Do you recollect of describing Mr. and Mrs. Wentworth, and especially the peculiarities of the lady, in the book? A: No, I had forgotten it.

Tilton's lawyer then quoted the passage from the novel, and asked whether Beecher remembered writing it. "I do not, Sir," Beecher replied. "I have never read the book since the day it came out of the press." The lawyer tried once more: "Won't you be kind enough to explain what you understood . . . nest-hiding to mean?" But Beecher was immovable: "No, Sir, I cannot."[20]

BEECHER WAS CLEARED of all wrongdoing by the Plymouth Church investigating committee, whose membership he had selected. The decision of the civil trial brought by Tilton was less than unanimous. The trial lasted for six months, from January 11 to July 2, 1875, the deliberations for eight stiflingly hot days. After fifty-two ballots, only one juror had shifted position. From eight to four against a verdict for Tilton the numbers were finally nine to three. Beecher's supporters considered the hung jury a vindication.

Then, on April 13, 1878, Elizabeth Tilton, separated from her husband, confessed again: "The charge brought by my husband, of adultery between myself and the Reverend Henry Ward Beecher, was true . . ."[21] Every newspaper in the country carried her confession. But by then she had changed her story so many times that this latest—and final—declaration seemed hardly to ruffle the great man's reputation, which was again on the rise. Beecher, of course, had not confessed.

7·

During the trials and after, public opinion remained divided, with Beecher's supporters concentrated in the liberal Northeast, while much of the rest of the country assumed that something suspect had transpired between the flamboyant preacher and Elizabeth Tilton. For his defenders, Beecher's innocence was almost a point of faith; for his opponents, Beecher's silence was as damning as a confession. There were even divisions within the far-flung Beecher family. Harriet Beecher Stowe, for her part, was never in doubt about her favorite brother's innocence; she came down from Hartford and attended the trial each day, sitting in the front row.

Other Beecher siblings were just as convinced of his guilt. Henry's half-sister Isabella Beecher Hooker wrote Thomas Beecher in Elmira, "Now, Tom, so far as I can see, it is he who has dragged the dear child into the slough, and left her there." Thomas Beecher agreed, adding, "Of the two, Woodhull is my hero and Henry my coward."[22]

Mark Twain, from his new home in Hartford next door to Harriet Beecher Stowe, sided with his friends Hooker and Thomas Beecher: "*I* think the silence of the Beechers is a hundredfold more of an *obscene publication* than that of the Woodhulls." He added that "the general thought of the nation will gradually form itself into the verdict that there is *some* fire somewhere in all this smoke of scandal."[23]

The *New York Daily Graphic* reported on March 10, 1875, that George Sand—crusading French novelist, fervent admirer of *Uncle Tom's Cabin*, and famous lover of Alfred de Musset and Frédéric Chopin—was planning to write a novel about the "profound spiritual tragedy" revealed in the Beecher-Tilton affair. According to the report, Sand "has written of many profound spiritual tragedies in her day, but never has found one in real life at all comparable for psychological effects with that with which she will deal in her new book."[24] Alas, Sand died the following year, depriving the world of what would have been a fascinating book.

8.

The view from Amherst College, of which Beecher was easily the most famous alumnus, was conflicted. Beecher had included an idyllic chapter set at Amherst College in *Norwood*, but his trials were hardly a good thing for the status of the college. If his fellow alumnus Judge Otis Lord had been waiting for revenge since that July afternoon in 1862, when Henry Ward Beecher bested him in the contest of commencement speakers, he seized his chance during the Plymouth Church investigation. In an article entitled "A Boston Judgment of the Case," printed in the *Springfield Republican* on September 24, 1874, Lord scoffed at the idea of Beecher's innocence. He wondered why the church had paid so little attention to Beecher's threat of taking poison, and was amused at Benjamin Butler's unsavory role in the proceedings.

While others saw the scandal as a religious or moral conflict, Lord concentrated on its political repercussions. Amid the Andrew Johnson impeachment, the old Whig didn't conceal his pleasure at the downfall of yet another conspicuous Republican; the embattled party, according to Lord, couldn't help but cling to Beecher's supposed innocence "with the tenacity of a drowning man to his last plank." As a seasoned judge, Lord ridiculed the church's claim that there was no "written evidence" of improper relations between Beecher and his paramour, "as if every man of pleasure, like Richardson's Lovelace, sat down and wrote out, each day, an exact account of his intrigues."

But perhaps, as we shall see, there was something more than rivalry at work here. We may wonder whether the judge was truly the guardian of old New England values. Is it possible that he was concealing an "intrigue" of his own, involving the daughter of one of his staunchest supporters in the old Whig circles? Was the unimpeachable Judge Otis P. Lord of Salem something of a "man of pleasure" himself?

9·

So well hidden were Henry Ward Beecher's covert flowers that some of them are still coming to light. In early 1860, as the biographer Debby Applegate recently revealed, Beecher became very close to Chloe Beach, one of his wealthiest parishioners.[25] Beach's husband, Moses, owned and edited the New York *Sun*; it was Beach who had first urged Mark Twain to hear Beecher preach, had traveled with him aboard the *Quaker City*, and had secured a dinner invitation for Mark Twain at Beecher's table.

When the extent of Chloe's affection for Beecher became clear to Moses, he bought a house up the Hudson to get as far from Plymouth Church as possible. Chloe, however, was miserable, and the couple returned to Brooklyn sixteen months later. The reserved and sensitive Chloe, always a favorite of Eunice Beecher, became a fixture in the Beecher household, and accompanied them to Fort Sumter for Beecher's address there in 1865. Since Eunice spent the winter months in Florida, Henry had ample time for Chloe. The intimacy finally became intolerable to Moses in early 1866, but his confrontation with Beecher came too late: Chloe Beach was pregnant.

Separated for the moment from Chloe, and uncertain about the progress of his novel, *Norwood*, Beecher took refuge in the Tilton household, with the explosive results known to all the world. But the Chloe Beach affair remained secret, until now.

Violet Beach was born on January 29, 1867. In the absence of DNA evidence, her paternity remains in question, but Applegate makes a strong case that Violet was Henry Ward Beecher's child. The violet, as Applegate notes, was one of Beecher's favorite flowers; he loved the way it bloomed in "shady, sheltered spots." For Applegate, however, the strongest evidence lies in photographs taken of Violet as a child, including an extraordinary studio portrait of Beecher and Violet dating from the early 1870s. "Already," as Applegate notes, "her face shows hints of Henry's moon shape and ample mouth."[26] As she grew older, the resemblance increased.

"Covert in April, candid in May," as Emily Dickinson wrote of the shade-seeking flowers of spring.

Part Three

TRANSITS

OF

VENUS

Chapter Eight

FOGGY BOTTOM

His whole conception of the place of man in the universe
had been upset at some point in his childhood by seeing the
planet Venus through a telescope.

❧ EDMUND WILSON

I.

WASHINGTON, D.C., DURING the late fall of 1881 was an unlikely place to go in search of Venus. The goddess of love was
more likely to be lurking in places where beautiful women were
known to congregate—Paris and Rome, for example, or tropical islands
deep in the South Seas. Why would she be wasting her time amid the dusty
haunts of office seekers and congressmen along the Potomac? America itself seemed hostile to Venus in those days. Henry Adams, the displaced
Bostonian who lived a few blocks from the White House, where his grandfather and great-grandfather had once held sway, looked for Venus in vain
in American art and society. "An American Venus would never dare exist,"
he wrote in the chapter titled "The Dynamo and the Virgin" in his *Education
of Henry Adams*. Adams wondered whether any American artist "had ever
insisted on the power of sex, as every classic had always done." He could

think of only Walt Whitman. Predictably, authorities in Boston had sought to suppress Whitman's erotic poetry. Adams concluded that "American art, like the American language and American education, was as far as possible sexless."[1]

Henry James visited Washington that winter of 1881 and stayed with Henry Adams and his clever wife, Clover. James described the carefully planned and oddly abstract city, so lacking in sex appeal, as "bristling and geometrical; the long lines of its avenues seemed to stretch into national futures." It remained an open question whether Venus in her sexual glamour was part of those futures. James, for the fun of it, set one of his stories in Washington, with a magnetic young woman—a sort of grown-up Daisy Miller—stirring things up among ambassadors and congressmen. He called her Pandora Day and had an inquisitive young German count named Vogelstein ("Birdstone") fall in love with her.

In "Pandora," Mrs. Bonnycastle (modeled on Clover Adams) subjects the American girl to a Darwinian analysis: "The American girl isn't *any* girl; she's a remarkable specimen in a remarkable species." Vogelstein asks for clarification and Alfred Bonnycastle obliges: "My dear Vogelstein, she's the latest freshest fruit of our great American evolution. She's the self-made girl!" Vogelstein is even more confused. "The fruit of the great American Revolution?" he asks. Later, on the terrace of the Capitol, as they look out on "the yellow sheen of the Potomac, the hazy hills of Virginia, the far-gleaming pediment of Arlington, the raw confused-looking country," Pandora asks Vogelstein "whether the eminence on which they stood didn't give him an idea of the Acropolis in its prime."[2]

2.

Washington's fog-infested river basin, whatever its picturesque charm was from afar, was hardly ideal for viewing the planet Venus. Nevertheless, the leading astronomers in the United States congregated in the United States Naval Observatory in Foggy Bottom and in office buildings nearby, where so-called "calculators" prepared statistics on the perambulations of heavenly bodies. The imposing astronomer Simon Newcomb, with his full beard and piercing eyes, ruled this demesne, surrounded by a phalanx of bright young men. A recent Amherst College graduate named David Todd had been at Newcomb's side in August 1877 during the opposition of Mars, when the red planet was closest to Earth. It was Todd who first recognized that a point of light near Mars was in fact an unknown satellite orbiting the planet, the moon that Newcomb named Phobos.

Despite this remarkable discovery, David Todd's true talents did not lie in observation—he had weak eyes and little patience—but rather in the machines and mechanisms for viewing heavenly bodies. Todd's promise was recognized early; Thomas Edison offered him a job in 1876, to join him in New Jersey in his experiments with electricity. Excited by the prospect of the new twenty-six-inch refractor at the Naval Observatory, at that time the largest lens in the world, Todd went to Washington instead, and a year later had his rendezvous with Phobos.

Mechanical gadgetry had fascinated David Todd ever since his childhood in Brooklyn, when he sat in Reverend Henry Ward Beecher's Plymouth Church and marveled at the great organ there. A direct descendant of the great Puritan minister Jonathan Edwards, Todd was baptized at age ten by Beecher himself. But as Polly Longsworth notes, "The most fascinating thing about Plymouth Church in David's eyes was not Rev. Beecher but the church's huge new hand-pumped Hook and Hastings organ."[3] Todd was a small boy—he never grew taller than five and a half feet tall when fully grown—and morbidly shy; the organ appealed to him as a magical source of power. He befriended the Plymouth Church organist and was allowed to work the bellows and look inside the instrument; he confided that on that day he "fell in love with organs." His parents bought him a secondhand organ which he learned to play. When he entered Amherst College in 1873, Todd was still uncertain about whether he wished to be a professional organist or an astronomer.

Todd's work at Amherst on the planet Jupiter attracted Newcomb's notice, and Todd was offered upon graduation an appointment on the U.S. Transit of Venus Commission. "Transit" refers to a rare astronomical event, when the planet Venus passes directly between Earth and the sun; the transit is observable as a tiny shadow—like a beauty spot—crossing the sun's broad face. The commission was charged with interpreting the observations made during the 1874 Transit of Venus, in anticipation of another Transit of Venus projected for December 1882. While the transits of 1874 and 1882 were only eight years apart, fully 122 years would pass before the next Transit of Venus, in the year 2004 (with another to occur in 2012). Newcomb and Todd knew that the 1882 Transit of Venus would be the last one they would view in their lifetimes.

3.

On a rainy June day in 1877, David Todd achieved another sighting, no less momentous for his future career than his glimpse of the satellite of Mars later that same summer. He had stopped by the Nautical Almanac Office to borrow a telescope, and there, standing in the pouring rain, stood an elderly man and a beautiful young woman wrapped in an old blue raincoat. It was the woman who arrested David Todd's attention. He made inquiries, and learned that her name was Mabel Loomis, and that she had already gone back to her home in Concord, Massachusetts. When she returned to Washington in November, Todd paid her a visit at the boardinghouse where she stayed with her father, Eben Loomis, a "calculator"—or statistician—in the Almanac Office as well as a nature writer.

After a courtship of two years, David and Mabel were married in March 1879. It was customary for nineteenth-century couples to confess their darkest deeds; for the male in particular, shady secrets seem to have added a Byronic allure to courtship. David Todd was at pains to suggest, without being explicit, that there was a "dreadful thing" in his past that might mar their perfect happiness. He hinted that it involved his passion for young girls; Todd also recorded in his journal, along with astronomical observations, his habitual recourse to masturbation. Despite these ominous shadows, the early married life of the Todds was by all accounts quite happy; their only child, a daughter named Millicent, was born on February 5, 1880.

In June 1881, David Todd was invited to return to Amherst College to teach astronomy. To sweeten the deal, there was talk of an alumnus who had pledged money for a new observatory to replace the outdated octagonal structure on the college grounds. Over Mabel's mild objections (she noted David's burgeoning career in Washington and her own reluctance to leave her father), David accepted the offer. So it was that on August 31, 1881, Mabel and David Todd arrived in the quaint New England village of Amherst, Massachusetts.

4·

Just as the Todds were preparing to leave Washington, Martin Johnson Heade set his sights on the capital. An attractive studio was available in the Corcoran Building, a few steps from Eben Loomis's office. By November, Heade was hard at work in his new surroundings, and had established a very close friendship with Loomis, based on many shared interests, including nature writing and botany. It was only a matter of time before Mabel Todd would pay a visit to her father, and come to know the fascinating and eccentric artist who painted salt marshes and hummingbirds while Eben Loomis calculated planetary wanderings.

Heade was on the move. For ten years this habitual drifter had led a fairly settled life in New York, holed up in the Tenth Street Studio Building, with summer campaigns to Newport, Newburyport, or the Connecticut shore. His work fit well enough into the broad category of "realism" that his paintings seemed at home among the canvases of Kensett and Church in the exhibitions at the National Academy of Design. With Church in particular Heade had established a relationship of mutual trust, affection, and inspiration. They shared studio space in the Tenth Street building, where Church held the central place of honor, and exchanged letters and ideas.

Why Heade left New York remains a mystery. A shift in artistic taste probably contributed. French Impressionism was making incursions in New York, and American painters such as William Merritt Chase, who took over Church's studio, found ways to portray American life with the fluent brush-strokes and splayed light of Monet and Pissarro. Heade stood firmly against such innovations, but his stubbornness was less provincial or nationalistic than it was visionary. His idiosyncratic art had its own logic and its own path of development.

If Heade's life was relatively settled during his decade in New York, he had not stood still as an artist. Three big ideas had come his way, and he knew exactly what to do with them. He absorbed each idea, let it settle into his artistic practices. Then he found a way to synthesize all three into the great canvases of his mature phase: the hummingbirds and orchids; the recumbent magnolias; the Florida swamps.

5 ·

The first idea was the conviction that the origins of life could best be viewed in the tropics. Drawn from paintings such as Church's *Heart of the Andes*, this idea partially inspired Heade's journey to Brazil in 1863. His concept of nature in those days was a fixed hierarchy of species, each in its place as God created them. As the self-appointed Audubon of hummingbirds, Heade aspired to collect and identify each species, and fix it for all time.

The second big idea that Heade absorbed during his New York sojourn was a different and competing version of the first, namely, Darwinian evolution. Yes, the origin of life (as well as its destruction) was best viewed in the tropics, but not because God's immutable creation was best viewed in its profusion there. The reason was that intensity of heat and diversity of climate accelerated species change. According to Darwin, the creation of species had not occurred at some distant moment in the past, when God's finger commanded by fiat the full range of creation. Creation, Darwin argued, was *ongoing*. Life in its diversity was not fixed for all time but in flux. Each species of hummingbird did not exist in a timeless universe; it adapted itself over time to change. The world of nature was a world of flux and interface: birds and flowers were in a dynamic and ever-changing relationship.

The third idea that Heade absorbed was the visionary treatment of birds and flowers in Asian art. The galvanizing impact of Chinese and Japanese bird-and-flower painting came to Heade through several channels. By the late eighteenth century, Chinese bird-and-flower decoration had migrated to New England on the surfaces of porcelain, prints, and folding screens. In Harriet Beecher Stowe's *The Minister's Wooing*, a romance set in Newport around 1800, "some curious Chinese paintings of birds and flowers gave rather a piquant and foreign air" to the heroine's "quiet, maiden-like" little room.[4] Heade was familiar with Whistler's imitations of Asian art, and Stowe herself painted flowers in a chinoiserie mode, decorating folding screens with ragweed and painting tropical flowers on a black ground. What Heade learned from Chinese painting was that ornithological accuracy was not sufficient to produce a satisfying painting. As James Cahill, a scholar of Chinese painting, observed of an influential twelfth-century painter of birds and flowers: "Hui-tsung's strength is more in getting it right than in making it live."[5] During his decade of development in New York, Heade wanted to make it live.

6.

To see how Heade synthesized all these ideas in his work, look for a moment at his mesmerizing *Cattleya Orchid and Three Brazilian Hummingbirds*, painted in 1871. The painting could be an illustration of that codependence of bird and orchid that Darwin wrote about the same year in his *Descent of Man*. What first draws the eye is the great pink orchid fully unfurled, as though inviting us into its florid embrace. We almost miss the three hummingbirds, a pair of rubythroats and a swallowtail, arrayed around a

Heade, Cattleya Orchid and Three Brazilian Hummingbirds
(National Gallery, Washington)

nest beside it. The male rubythroat turns his gorget toward us, which picks up the pink of the orchid. Across the nest, beak to beak, is the contrasting form of the swallowtail, the serpentine shape like a spectrum from yellow through green to red. The evanescent nest, like something woven of gossamer and beads, seems to be vanishing before our eyes. Two tiny white eggs shine inside; the three far-traveling birds could be Magi come from afar to pay homage.

But there's a countervailing body of imagery in this beguiling picture. The birds and flamboyant flower overflow with life. But notice how gothic the branches are, these rotting limbs decked with lichen and dripping with moldering vines. The orchid leaves and seedpods are mottled with rot; they seem a morbid mirror for the vital flower above. The whole mysterious cycle of procreation and destruction flows through this painting; it speaks deeply to us of the ephemeral, the evanescent.

Now look closer. Allow your eye to be drawn to the mysterious emanation of light, the strangest light ever seen in heaven or on earth, under the gothic branches. Somewhere back there the sun is shining, though the flower has turned away from it. What we feel is some other kind of light, an inner light or spiritual emanation, found nowhere else in American art. It's the light we divine in certain paintings of Vermeer or Caspar David Friedrich, or in the mystical array of deer or birds in Chinese classical paintings. We are in another world, a world that doesn't know us.

7.

The value of Washington for Heade was that it was *not* New York, that he was insulated from pressure to paint in the French way. In the quiet confines of his studio, he could paint as he wished to paint, and consolidate the hints and intuitions that were shaping his new paintings. With his neighbor in the Corcoran Building, the charming and kindly polymath Eben Loomis, Heade found a kindred spirit. Like Heade, Loomis preferred to be outdoors, and spent his indoor hours thinking about the woods and flowers and birds. Both men had a philosophical bent; both followed politics and literature. And both felt underappreciated by their contemporaries, shunted to the side as lesser talents won recognition and status. Heade had failed to win election to the Academy of American Artists. Loomis, after a brilliant undergraduate career at Harvard in mathematics and the sciences, had stalled among the other calculators in government offices. His own son-in-law, David Todd, had passed him by, and was briefly his superior in the Almanac Office.

As a young man growing up in Concord, Massachusetts, Eben Loomis had known Thoreau and Emerson; he now turned for respite and refuge to nature writing. In his rambles in the woods on the fringes of Washington, he had identified a red fern unknown to the botanists; the discovery impressed Darwin. Heade too was an aspiring poet in his youth; in 1881, at the time he arrived in Washington, he had begun writing essays for the sporting magazine *Forest and Stream*. Finding so much in common, the two men formed a deep and lasting friendship. They visited each other in office and studio on workdays; on weekends they rambled into the woods of Rock Creek Park and rural Virginia in search of rare plants.

8.

During her scant four months in Amherst, Mabel Loomis Todd had found little to amuse her. She had arrived in the sleepy college town expecting to dazzle. Wife to a brilliant astronomer, she swam into view like Venus herself. And yet she found that the proper Congregationalists of Amherst shied away from her, as though she were too bright and flashy for their eyes. Mabel aspired to be a woman of fashion, and she had found that the professors and their wives had little appreciation for her accomplishments.

Things were different in Washington, where she returned in early 1882. When she was introduced to Martin Johnson Heade, she knew immediately that she had made a conquest. On January 23, 1882, she first visited Heade's studio in the Corcoran Building, downstairs from her father's office. The following day, Heade called on Mabel, and asked to see her own paintings. "Mr. Heade admired my trumpet vine in the shaped jar, intensely," she wrote in her diary, "and praised me a great deal."[6] The intensity of his praise—was it for her or for her art?—remained with her after her return to Amherst the next day.

By early spring, Mabel's social status in Amherst had changed dramatically. "What is there in me which so attracts men to me, young and old?" she wrote in her journal on March 2. She had become a particular favorite of the Dickinson family and a fixture in the social scene at the Evergreens, Susan and Austin Dickinson's elegant house on Main Street, with its grounds of magnolia and gingko laid out by Frederick Law Olmsted.

When she returned to Washington in April, she visited Heade's studio daily, copying his paintings of salt marshes and hummingbirds, and submitting her own flower sketches to his scrutiny. Nothing in this dutiful apprenticeship quite prepares us for what followed. Susan Dickinson had invited Mabel and David Todd to her Amherst College commencement party, the biggest social event of the year, and Mabel was determined to make a striking impression. A delirious idea was germinating in Mabel's imagination. Not content to paint flowers on canvas, she wanted, somehow, to become a flower, and she enlisted Martin Johnson Heade, the master painter of birds and flowers, to help her realize her dream.

She began painstakingly painting sweet-pea designs on the satin shoulder panels and cuffs of a white camel-hair dress. Heade came to dinner a few days later. "I finished the sweet peas," Mabel reported. "Mr. Heade put in a leaf or two." We can imagine how titillating the dress-painting occasion must have been for Heade, and how flirtatious Mabel was in inviting him to add a leaf or two to her dress. It was as though he were painting *her*, and completing the metaphor of flowers-as-women that was a major theme in

Mabel Loomis Todd in hand-painted dress (Yale University)

his own work. Heade was sixty-three; Mabel was twenty-six. He began to think seriously about following her back to Amherst.

During the weekend of April 29, Mabel's relationship with Heade intensified. She had intended to leave Millicent with either her father or her husband in the Corcoran Building, but both were busy elsewhere. So

Mabel took her daughter into Heade's studio "where she had a good time for an hour."

Heade never forgot what happened the next day, a Sunday. He and Mabel joined Eben Loomis for a "ramble" in the woods. It was arbutus time, the romantic quest for the elusive and shade-seeking trailing arbutus. During the months that followed, Heade would remind her many times of this outing, which proved particularly exciting for him. This flower that meant so much to him, and that he had painted in several ambitious canvases, had merged in his mind with this magnetic woman.

9.

As Mabel returned to Amherst to impress the Dickinsons, Martin Johnson Heade, after barely six months in Washington, was feeling restless again. On June 1, 1882, he poured out his bile on the nation's capital. In an article in *Forest and Stream* titled "'Didymus' Criticizes Washington," he conceded that the "political city" had some charm. He called it "a half-civilized Garden of Eden" and "a delightful city for a permanent home," as though he were considering such a thing. "The streets are very broad, and it has miles upon miles of beautiful concrete pavement . . . so that driving around the city is really a delight." While an occasional wild turkey wandered the streets, "the principal game," Heade wryly observed, "is the English sparrow, but they are not allowed to be shot, as they will some day be needed as a substitute for pigeons at shooting matches."

Heade reserved his rage for two topics: Washington's black people and its trees. Heade's distaste for the black people of Washington is a reminder that abolitionists could also be racists. Heade's racism was of the populist variety; he felt that freed slaves were given a free ride while workingmen like himself had to labor for their livelihood. "A huge chunk of our national wisdom once took this form," he wrote of post–Civil War policy. "They set apart 10,000 dollars to feed the negroes, which in one light looks very well, for negroes must eat; but unfortunately, as long as they are fed they will not work, and a city where it's all eat and no work, is equal, in their eyes, to the New Jerusalem. So the lazy rascals flock in from all parts of the South to feed at the public crib."

Heade the itinerant painter, financially insecure, may have felt uncomfortably close to the fate of the homeless blacks. As bohemian transients living in makeshift hotels and boardinghouses, he and his friend Eben Loomis might easily have been mistaken for bums on the dole themselves.

Heade's tirade against trees also had private meanings. "There are trees in abundance all over the city," he wrote, "and at surface glance they seem to clothe the city in a garb of beauty, but there is probably no city in these United States where such utter ignorance is shown in the planting of trees." The silver maple was the big offender since "the foliage is thin and pale, the limbs are long, slender, and brittle, and liable to be split or broken off." He pointed out that "strong and lasting" trees with denser, darker foliage, such as the sugar maple, would have made the city more alluring. In this comparison of thin and pale foliage to what was strong and lasting, it was as though he were contrasting the brittle brushwork of the Impressionists to his own denser palette.

In his persona of Didymus, or Doubting Thomas, Heade was building a case, however flimsy, for leaving Washington. One reason was to pursue Mabel Loomis Todd, in whose company he had glimpsed, for a fleeting moment, the potential joys of a more domestic life. In a rare confessional moment, Heade jotted down some thoughts about passion in a notebook:

> Every man who possesses a soul has loved once, if not a dozen times, for passion was created with man, and is a part of his nature. . . As soon as the affectionate and sensitive part of my nature leaves me, I shall consider the poetry of my existence gone, and shall look upon life as a utilitarian, bargain-and-trade affair; for that poetry is the only source of real happiness we have, and I care not whether it is laughed at or acknowledged.[7]

Roaming the woodland paths with Mabel in quest of the first arbutus in spring, or painting a sweet-pea leaf on her collar—such things were all that was missing to make his half-Eden whole. New England was where sugar maples cast their dense, dark foliage on the landscape. It was time for the migration northward, to cooler climes. And so, in early July 1882, Martin Johnson Heade packed his bags and headed for Amherst and Mabel Todd.

Chapter Nine

A ROUTE OF EVANESCENCE

What is more gentle than a wind in summer?
What is more soothing than the pretty hummer
That stays one moment in an open flower,
And buzzes cheerily from bower to bower?

❦ JOHN KEATS

I.

THE AMHERST SUMMER of 1882, a summer of hummingbirds, began with the Amherst College commencement and its associated festivities and frolics. Susan Dickinson's party, the highlight of the season, was held on June 15 in the front parlor and veranda of the Evergreens, overlooking the flowering magnolias on the lawn. Among the guests, chiefly conservatively attired professors and their students, Mabel Loomis Todd was resplendent in her camel-hair dress, decorated with the vivid sweet-pea blossoms that she had painted, with Martin Johnson Heade's eager assistance, on her collar and cuffs.

The next day, a euphoric Mabel informed her husband, who had remained in Washington, that the dress had had its intended effect. "I was quite the center of attraction . . . and had nearly all the gentlemen around me at once," she wrote. "All spoke of my magnificent painted dress."[1] A photograph of Mabel wearing the dress that she had designed specifically to impress the Dickinsons shows that the panels on the collar extended down toward her breasts. Enveloped in sweet-pea blossoms and still in the bloom of youth, she resembled a goddess of summer come to earth.

After her triumph at the party, Mabel became a fixture at the Evergreens, singing and playing the piano for Susan Dickinson's frequent guests and taking part in amateur theatrical productions and impromptu outings into the countryside. She had an admirer. During the first weeks of the summer, Mabel was courted assiduously by Austin and Susan Dickinson's twenty-year-old son, Ned, who called on her almost every day. Ned was shy and sickly, awkward and decorous. It was felt—by both Ned's parents and the Todds—that such a sentimental attachment to a mature woman was good for the young man and harmless for Mabel herself. It was an apprenticeship of sorts. "He likes Ned," Mabel wrote of her husband, "and he thinks it a good thing for *him* to be under my influence."[2]

Photographs commemorate this midsummer moment, when Mabel and her adoring entourage took a pleasure trip into the woods of nearby Shutesbury in July. Riding jauntily on top of the Amherst stagecoach, bristling with parasols and walking sticks, they seem to have entered a fairy-tale world of magic and metamorphosis. A group photograph taken on their return, at John Lovell's studio on Main Street, commemorates the occasion. All eleven participants are carefully arrayed in what they called "The Shutesbury School of Philosophy"—an allusion to Raphael's famous fresco of "The School of Athens"—with appropriate props and gestures.

Five women pose behind five seated men. Mabel, dressed in white with a large feathered hat, presides. Seated next to her is Susan Dickinson, entirely maternal, with her younger son, Gib, in her lap. The studio backdrop features a light-filled French window opening to the left and a contrasting dark fireplace to the right. A young woman stands in the window, with a

John Lovell, "The Shutesbury School of Philosophy"
(Yale University)

Colt revolver in her hand, pointed playfully at Mabel. David Todd sits hunched in front of the fireplace, as though he has just crawled out of it. In front of him Ned Dickinson lies propped on the floor, mimicking Raphael's Diogenes, his tennis racket in front of him. Another Amherst student, William Clark, sits guarding the large picnic basket, slightly open like Pandora's box.

Missing from the photograph is Austin Dickinson, who by midsummer was spending more and more time with Mabel Todd, on private drives and walks into the countryside. A decisive change was taking place in her relations with father and son. She described the moment of her shifting allegiances as "the middle of last summer"—i.e., 1882—when she and Austin realized the extent of their attraction for each other. And just to complicate matters, another suitor arrived in town that July.

2 .

Martin Johnson Heade checked into the Round Hill Hotel in Northampton, across the Connecticut River from Amherst, on July 5, 1882. Once a "water cure" for invalids like Emily Dickinson's mother, the Round Hill Hotel, in a suite of buildings on the edge of Jonathan Edwards's old village—now a bustling manufacturing town—was the best hotel in the area, and Heade made himself at home. "I am here, within sight of Amherst," he wrote in a postcard to Eben Loomis, "and I shall stay some time." Mabel had been on Heade's mind all summer. "If I should find myself near Amherst," he had told her father in mid-June, "I'll certainly go to see Mrs. Todd and her little pet [Millicent]. The fact is—to put it in a mild and delicate form—I like your whole family *to excess*."[3]

The Connecticut River Valley was familiar to Heade from earlier painting campaigns, and a favorite locale for American landscape painters. Artists of the Hudson River School had followed their master, Thomas Cole, to paint the Holyoke Range, a picturesque spine of small mountains rising above the river. Just below Northampton, the river turned upon itself in the so-called "Oxbow" that Cole had made famous. Cole's painting of the view from Mt. Holyoke, with a thunderstorm approaching, was the best known landscape painting in the United States. More recently, Henry James had checked into the Round Hill Hotel, in search of healing waters to cure the constipation that had plagued him since the Civil War. James had been sufficiently charmed by his surroundings, especially the lovely elms in the meadows along the river, to set the opening of his first novel, *Roderick Hudson*, in Northampton.

Heade kept his arrival a secret from Mabel. On July 13, 1882, she noted in her journal: "After dinner I was reading Cape Cod Folks [an 1881 novel by Sarah Pratt McLean] when our dear Mr. Heade arrived! He is staying at the Round Hill Hotel in Northampton for a little while. I took him about the town & college and he remained to tea with me. A letter came from my dear David [in Washington]; & Ned [Dickinson] overtook us & asked to go rowing this evening. He came for me at seven, I said good bye to Mr. Heade and drove off."

We learn a bit more about the visit from Heade's account to Mabel's father, dated July 18, from the St. Denis Hotel in New York. It is clear from the opening that Heade had hoped to stay longer in Northampton, had Mabel's welcome been warmer.

> I am here. Consequently I am not in Northampton. Before leaving there I went over to Amherst & called on Mrs. Todd, & had a most delightful visit.
>
> She was as bewitchingly enthusiastic as ever, but the little one [Millicent] was timid & would not have much to do with me. I rec'd a brief letter from Mrs. Todd since I came—forwarded from Northampton.
>
> [Amherst is] a lovely place, & I'd much rather pass a few weeks there than in Northampton. Mrs. Todd was kind enough to show me around the city & took me up to the top of an exceeding high tower & showed me all the farms of the earth, (that's as true as the other story) but she didn't offer to give them to me if I fall down & worship her.[4]

The tower was in Johnson Chapel, the main building of Amherst College, on a hill above the town. The meadows below belonged to the Dickinsons. Heade's little joke about the temptation of Christ lightly conceals both his own sense of temptation in Mabel's radiant presence and his disappointment that his worship didn't mean more to her. He found himself third in line behind two Dickinson men, father and son.

Heade cut his losses. Having failed to elicit more of a response from Mabel Todd, he turned his attention to reestablishing contact with the Beechers.

3·

It was a momentous summer for Henry Ward Beecher and his famous sister. In honor of Harriet Beecher Stowe's seventieth birthday, the *Atlantic* editors hosted another of their famous parties in June, on the outskirts of Boston. It was only the second such occasion to which women had been invited—the first was in 1859, when Thomas Wentworth Higginson had made the awkward introduction of Stowe and Harriet Prescott Spofford. After toasting his sister, Henry Ward Beecher crossed the state, where he met up with Heade in Greenfield, just north of Amherst on the Connecticut River.

Beecher, who spent his summers in Brattleboro, Vermont, trying to ease his hay fever, was preaching around New England on his great new subject, evolution. He had survived the storm of opprobrium arising from his trial for adultery with Elizabeth Tilton, but his old gospel of love raised ironic eyebrows after the scandal. In the intervening years, he had found in the controversy surrounding Darwin, who had just died on April 19, 1882, a new platform for his optimistic ideas.

Never much of a student of science since his Amherst College days, Beecher neglected to master the details of Darwin's scheme of the struggle for existence. Instead, he discerned in the theory of evolution a striving for perfection consistent with his own Christian views—he called himself "a cordial Christian evolutionist."[5] The resulting amalgam—resembling twentieth-century assertions of "intelligent design"—proved appealing to progressive Protestant churches in the Northeast. Beecher publicly endorsed Darwin in 1882, proclaiming, "Slowly and through a whole fifty years I have been under the influence, first obscurely, indirectly, of the great doctrine of evolution."

Heade made arrangements to meet his old friend and patron at a point between Northampton and Brattleboro. "I met Beecher at Greenfield," he wrote Eben Loomis, ". . . & had a long fight with him on Nature's cruelty." Barnum's circus was in Greenfield that July, with reduced train fares for "Jumbo-day." "Well," Heade continued, Beecher "went home & preached (a day or two after) on the subject, but I saw only a slight sketch of it in the Tribune." The bone of contention was still on Heade's mind twenty years later. In an article titled "Big Game vs. Birds," Heade wrote: "There is no doubt that greater interest is felt in the suffering of an elephant or a moose than in that of smaller game, though they suffer no more, but we may carry that idea down to our daily walks where we crush out the lives of insects by the thousand, but it can't be helped, and we give ourselves no trouble about it."[6]

4·

After Heade's departure, it became clear to Mabel Todd that her affection for Austin Dickinson excelled anything she had felt for Ned. Austin found excuses to accompany Mabel home after her visits to the Evergreens, and they went for romantic drives in the countryside around Amherst. They found that they shared a passion for nature and poetry. "He is almost in every particular my ideal man," she confided in her journal.

> The autumn chirp of crickets thrills him inexpressibly, & the misty hills & the first red leaves. The first thing which made me sure he was a true, if silent, poet, was his saying one day up in Sunderland Park [a rural village north of Amherst that was the destination for many outings] that when he died he wanted to be buried where the crickets could constantly chirp around him.

On September 11, 1882, Austin and Mabel reached a romantic understanding, commemorated in their respective diaries with the single word *Rubicon*. According to Polly Longsworth, chronicler of the affair, another year passed before "Consummation of Mabel and Austin's love occurred at the Homestead, Emily and Vinnie's dwelling, the evening of December 13, 1883, in the dining room, where they often met before the fire."[7]

5.

In late September 1882, Mabel Todd sent Emily Dickinson a painting of Indian pipes, a white woodland plant common in New England. Dickinson sent in return an oblique poem with an explanatory note: "I cannot make an Indian Pipe but please accept a Humming Bird." The exchange of gifts had lasting repercussions for American literature. Here is the eight-line poem Dickinson sent:

> *A Route of Evanescence*
> *With a revolving Wheel—*
> *A Resonance of Emerald—*
> *A Rush of Cochineal,*
> *And every Blossom on the Bush*
> *Adjusts its tumbled Head—*
> *The Mail from Tunis probably,*
> *An easy Morning's Ride—*[8]

It is an exchange of enigmas: a riddle poem about an elusive bird that bats its wings in order to stand still, and a painting of a spectral plant without chlorophyll, like an image of the shade-seeking Emily Dickinson herself, all dressed in white.

On September 10, the day before the "Rubicon," Mabel Todd had sung and played the piano for the Dickinson spinster sisters, fifty-two-year-old Emily and her younger sister, Lavinia, in the Homestead. Mabel Todd noted in her diary: "Before tea I had a walk with dear Mr. D. Senior, & called at the other house to see Miss Vinnie Dickinson. I sang there, & the rare, mysterious Emily listened in the quiet darkness outside." The "Mr. D. Senior" Mabel Todd refers to is Austin. (No mention is made of Emily's invalid mother, confined to her bed in the Homestead.) Mabel Todd did not actually meet Emily Dickinson that day, as she played Beethoven and sang a few arias for the mysterious recluse upstairs. It is a startling fact that Mabel never did set eyes on Emily—never, that is, while Emily was alive. Their friendship, such as it was, was destined to be played out at a discreet distance.

Soon after her Sunday recital at the Homestead, Mabel Loomis Todd traveled with her daughter, Millicent, to Washington to visit her father. Her recital at the Homestead was still vivid in Mabel's mind. "It was odd to think," she wrote in her journal on September 15, "as my voice rang out through the big silent house that Miss Emily in her weird white dress was outside in the shadow hearing every word." The same journal entry includes Mabel Todd's well-known description of Emily Dickinson as the eccentric "myth" of Amherst:

> She has not been out of her house for fifteen years. One inevitably thinks of Miss Haversham in speaking of her. She writes the strangest poems, & very remarkable ones. She is in many respects a genius. She wears always white, & has her hair arranged as was the fashion fifteen years ago when she went into retirement. She wanted me to come & sing to her, but she would not see me. . . No one *has* seen her in all those years except her own family.

On September 22, still in Washington, Mabel painted her present for Emily. It was, Todd recalled, a "sudden inspiration," as she "looked about over my [flower] studies," to paint "the Indian pipe (monotropa) on a black panel for her." Todd grouped the graceful white flowers in a sort of frieze, like danc-

Mabel Loomis Todd, Indian Pipes

(Amherst College Archives and Special Collections)

ers bowing to an audience, against a black background. The uncanny effect is that of a photographic negative.[9]

Emily Dickinson's extravagant written response, on September 30, 1882, confirmed Mabel Todd's intuition of a resemblance between the ghostly white flower and the reclusive poet dressed in white:

> That without suspecting it you should send me the preferred flower of life, seems almost supernatural, and the sweet glee that I felt at meeting it, I could confide to none—I still cherish the clutch with which I bore it from the ground when a wondering child, an unearthly booty, and maturity only enhances mystery, never decreases it—[10]

The whole passage is imbued with the sorcery of death and resurrection: this "flower of life" lives on rotting wood and comes from the underworld; the "unearthly booty" is also an unearthly "body."

6.

Before Mabel Todd entered the gate of the Dickinsons' picket fence that September, and mounted the stone steps to the Homestead, she had received a surprising warning from Susan Dickinson next door. The Dickinson sisters, Sue informed her, "have not, either of them, any idea of morality." She added, "I went in there one day, and in the drawing room I found Emily reclining in the arms of a man."[11] It was Emily Dickinson's strange fate to be granted two long-cherished wishes at a time in her life when it was no longer clear that she wanted either one. The summer of 1882 brought fulfillment of both wishes, marriage and publication, within the realm of intoxicating possibility.

For Emily Dickinson was in love that summer, passionately in love, and she was loved in return. At first, there was every reason to keep the love affair private, because Dickinson's lover was a married man, and second, because he was a close friend, the closest friend, in fact, of her own father. The secrecy makes it difficult to reconstruct the origin of the affair, but it seems reasonable to look back twenty years, to the summer of 1862, when Judge Otis Lord went up against Henry Ward Beecher at the Amherst College commencement.

Lord was a frequent visitor in Amherst throughout the intervening years. He regularly visited his alma mater, and paid calls on both Dickinson houses. In 1875, he was elevated to the Massachusetts Supreme Court, and for a part of each year he presided over sessions in Northampton. On December 10, 1877—Emily Dickinson's forty-seventh birthday—Lord's wife died, clearing one obstacle to what may already have become an intimate relationship. The death of Dickinson's father in 1874 had cleared another. Within months of Mrs. Lord's death, Emily Dickinson's letters had reached an ecstatic pitch:

> My lovely Salem smiles at me. I seek his Face so often—but I have done with guises.
>
> I confess that I love him—I rejoice that I love him—I thank the maker of Heaven and Earth—that gave him me to love—the exultation floods me. I cannot find my channel—the Creek turns Sea—at thought of thee—[12]

Lord's visits at the Homestead intensified; he practically lived in Amherst during August and September 1880, and it was presumably around this time that Susan Dickinson saw Emily reclining in his arms.

By the spring of 1882 Dickinson and Lord had reached an understanding. On April 16 there was a momentous visit, followed, on April 30, by a remarkable letter from Emily Dickinson. "Our Life together was long forgiveness on your part toward me," she wrote. "I never knelt to other."

She mailed the letter on May 1. "I shall never forget 'May Day,'" she wrote a week later.[13] Lavinia had returned to the Homestead that day, having seen Austin on his way to the train. He had bad news. Otis Lord was gravely ill, and not expected to live. Dickinson remembered the terrible moment. "I grasped at a passing Chair. My sight slipped and I thought I was freezing."[14] She dropped into the arms of Tom Kelley, her beloved servant. "He will be better," Kelley said. "Don't cry Miss Emily. I could not see you cry." Kelley was right. Lord did recover, though this proof of his fragility was a reminder of the transience of earthly things. Meanwhile, the birds were returning, the flowers were blooming, and New England was rounding into summer.

7·

It was the rekindling of Dickinson's childhood friendship with the novelist Helen Hunt Jackson that opened up the possibility of publication. Jackson was another protégée of Thomas Wentworth Higginson; the two had met in 1866 as fellow boarders in a rooming house in Newport, Rhode Island, where Higginson was recovering from the trauma of the war. At that time, Higginson had shown Jackson some of the poems Dickinson had sent him during his months of active duty in Florida and South Carolina. A sporadic correspondence between Dickinson and Jackson, Amherst girls born during the same year, ensued, and intensified after Jackson sent Dickinson a letter in 1875:

> I have a little manuscript volume with a few of your verses in it—and I read them very often—You are a great poet—and it is a wrong to the day you live in, that you will not sing aloud. When you are what men call dead, you will be sorry you were so stingy.[15]

"You are a great poet." No one had ever written such a thing to Dickinson before, not Higginson or Susan Dickinson or anyone else. It must have given her indescribable joy. But when, a year later, Helen Hunt Jackson asked for Dickinson's permission to allow some of her verses to be published anonymously, in a volume of poetry in the "No Name Series" launched by Roberts Brothers of Boston, Dickinson hesitated. Jackson, who was staying at the Hartford home of Mark Twain's friend and collaborator Charles Dudley Warner, visited Dickinson in Amherst that October, and again sought Dickinson's consent.

In desperation, Dickinson wrote to Higginson, asking him this time, in an ironic twist, to discourage publication, just as he had in the past. "She was so sweetly noble, I would regret to estrange her," Dickinson wrote of Jackson, "and if you would be willing to give me a note saying you disapproved it, and thought me unfit, she would believe you."[16] But Jackson persisted ("Could you not bear this much of publicity?"), and Dickinson's "Success is counted sweetest" was included in *A Masque of Poets,* published in 1878 to great acclaim. Critics trying to guess the identity of the author most frequently settled for Emerson.

It was within this frame, Helen Hunt Jackson the successful writer trying to coax a bashful and reluctant Emily Dickinson to join her in the limelight, that Jackson, in 1879, solicited a poem from Dickinson. Jackson particularly liked Dickinson's bird poems. "What should you think of trying your hand on the oriole?" she wrote.[17] It was a commission of sorts, and Dickinson accepted, responding not with one poem but with two. Along with "One of the ones that Midas touched," her portrait of the oriole as drunken prodigal, she also sent Jackson "A Route of Evanescence."

8.

Among Dickinson's nearly two thousand poems, "A Route of Evanescence" has unusual claims on our attention. It was her "signature poem" in more ways than one. She sent it to more correspondents, seven in all, than any other poem. She used it as a calling card, as in her exchange with Mabel

Todd, and sometimes signed it "Humming-Bird," as though she herself were its evanescent subject.

For this most private of poets, "A Route of Evanescence" is unusually public in its purposes. Dickinson wrote it for a particular audience, Helen Hunt Jackson and her circle. When she was asked in November 1880 to contribute a poem for a missionary benefit for children in foreign lands, this was among the poems she sent, first asking Higginson, as usual, for his advice. And when Thomas Niles, an editor at Roberts Brothers, continued to express interest in publishing a volume of her poems, she sent him a copy of her hummingbird poem in April 1883. If she were ever to publish—a big *if*—this was the poem under the sign of which she would do so.

Why did the poem mean so much to Dickinson? It is unusually abstract, a poem of elusive aftermath rather than concrete description. The whirring bird is all rush and resonance, its presence felt only by its lingering effect on flower and bush. And what should one make of those mysterious closing lines about the mail from Tunis? She means that the bird moves at incredible speed, of course, but she is also saying something about the miracle of mail for her. Dickinson loved letters; they were her major way of "publishing" her poetry to her intimate circle of readers. Letters themselves were like migratory birds, humming with words. An easy morning's ride is also an easy morning's *read*.[18]

"A Route of Evanescence" is the culmination of two kinds of poems that Dickinson had been writing for twenty years. It is, first of all, a riddle in verse. Dickinson's riddles tend to be about elusive things that vanish under scrutiny: snakes, snow, and sunsets. Dickinson once wrote that "The Riddle we can guess, / We speedily despise."[19] As riddles go, "A Route of Evanescence" is perhaps unguessable. First-time readers may surmise that it is about time or the earth or the passage of seasons; other possible guesses include the sun, the sunset, or, getting warmer, the butterfly. It is quite possible that Dickinson supplied the "answer"—as she did to Todd, Jackson, and Higginson—to minimize confusion.

Dickinson's other favorite poetic genre is the definition poem. Like many poets, Dickinson loved the dictionary. She told Higginson that when she was young "for several years, my Lexicon—was my only companion."[20] She lived across Main Street from Noah Webster, the famous compiler of dictionaries who, along with Dickinson's own grandfather, founded Amherst College. But Dickinson's definitions are hardly the kind found in dictionaries. She almost always chooses an abstraction and defines it with something concrete. "Hope is the thing with feathers." "Doom is the house without the door." Dickinson's definitions often have a built-in riddle. What is a house without a door? Answer: a prison. What is the thing with feathers? A bird.

In some ways, a riddle is the opposite of a definition. Riddles ask: "What is X?" Definitions say, "X is . . ." If Dickinson's definitions tend to define abstract things with concrete ones, her riddles attempt the reverse, rendering concrete things intangible. Just as Dickinson's definitions often have built-in riddles, her riddles tend to have built-in definitions. Thus, Dickinson's famous riddle about the snake, "A narrow fellow in the grass," ends with the words "zero at the bone," a pretty good definition for fear. Dickinson's hummingbird poem fits all these strictures. Its concrete subject is famously elusive, so much so that the poem registers only its aftereffects. And the poem seems to attempt a definition of *evanescence* itself.

If the poem was meant to beguile its influential readers, it amply served its purpose. By April 1882, Dickinson could have published a volume of her poems had she wished to do so. Thomas Niles was so impressed with "A Route of Evanescence" and the other poems he had seen that he wrote Dickinson:

> "H.H." [Jackson] once told me that she wished you could be induced to publish a volume of poems. I should not want to say how highly she praised them, but to such an extent that I wish also that you could.[21]

"A Route of Evanescence" was a favorite poem of the two correspondents destined to be Dickinson's posthumous editors: Higginson and Todd. Higginson's pleasure in the poem is hardly surprising, for it has long been assumed that its immediate source is his own essay "The Life of Birds," in which he quotes a sexually charged passage from Harriet Spofford.

Mabel Todd liked the poem so much that she set it to music, in her year of diary entries titled *A Cycle of Sunsets* (1910). The little book described a year of sunsets in Amherst, a very Heade-like subject. For her entry of June 4, Todd noted the arrival of a hummingbird in her garden: "In and out, flashing here, shining there, a humming-bird has spent the day with us, in the vines, in the garden, scintillating bit of prismatic wealth, concentrating all the day's brightness in his tiny body. His wings gave a swift, definite, wave-like sound as he approached or receded from us." Todd appended, as a tune for the first two lines of "A Route of Evanescence," an upward run of sixteenth notes, separated by half steps, then two quarter notes, followed by an inverted descending run.

The scholar Jay Leyda once pointed out that if Mabel and David Todd hadn't come to Amherst during the fall of 1881, no one today would know the name "Emily Dickinson." Almost alone among her contemporaries, Mabel Todd recognized the genius of Emily Dickinson's poems and shep-herded them to a wider public. That recognition was shaped and nurtured by her apprenticeship with Martin Johnson Heade. It was in Heade's studio in Washington that Mabel saw what could be done with a few hypnotic images—flowers, mysterious light on meadows, hummingbirds. During the summer of 1882, she met these images again in Emily Dickinson's poetry.

9·

The painter of hummingbirds and the poet of hummingbirds hovered in each other's proximity for a tantalizing summer afternoon in Amherst. But was Emily Dickinson aware of Heade's visit? If so, would she have recognized his name? Did she know that he painted hummingbirds? Is that why she gave Mabel Todd a poem about a hummingbird, as a sort of commemoration of his visit?

Dickinson's attention to the effects of light on landscape has seemed to some scholars to have analogies with American painters of her time.[22] Austin Dickinson was an avid collector of American landscape paintings, including a work by John F. Kensett, although, as Barton St. Armand notes, Austin's "fever for art appears to have burned itself out soon after Mabel Loomis Todd arrived in Amherst" in 1881. Judith Farr followed St. Armand's lead in *The Passion of Emily Dickinson* (1992), comparing specific poems of Dickinson to works of Kensett and Heade. Farr noted that Heade and Dickinson shared a fascination with hummingbirds. "Behind the precise subjects of Heade's painting, mists recede and light is clouded over," she writes. "Dickinson's poems about hummingbirds . . . also present a fusion of realistic detail and vaporous suggestion."[23]

In *The Gardens of Emily Dickinson* (2004), Farr goes into greater detail about the parallels she finds between Heade's bird-and-flower paintings and Dickinson's poems, noting in particular Dickinson's taste for "tropical" and "Edenic" imagery of the kind found in depictions of South America by Heade and Church. Farr plausibly suggests that Dickinson might have followed Heade's career in the Boston newspapers. "Heade's decision to live in Boston for two years (1861–63)," she writes, "caused him to be favorably reviewed in Boston newspapers received by the Dickinsons long after he had ceased to live there." One of those newspapers, the *Boston Transcript*, reported Heade's departure for South America, in April 1863, to pursue his work on the hummingbirds of Brazil.[24]

10.

It is likely, however, that Emily Dickinson first heard of Heade through the literary and artistic circles of Newburyport, centered around Thomas

Wentworth Higginson and his protégée Harriet Prescott Spofford. Years afterward, Susan Dickinson remembered how Samuel Bowles would sometimes take a poem from his pocket to share with his Dickinson friends. One such poem, according to Sue, was Spofford's "Pomegranate-Flowers," published in the May 1861 issue of *The Atlantic*, which Dickinson would have read in any case.[25] In the closing stanzas of the poem, Spofford described a hummingbird. Or rather, she described (like Dickinson in "A Route of Evanescence") an *absent* hummingbird—an absence that turns out to be more imaginatively exciting than the flowers left behind:

> *As if the flowers had taken flight*
> *Or as the crusted gems should shoot*
> *From hidden hollows, or as the light*
> *Had blossomed into prisms to flute*
> *Its secret that before was mute,*
> *Atoms where fire and tint dispute,*
> *No humming-birds here hunt their fruit.*

Harriet Prescott Spofford was herself drawn to Heade's work, and in the July 1875 issue of *Harper's New Monthly Magazine*, she wrote of the salt meadows of Newburyport:

> He who desires to see a meadow in perfection, full of emerald and golden tints and claret shadows, withdrawing into distance till lost in the sparkle of the sea, must seek it here, where Heade found material for his dainty marsh and meadow views.

In the same article, Spofford mentioned both Higginson and "the Rev. J. C. Fletcher, of Brazilian fame."[26] Since Emily Dickinson was a devoted reader of both *Harper's* and Spofford, and noticed any published mention of Higginson, this article is probably the single most likely source for her awareness of Martin Johnson Heade as a kindred spirit.

II.

On November 10, 1882, David Todd and the photographer John Lovell set off on a train for California to photograph the Transit of Venus. Lovell, for several decades the class photographer at Amherst College, was a beloved figure in Amherst, close to both the Dickinsons and the Todds. Many years earlier, he had photographed Henry Ward Beecher's stuffed owl. He had photographed, in his Amherst studio, the picnickers who made up the "Shutesbury School of Philosophy." He was a pallbearer at Edward Dickinson's funeral; after his own death in 1903, Mabel wrote a short biography. Lovell had a special interest in scientific uses of photography. He had worked closely with the great Amherst geologist Edward Hitchcock in recording the geology of the Connecticut River Valley. Lovell's professional practice had moved from the daguerreotype, in 1849, through the dry-plate process, in which he specialized after his return from the California trip.

The Transit of Venus was expected on December 6, 1882. Astronomers like David Todd, aware that this would be the final Transit of Venus until 2004, needed no outside stimulus to take a special interest in this dramatic event. But there was intense popular excitement as well. With improvements in telescopes and the new invention of photography, astronomers, both professionals and amateurs, were tremendously excited by planetary transits. From an observatory in Pernambuco (Recife), Brazil, Dom Pedro II planned to view the Transit of Venus.

New England readers were enchanted with Thomas Hardy's novel about astronomers in love, *Two on a Tower*, serialized in *The Atlantic Monthly* between May and December 1882, with the final installment coinciding with the transit itself. Fittingly, the novel followed the progress of a May-December romance between the budding but impoverished young astronomer Swithin St. Cleeve and the older, wealthier Viviette, Lady Constantine, who supports him and falls in love with him. Swithin spends his days reading technical journals on astronomical apparatus, including the very journals that David Todd published in. A May-December romance was building in Amherst as well, between Mabel Todd and Austin Dickinson.

David Todd, to his intense disappointment, was closed out of the official Transit Commission plans directed by his old mentor, Simon Newcomb. Todd's decision to take the job at Amherst College, leaving the inner astronomical circles in Washington for a small college with an outdated observatory, must have seemed increasingly shortsighted. At the last minute, however, Todd received an invitation from a maverick benefactor named James Lick, who was building an observatory on Mount Hamilton, in California. Having failed to lure Newcomb to Mount Hamilton, Lick's trustees approached David Todd, who eagerly accepted, despite the half-finished observatory and uncertain prospects of the often cloud-covered site.

For recording the Transit of Venus, Lovell and Todd elected to use the older technique of fine-grained gelatin wet plates rather than the newly developed dry plates used on the other expeditions. It turned out to be a brilliant decision. As the sun rose on December 6—"as perfect as a June day in New England," Todd wrote in his diary—Venus was already visible crossing its expanse. Todd and Lovell took 147 plates in all as Venus moved across the sun's disk. He telegraphed Mabel jubilantly, "Splendid day. Splendid success." Though he could not know it, the photographs Todd took that day were to be the pinnacle of his career as an astronomer. His later attempts to photograph eclipses of the sun, in Japan and Tripoli, were doomed to failure; he once told his daughter that "what saddened his life were three cloudy eclipses of the Sun."[27] But his photographs of Venus excelled any images from the other expeditions; displayed at the Chicago World Exposition in 1893, they were one of the major attractions of the fair.

There was sunshine in California but clouds in Amherst. Sue's suspicions about Mabel and Austin were aroused, and the transit coincided with her rising rage. On the morning of December 6, the day of the transit, Mabel wrote to Austin that Sue's coldness the previous night "was dreadful, but I should not have cared so much if I could have thought it accidental. . . . Things look to me of much the same color as the leaden sky, but I love you." That afternoon, Mabel invited four women, including Sue, to go to the college observatory and look through the telescope, but there were clouds to the northeast, obscuring the spectacle. That evening, Mabel and Austin took a walk toward Mill Valley, south of Amherst, as the sky cleared. Later that night, Mabel wrote Austin again, to tell him that "*my* sky has changed from leaden clouds to sunshine, as the day did."[28]

I 2.

On December 9, three days after the Transit of Venus, Martin Johnson Heade wrote to Mabel, expressing the fervent hope that he might see her again in the spring. "Your father," he reported teasingly, "wrote me that your truant husband had, like many others, become fascinated with Miss Venus Hesperus, and had gone all the way to California to feast on her beauties through his opera glass—Why do you allow it?" "Well," he concluded, "I'll probably see you soon, and when we make up another party to gather flowers I know just where to go for *oceans* of arbutus. I have just finished one of the most beautiful flower pieces that I ever painted."

Heade wrote to Mabel's father that he had received a "very interesting (of course) letter from Mrs. Todd" and lamented, with a clear double meaning, having missed the Transit of Venus. He regretted that he would have to "wait till 2002 before I can see one." On the other hand, he had discovered in his boardinghouse "a setter of sublime beauty" that he was seriously considering buying, for twenty-five dollars, to hunt with.[29]

I 3.

Emily Dickinson continued into the fall of 1882 to banter with Judge Lord about their engagement, using his pet name for her who felt so small in his presence: "Emily 'Jumbo'! Sweetest name, but I know a sweeter—Emily Jumbo Lord." (Barnum's famous elephant, Jumbo, had been exhibited in Greenfield earlier that summer.[30]) But the deaths and threats of further deaths were taking their toll on Dickinson, and the promise of marriage—so palpable before Judge Lord's stroke on May Day—receded.

For Emily Dickinson, the six months between April 1, 1882, when Reverend Charles Wadsworth died, and November 14, 1882, the date that her invalid mother finally passed away, were almost unbearably painful. She noted Emerson's passing (he had "touched the secret Spring. Which Earth are we in?") on April 27; in May she learned that Judge Lord was seriously ill; Higginson fell ill in August; in September, her beloved servant, Margaret Maher, contracted typhoid—without her watchful eye, Dickinson wrote, "The pussies dine on sherry now, and humming-bird cutlets."

Under this onslaught, Dickinson came to think of each month as having a certain character. "It sometimes seems as if special Months gave and took away—" she wrote to Mrs. Holland on October 29, when Lord had recovered. "August has brought the most to me—April—robbed me most—in incessant instances." Writing on the eve of the Transit of Venus, she was feeling a kindred transit in her own life. "The Dyings have been too deep for me," she confided in the fall of 1884, "and before I could raise my Heart from one, another has come."[31]

Fate held one more death in store for her, and she never recovered from it. Austin and Susan's youngest child, Thomas Gilbert, was barely eight years old when he contracted typhoid during the fall of 1883. "Gib," as he was known to everyone, was a lively child with a gift for words, and a special favorite of Emily's. The night he died, on October 5, Dickinson made her first visit to the Evergreens in fifteen years. Overwhelmed by the sadness and horror of the scene, as well as the smell of disinfectants, she returned to the Homestead at three A M, vomited, and collapsed.

She was ill for several weeks thereafter, and never fully recovered from the blow. To Susan Dickinson, the grieving mother, she wrote one of her most beautiful letters, which was also a summation of her growing sense of human transience. Many of the lines fall into the rhythm of her poems:

ejoiced in Secrets—

His Life was panting with them—With what menace of Light he cried "Don't tell, Aunt Emily"! Now my ascended Playmate must instruct *me*. Show us, prattling Preceptor, but the way to thee!

He knew no niggard moment—His Life was full of Boon—The Playthings of the Dervish were not so wild as his—

No crescent was this Creature—He traveled from the Full— Such soar, but never set—

I see him in the Star, and meet his sweet velocity in everything that flies—[32]

14.

In the face of these accumulating losses, we see two related insights working themselves out in Emily Dickinson's poems and letters of 1882 and after. One is the fleeting nature of all life. "All we secure of Beauty is its Evanescence—" she wrote in late December, echoing a line from a poem contemporaneous with "A Route of Evanescence":[33]

> *To see the Summer Sky*
> *Is Poetry, though never in a Book it lie—*
> *True Poems flee—*[34]

This idea was always implicit in her poetry, and was closely linked with her love of flowers.

But we also see in Dickinson's late letters an emerging theory of biography. Even as she labored to secure traces and documents of loved ones like Wadsworth, she recognized the futility of the endeavor. "Memory is a strange Bell—Jubilee, and Knell," she wrote after her mother's death. And her most stringent judgment on trying to pin down a human life came a few months before her own. "Biography first convinces us of the fleeing of the Biographied—" she wrote Higginson in February 1885.[35]

All riddles in Dickinson have two answers, a physical and a spiritual one. The physical answer to the poem she sent to Mabel Todd in October 1882 is the one she helpfully provided: "please accept a Humming-Bird." But the spiritual answer is clear as well. Human life, all life, is a route of evanescence.

Chapter Ten

FLORIDA

I was a little uncertain, afterwards, as to when I had become distinctively aware of Florida. . . . I had come out to smoke for the evening's end, and it mattered not a scrap that the public garden was new and scant and crude, and that Jacksonville is not a name to conjure with; I still could sit there quite in the spirit, for the hour, of Byron's immortal question as to the verity of his Italian whereabouts. . . . I projected myself, for the time, after Byron's manner, into the exquisite sense of the dream come true. . . . I was meanwhile able, I found, to be quite Byronically foolish about the St. Johns River.

HENRY JAMES

I.

IT IS DIFFICULT, a hundred years and more after the fact, to capture the sheer magic of the moment of arrival at one of the grand hotels of the Gilded Age. Today, all hotels are pretty much alike, differing only in the degree of luxury rather than in their essential aura; a certain level of agreed-upon "excellence" is guaranteed by the commercial chain to which they belong. But in the Gilded Age, a hotel was a world unto itself, a vivid destination rather than a mere convenience. Everything conspired to translate the moment of arrival into a dream or fairy tale.

As you stepped down from the horse-drawn hotel-coach that had met you at the railway station, you found arrayed before you the manifold helpers, clothed in fantastic garments and velvet hats, anticipating your every need. Professions that existed nowhere else—the bellman, the doorman, the concierge—lined up like soldiers at your beck and call—as you were ushered through the great doors. Your trunk, bearing the brightly colored labels of its past exotic itineraries, followed. Your credentials checked and your respectability confirmed, you were welcomed into a single extended family, your party distributed among far-flung bedrooms to reassemble, at the proper time and in proper attire, at dinner. It was all a public performance, choreographed and scripted, in which you were the player as well as the audience.

The spectacular development of one corner of Florida as a luxury resort for upscale northern travelers presented special challenges during the final decades of the nineteenth century. In the absence of mountains or other dramatic features of the landscape, everyone agreed that the magnificent St. Johns River, flowing north from an interior lake and emptying into the ocean at Jacksonville, should be a focal point for visitors. The ancient Spanish port of St. Augustine was down the coast nearby, with its picturesque streets and houses, and could be reached either via a short rail link from the river, by railroad from Jacksonville, or by ocean. So it was that this triangle of two small cities and a broad river became the first destination in Florida for the mass winter exodus from the North.

There was historical justice in the arrangement, for the area had been staked out in the imagination by northern explorers and artists. William Bartram, the Philadelphia Quaker and visionary artist, had explored the region during the 1760s, locating underground rivers and singing alligators that stoked the feverish brain of Samuel Taylor Coleridge, who extracted details of Xanadu from Bartram's reports. A century later, Colonel Thomas Wentworth Higginson had journeyed upriver into Rebel territory, occupied Jacksonville, then watched it burn, a salvaged red rose in his uniform lapel. Immediately after the war, Harriet Beecher Stowe had found on these same war-ravaged shores a temporary refuge for her son Freddy, wounded at Gettysburg, before he boarded a ship bound for San Francisco and vanished into thin air.

Among these northern wanderers, Stowe had stayed. Like some deep-rooted symbol of her commitment, the tree that impinged on the porch of her gingerbread cottage in the hamlet of Mandarin, fifteen miles from Jacksonville on the eastern shore, had grown through the 1870s, dwarfing the dollhouse below it. It conferred an Alice in Wonderland scale to the scene that greeted hundreds of visitors steaming up the St. Johns. Orange groves came to the water's edge, and through the trees one could glimpse from the water the gleaming white cottage. There on her porch for all to see sat Harriet Beecher Stowe, spectacles perched on her nose, writing writing writing in her rocking chair. Edward King, hired by Emily Dickinson's friend Josiah Holland to write a series of articles later collected in his book *The Great South*, wrote that the visitors "do not seem to understand that she is not on exhibition."[1] But the popularity of his book only made her even more of a tourist attraction. Artists, including King's gifted illustrator J. Wells Champney, avidly painted Stowe's Florida refuge.

No one had done more to dream Florida into its modern mode than Stowe herself, and it was perfectly fitting that she should be, so to speak, on view. Before the Civil War, the whole Beecher clan had been involved in securing the Midwest—especially Ohio, Wisconsin, and Illinois—for the Northern cause. During the years just after the war, Stowe and her friends had envisioned Florida as a Northern colony in an unregenerate South, where freed slaves would find, among Yankee transplants like Stowe, inspiring models of industry, piety, and thrift. Through books like *Palmetto*

*Stowe (second from left) with her husband (seated) and Eunice Beecher
(seated to his left) at Mandarin*

Leaves, an atmospheric series of letters addressed to potential visitors, Stowe had advertised the lazy charm and health-promoting climate of the state. Her oranges, crated and sent north with the words "Sent to you from Mandarin by Harriet Beecher Stowe" on the label, were proof of the existence of this American Eden—a country promising, as Ponce de León had predicted, eternal youth.

2.

Martin Johnson Heade arrived in Jacksonville in January with none of the pomp of the luxury traveler. He carried his guns and his easel, as well as the hunting dog he had purchased in Boston a few months earlier. Heade was feeling sorry for himself. After lingering in New England through the summer, hoping against hope that Mabel Todd might show him more than a respectful affection, the thought of returning to Washington was depressing. "I'm convinced that Washington will not do for me," he wrote Mabel's father, Eben Loomis, in early December. And then, with an uneasy mixture of irony and histrionics, he added: "It looks as if I was never to be settled again. I've been a wanderer on the face of the earth ever since I left that studio in 10th St." in New York.[2]

Having glimpsed domestic happiness during his visit with Mabel Todd in Amherst, Heade was increasingly troubled by his own "unsettled" existence. He struck the Byronic note, part arrogance and part self-pity: "I've rambled about so long that I'm in a very unsettled state of mind & can't be contented anywhere." And then, in a letter a week later to Loomis, comes a hint of a new direction: "I've had a sort of Florida fever but I'm getting over it."

Evidently, he didn't get over it. In late December Heade informed Loomis, "I'm going to Florida immediately after New Years." He went there to hunt and fish, and also to paint, drawn by the allure that the tropics had always held for him. "It looks like June here," he wrote Loomis on February 12 from the sporting resort at Enterprise on Lake Munroe. "The orange trees are in full bloom, & strawberries are ripe." The St. Johns River, which fed Lake Munroe, was also ripe for painting: "The Upper St. Johns is perfectly beautiful & I have prepared for lots of pictures from the scenery along the river—leaving out the alligators." Heade's enthusiasm for northern Florida must have been bittersweet to Loomis, who knew the area well; right after the Civil War, he had invested heavily in a cotton plantation near Jacksonville, an endeavor that was no more successful than Captain Fred Stowe's ill-fated plantation nearby.[3]

Heade made a point of visiting Harriet Beecher Stowe in her picturesque tree-house in Mandarin. It was almost the first thing he did in Florida. Stowe had recommended Heade's landscapes to her readers, after all, and he had recently had a visit with her brother in Greenfield. They were also linked by their passion for hummingbirds, and their concern for the endangered avian population of Florida. "When I landed at Jacksonville," Heade reported to Loomis on February 12, "I took a run down to see Mrs. Stowe, but had only a few minutes. I found her (& also her daughter) in a delightful mood, & could hardly get away. They made me promise to pay them a visit before leaving Florida, which I mean to do, if I can." Stowe was unable to produce Heade's other quarry. "I've not seen a humming bird since I came," he told Loomis. "I wonder where the little rascals are?"

Stowe was coming to the end of her own Florida days. Her husband's health was declining, and Fred's disappearance was again on her mind. Soon after Heade's visit, Harriet wrote to her sister Isabella, who dabbled in spiritualism, for news of her lost son. Victoria Woodhull, Henry Ward Beecher's nemesis, had persuaded Isabella that she, Isabella, had spiritualist powers. On hot summer days in Hartford, Isabella would lie dozing on the tin roof outside her window. Tappings on her parasol alerted her to the presence of spirits, whose messages were conveyed through inspired utterance or automatic writing. Sometimes, Isabella in a trance adopted the handwriting of absent friends like Samuel Bowles, editor of the *Springfield Republican* and a longtime ally in the fight for women's suffrage. "I wish dear sister you would do me one favor," Harriet wrote Isabella. "Copy and send to me the supposed communication from my poor Fred . . . Mr. Stowe wants to see [it] and I want to see [it] again."[4]

Heade's immediate aim was to find a place in Florida that suited him, with a good enough hotel to allow him to "live comfortably at a reasonable price." Heade was, by his own account, "fastidious"; having found the hotel at Ocala "abominable" and Enterprise too expensive, he set his sights on St. Augustine. "I *think* I'll like it at St. Augustine," he told Loomis, "but *don't* think I'll like the hotels, & I understand the boarding houses are crowded with invalids."[5]

The old rail link Heade took from Tocoi on the St. Johns to St. Augustine was primitive—a streetcar drawn by a pair of horses. "The journey is made partly on iron, partly on wooden rails; but it is comfortable," as Edward King described it, "and affords one an excellent chance to see veritable Florida back-country."

> There is not a house along the route; hardly a sign of life. Sometimes the roll of the wheels startles an alligator who has been napping on the track; and once, the conductor says, they found two little brown bears asleep in the run directly in their path. It is night ere you approach the suburbs of the old city. The vegetation takes on a ghostly aspect; the black swamp canal over which the vehicle passes sends up a fetid odor of decay; the palm thickets under the moonlight in the distance set one to tropical imaginings. Arrived at the Sebastian river, an arm of the sea flowing in among long stretches of salt-marsh clad in a kind of yellowish grass and inhabited by innumerable wild fowl that make the air ring with their cries, the horse-car stops, you are transferred to an omnibus, brown-skinned Minorcans and French touters for hotels surround you; the horn sounds ta-ra! ta-ra-ta-ra! and you rattle through the streets to the hotel.[6]

3.

And there in the ancient Spanish town of St. Augustine, amid the moldering cottages built of shell-based coquina with their wide, overhanging balconies, Heade's wanderings came to an end—for life, as it were. "I have wandered in an unsatisfactory sort of way nearly all over the State without finding a spot where I cared to stop until I reached St. Augustine," he wrote in a report for *Forest and Stream* published that spring, "and that I find a fascinating, quaint old place."[7]

Heade worked fast. Having found a place to settle, he was determined to leave any trace of his "unsettled" status behind. In early March, he bought a "pretty little cottage" on San Marco Avenue, the old "Shell Road," from General Frederick T. Dent, brother of Mrs. Ulysses Grant.[8] The house was a few blocks from a new hotel called the San Marco, just north of the old city gates. Heade then made a quick trip to the Northeast, presumably to retrieve paintings and other possessions, and stopped in Washington on his return, when Mabel Todd happened to be there. On March 24, Mabel noted in her diary that "our well beloved Mr. Heade" had visited, noting with surprise that he had "bought a place in St. Augustine." In May, with carpenters and painters at work on the house, he headed north again, making sure to visit Mabel, who was still in Washington (and madly in love with Austin Dickinson). Heade was assiduously assembling the pieces of the settled life he craved, but it was abundantly evident that Mabel Loomis Todd wasn't one of them.

What happened next astonished Heade's friends. There is no record of how he spent the summer of 1883; but in early September he announced his engagement to Elizabeth Smith of Southampton, Long Island. To those who had known Heade's wandering ways from up close, the news was incongruous. Frederic Church wrote Heade: "I'd heard that . . . you had bought a house in St. Augustine and wondered at it. That surprise gives way to the greater one of your engagement." On October 8, Martin Heade and Elizabeth Smith were married in New York. Heade was sixty-four; his bride was forty. "*Of course* I'm as happy as a possum in a persimmon tree," he wrote Eben Loomis at the end of the year.[9]

Heade was confident that he had made good investments, for St. Augustine, as he informed his readers in *Forest and Stream*, "is bound to be the winter Newport of this country. The great obstacle in the way of settling up this place rapidly has been the difficulty of getting here and the atrociously kept hotels; but both these difficulties are about to be removed."

4 ·

At that very moment, in December 1883, another traveler arrived in St. Augustine. At age fifty-three, Henry Morrison Flagler, honeymooning with his own much younger wife, was destined to do more than anyone else to transform St. Augustine into the winter Newport. Flagler, John D. Rockefeller's partner in Standard Oil, had both the energy and the means. On an earlier trip with his ailing first wife, Flagler had found St. Augustine "depressingly full of consumptives and other invalids." Now, a widower with a second wife almost twenty years his junior, he found the city "rejuvenated by an influx of Northern visitors who enjoyed both good health and affluence."[10]

Just as Heade had glimpsed new possibilities for pictures in the scenery along the St. Johns, Flagler saw something in the broad beaches and narrow streets of St. Augustine that appealed to his imagination. A pageant Flagler attended two years later, celebrating the landing of Juan Ponce de León, the aging Spanish conquistador who had searched for a legendary Fountain of Youth and who gave the peninsula the name "Florida," crystallized Flagler's vision. He would build a resort centered around a grand hotel, grander than any previously seen in the South, and call it the Hotel Ponce de Leon. He would lay new railroad lines, making it easy for visitors to get there. And he would engage other like-minded visionaries in his dream, including Martin Johnson Heade, whom he met that winter. [11]

The parallels are irresistible. Two middle-aged men with their young brides arrive during the same year in Ponce de León's city, and achieve together a vision of the Fountain of Youth.[12] Heade was excited about Flagler's plans. "Another big hotel is going up soon," he wrote Eben Loomis in June 1885, "larger and finer than the 'San Marco'—to be called the 'Paunch de León'—which means, being interpreted, the internal portion of a famous British animal." He suggested that Loomis should come down for the opening of the "monster hotel," which promised to be "the biggest thing in modern times."

Flagler had engaged two young architects, John M. Carrère and Thomas Hastings, with the design. Trained in the Beaux Arts tradition, they later designed the New York Public Library, with two more lions at the gate. For Flagler's Florida folly, they made use of local materials and local architectural ideas. Coquina-shell stone dug from the seashore on nearby Anastasia Island was the main building material. Balconies and arches topped with salmon-colored terra-cotta tiles echoed the Spanish style of old St. Augustine houses.

But the sheer scale of the hotel complex was what visitors noticed first. It was as though a child armed with bucket and shovel had created a gigantic sand castle, with turrets and towers, archways and fountains. There was a playfulness about the whole glorious construct, at once breathtaking and oddly intimate, that beguiled the eye. Journalists vied with one another to describe the effect. "Of course this marvelous creation, that has sprung up in Florida . . . is the wonder of everybody who comes here," wrote Flagler's friend Henry M. Field, "and it is amusing to observe the look of surprise of newcomers, and hear their expressions of astonishment." The well-traveled journalist Julian Ralph described the hotel in pictorial terms reminiscent of Whistler, as "a melody or a poem in gray and red and green. The pearl-gray walls of shell-stone lift their cool sides between billows of foliage and masses of bright red tiling. The graceful towers, quaint dormer-windows, airy log-gias, and jewel-like settings of stained glass, like the palms and fountains and galleries, all melt, unnoted into the main effect."[13]

ART WAS CENTRAL to the main effect Flagler was seeking. Newport was known for its artists, and he was determined that St. Augustine should have its artists too. He had a row of seven artists' studios built on the hotel prem-ises, and invited Heade to occupy the seventh and most prominent one. The artists moved in before the guests arrived, which was also part of the plan; as Heade explained to Loomis, the artists were meant "to please the hotel guests." The artists were part of the public spectacle on view. Heade in his studio, like Stowe on her Mandarin porch, was on display—a typical tour-ist sight.

At the same time, Heade and the other artists in Flagler's studio row produced scenes of Florida for tourist consumption, luxury souvenirs of a winter in paradise. It was a perfect economic arrangement, and fixed in the public mind a series of Florida scenes. "The St. Augustine painters traveled the same routes that the tourists took," as Frederic A. Sharf notes, "going down the St. Johns River . . . Travelers from all over the country brought pictures of St. Augustine, and those not sold on the spot were of-fered in Boston, New York, or Philadelphia by art dealers and at auction galleries. Eventually such Florida scenes became familiar throughout the country."[14]

5.

During his early months in Florida, Heade enlisted Eben Loomis's help in finding buyers in Washington for his Florida paintings. As expenses mounted during the outfitting of his new house in St. Augustine in early 1884, he wrote urgently to Loomis: "If you can effect any sales for me I'll hold you in everlasting remembrance." Heade enclosed a painting, adding, "I want you to get 200 for this one—if you can, but *sell* it."

Loomis had more pressing things on his mind, however, than selling his best friend's landscapes and orchid-sipping hummingbirds. On a visit to Amherst that fall, Loomis's wife, Molly, had made an extraordinary discovery about their daughter's private life. Mabel Loomis Todd had planned a housewarming party for the new house, right behind the two Dickinson houses, that she and David had moved into in June. She decked the rooms with daisies and with red and gold autumn leaves for a huge party, inviting seventy-five guests for an evening supper. But apart from the festivities, what Molly noticed most was that Austin Dickinson, early and late, had the run of Mabel's house. She saw that he stopped by the house every day, often entering through the back door, that he stayed at night after David Todd's departure for the observatory, and that Mabel and Austin took frequent drives into the countryside together.

Alarmed, Molly summoned Eben Loomis to come to Amherst immediately. Eben confronted Austin, who was indignant. "Ought he not to have something pretty well attested," he wrote Mabel, "before setting me down as a sneak, and an improper person, given to mischief, and treachery?"[15] But Eben Loomis's charges, as detailed in what Mabel called "a terrible letter from my father" that January, were quite accurate. Austin and Mabel were deeply in love, and even considered themselves married. Their defense, an old one for adulterers, was that their love was consecrated, and that convention was for lesser folk. "We are not to be frightened," Austin wrote, "we are not of that cheap stuff . . . Our life together is as white and unspotted as the fresh driven snow."[16]

Austin Dickinson was so confident of the sublimity of this love affair that he was eager to confide his passion, speaking of Mabel with his two spinster sisters next door—whom Molly Loomis had described as "cynical, carping, irreligious people."[17] Mabel had been painting again and giving art classes to Amherst girls. She had painted an extraordinary picture of barn swallows swooping through the sky, a vision akin in its profusion to her teacher Martin Heade's picture of many different species of hummingbirds congregating in a single tree. When Mabel traveled to Europe during the summer of 1885, her paintings were stored on the walls and in the closets of the Homestead, where Emily Dickinson admired them. "I see Vin and Em more than I did," Austin wrote to Mabel in mid-June, "and you are the constant theme. Emily has had great pleasure in looking over your pictures."[18]

Emily herself wrote to Mabel in July, telling her, apropos of one of Mabel's paintings, that "Your Hollyhocks endow the House, making Art's inner Summer." In the letter, Dickinson teased Mabel for traveling to Europe when New England's charms were so intense. She quoted Emerson's "The Humble-Bee," with its nationalist conviction that travel is pointless:

> *Burly, dozing humble-bee,*
> *Where thou art is clime for me.*
> *Let them sail for Porto Rique,*
> *Far-off heats through seas to seek;*
> *I will follow thee alone,*
> *Thou animated torrid-zone!*

The bee, as Dickinson imagined in many of her poems, brings the tropics home. "I write in the midst of Sweet-Peas and by the side of Orioles," Dickinson wrote Mabel, "and could put my Hand on a Butterfly, only he withdraws." She signed the letter "America."[19]

6.

This was to be Emily Dickinson's final summer. She had had a series of alarming symptoms and setbacks since the spring of 1884. Judge Lord had died on March 13, and she had collapsed unconscious to the floor in June. In August 1885, she had suffered another blow, when she learned of the death of Helen Hunt Jackson. "Life is deep and swift," she wrote in early 1886. "Spars without the Routes but the Billows designate."[20]

Then, in a poignant reprise of their famous exchange of a hummingbird poem for a picture of Indian pipes, Mabel Todd painted a bronze plaque of thistles for Emily Dickinson. Dickinson sent her a hyacinth with a cryptic cover note—"Or Figs of Thistles?"—alluding to Matthew 7:16, "Do men gather grapes of thorns, or figs of thistles?"

Twice in her final days, Dickinson compared herself to her beloved trailing arbutus—she had once signed a poem with the flower's name—that revived with the first hint of spring. Daphne, whom Zeus changed into a laurel, allowing her to elude Apollo's amorous pursuit, "always seems to me a more civic Arbutus," she wrote in late spring, adding, "If we love Flowers, are we not 'born again' every Day?"[21] And to her Norcross cousins in March, she wrote of how she had "lain in my bed since November, many years, for me, stirring as the arbutus does, a pink and russet hope."

She wrote a final note to Higginson, wondering if he was still alive, and one to her Norcross cousins:

> Little Cousins,
>   Called back.
>   Emily.[22]

Emily Dickinson died on May 15, 1886.[23]

Thomas Wentworth Higginson read Emily Brontë's "Last Lines" at the funeral four days later. Violets and a pink cypripedium fringed Dickinson's throat, with more violets covering her white casket. She was said to appear miraculously young, not a single gray strand in her red hair. According to her own request, the Irish laborers employed at the Homestead carried the casket out the back door of the house, through the open barn, and across a meadow full of wildflowers to the Amherst cemetery.

7.

Now it was Austin's turn to dream of travel: "Perhaps I will take to Mexico. I always had a romantic fancy that way. Or Peru. Something with a Spanish tang."[24] But Austin stayed in Amherst, fending off accusations from the Loomises and building a new house in the middle of the Dickinson meadow for the Todds (and, of course, for himself, the daily and nightly visitor). Mabel, meanwhile, circled the globe, following her husband on eclipse expeditions to Japan—twice—and to Libya, and journeyed to Peru to photograph Mars, too busy to accept Martin Johnson Heade's repeated invitation to join him in sunny Florida. Heade continued to think that Mabel might be drawn to the Florida scenery. To Loomis he wrote: "Tell [Mabel] to come down & paint some of her pictures in my studio by the edge of the salt meadow."[25]

8.

"There are men whom a merciful Providence has undoubtedly ordained to a single life," wrote W. Somerset Maugham in *Moon and Sixpence*, his fantasy of Gauguin's life in Tahiti. "There is no object more deserving of pity than the married bachelor." Married for the first time at the ripe age of sixty-four, Martin Johnson Heade struck his friends as a married bachelor, but he seemed a singularly happy one. Reports of the Heades in St. Augustine place them at the center of the resort's social life. They gamely performed the role of artist and artist's wife, on display at the hotel—part of the decor—and highly visible at art exhibitions and receptions. They seemed happy to be roped into Flagler's dream of the Florida "scene."

As Flagler's favorite painter, Heade was enlisted to decorate the grand hotel as well as perform in its studio row as artist-in-residence. Flagler commissioned two landscape paintings—at seven and a half feet wide and eight feet wide, respectively, monumental for Heade—to grace the rotunda. "My two big pictures, for the parlor of the hotel are nearly completed," he wrote Loomis on June 16, 1887. "One is a Jamaica picture, with tree ferns and things and I think it's a pretty neat thing—for me. The other is a Florida scene, a sunset. St. Augustine is going to be great fun!" *The Great Florida Sunset*, with its egrets and lily pads and bulbous palm stumps, drew on Heade's new preoccupation with the subtle sublimity of the Florida swamp.

"Our American Italy has not a mountain within its boundaries," Edward King wrote of Florida in *The Great South*.[26] The absence of dramatic features might have ruled out the "flowery peninsula," as King called it, for a more conventional landscape painter. For Heade, however, the featurelessness enhanced Florida's charm. Since his childhood along the Delaware, Heade had been a connoisseur of flatness. Faced with what Henry James would call "the great empty peninsula," "a void furnished at the most with velvet air," Heade felt perfectly at home, his imagination relishing the sheer barren extent of marsh and swamp.[27] While other painters, like his friend Church, traveled in search of waterfalls and mountain peaks, his own meandering quest had been for flatness. In this respect, Florida better suited his needs than New England. He wrote to Eben Loomis on December 3, 1883: "As the St. Johns River scenery is perfectly flat—as it is here [in St. Augustine]—I have neglected the northern meadows lately & taken to Florida."[28] Palms replaced haystacks.[29] Thunderstorms and crashing waves disappeared from his paintings; he never painted the Florida coast. A Quaker simplicity worthy of his old master, Hicks, ruled.

Heade's embrace of Florida's flatness constituted a new aesthetic vision in American art, rejecting, as Theodore Stebbins notes, "the old picturesque and valuing a different kind of landscape: murky, primeval, barren, and wet."[30] In this commitment, Heade was following Edward King ("One ceases to regret hills and mountains, and can hardly imagine ever having thought them necessary, so much do these visions surpass them") and Harriet Beecher Stowe, who waxed lyrical in her evocation of the "most gorgeous of improprieties, this swamp."[31]

King's gifted illustrator, J. Wells Champney, showed what could be done with a swamp at sunset, the great palms rising—"as so many rows of puzzled philosophers, disheveled, shock-pated, with the riddle of the universe," in Henry James's wonderful simile—against the cloud-streaked sky.[32] New visions required new formats, and Heade experimented with "an exaggerated horizontality" in his very Champney-like *Sunset: Tropical Marshes*, painted on a canvas whose width was three times its height.[33] Heade often seems to anticipate Monet, but never more so than here, where the canvas, like Monet's late water lilies, can be imagined to extend laterally forever.

9.

Henry James, touring the United States after many years in Europe, stayed for four days in the Ponce de Leon in February 1905. The whole phenomenon of such pleasure palaces was still relatively new, and James tried to capture the impression of a self-sufficient world unto itself, a "hotel-world," as he called it.

> St. Augustine proving primarily, and of course quite legitimately, but an hotel, of the first magnitude—an hotel indeed so remarkable and so pleasant that I wondered what call there need ever have been upon it to prove anything else. The Ponce de Leon, for that matter, comes as near producing, all by itself, the illusion of romance as highly modern, a most cleverly-constructed and smoothly-administered great modern caravansary can come . . . It did for me, at St. Augustine, I was well aware, everything that an hotel could do.[34]

The relentless theatricality of Flagler's resort, its incessant impression of high society performing on an artificial stage, seemed to leave little room for the private life—what James called "the comparative privacies and ancientries of Newport." Life at the Ponce de Leon, by contrast, was enclosed and exposed. From the moment one boarded the train, one had already entered the boundaries of what James called the "hotel-world." Guests arrived at the resort in luxury railroad cars designed by Flagler, bearing the same yellow trim—"Flagler yellow"—as the arches and windows of the hotel. The transition between railroad and hotel was seamless; the Pullman cars, as James noted, "are like rushing hotels and the hotels . . . are like stationary Pullmans." One felt enveloped by the Ponce de Leon, swallowed up in it.

It is difficult to render the intensity with which one felt the great sphere of the hotel close round one, covering one in as with high shining crystal walls, stretching beneath one's feet an immeasurable polished level, revealing itself in short as, for the time, for the place, the very order of nature and the very form, the only one, of the habitable world.

I O.

Martin Johnson Heade, destined to leave Flagler's hotel-world just a few months before James arrived in it, was an integral part of Flagler's vision. And yet, what strikes one most forcefully in the photographs of Mr. and Mrs. Heade that have survived is the unmistakable note of privacy in their Florida arrangements, of a shared intimate life kept to themselves.

Nowhere is the private note more poignantly sounded than in Heade's late, great series of paintings of magnolias. Magnolias too had been enlisted in the public image of Florida and its hotel-world. Ever since William

Bartram had admired the great white flowers and waxy leaves, "the most beautiful and tall that I have any where seen," as he sailed up the St. Johns during the 1770s, magnolias were a crucial part of the iconography of the flowery peninsula. Magnolia hotels dotted the state, a resort on the St. Johns was named Magnolia Springs, and magnolias in profusion filled the magnificent gardens of the Ponce de Leon.[35]

But Heade was after something entirely different in his paintings of magnolia blossoms arrayed on blue and red velvet cloth. The paintings are unmistakably erotic, as John Baur noted in his pioneering article of 1954: "the fleshy whiteness of magnolia blossoms startlingly arrayed on sumptuous red velvet like odalisques on a couch." Roberta Smith took the idea further, finding "an aura of post-coital dishabille" in the reclining blossoms.[36]

These paintings hint of a private realm, velvet-enshrouded, and one that is temporary and transient, evanescent like the magnolia itself. Harriet Beecher Stowe wrote of the difficulty of trying to paint magnolias in Florida: "Who would take the portrait of the white lady must hurry; for, like many queens of the earth, there is but a step between perfected beauty and decay,—a moment between beauty and ashes."[37]

Heade was happy enough to be an accessory of the Ponce de Leon, the sociable artist at work in his studio provided by Flagler. But in addition to his public studio, Heade kept a private one as well, on his own grounds at a comfortable remove from the social whirl. A late painting shows a man alone in a boat on the river, the hotel towers barely visible in the far distance. And a photograph has survived of Heade sitting indoors by the window, framed by a great profusion of vines and shrubbery. We see him as through a tunnel, holed up in his private, darkened space. The vines seem on the verge of closing up the window's opening altogether, cutting off our access to the reclusive painter.

Another photograph shows him sitting in his yard with Mrs. Heade; he wears a boater and his back is turned to us. Mrs. Heade, facing him, holds a parasol with her left hand and, with her right, feeds a tiny hummingbird with a tiny bottle.

Photo of Heade, Mrs. Heade, and pet hummingbird (private collection)

It was a shared obsession. In 1898, he summoned up this picture of domestic happiness:

Last spring, my wife and I were standing on the piazza and a pair of male ruby-throats—the first arrivals—came hovering round our heads, chasing each other in seeming play, and then lighting side by side on a star Jessamine vine within a foot or two of our faces, without the slightest fear of us, which meant, of course, that they knew their ground, and when I brought out the little bottle they always feed from, one of them came directly to it as if he had fed from it all his life. . . . This season at least two or three of my old pets have visited me, and all seem as tame as the previous year, but the early birds that are on the migratory move I cannot induce to stay. They nearly all go further north to set up house-keeping.[38]

Martin Johnson Heade died on September 4, 1904. His final article for *Forest and Stream*, dated July 20 and published August 6, was titled simply "Hummingbirds."

TOWARD THE BLUE PENINSULA

a moldering plume, an empty house, in which a bird
resided

𝄞 EMILY DICKINSON[1]

I.

ℰMILY DICKINSON THOUGHT that one of the supreme advantages
of being human was the writing and receiving of letters. "A letter is
a joy of earth," she wrote, "it is denied the Gods."[2] On another occasion, in a letter to Thomas Wentworth Higginson, she compared a private
letter to immortality, "because it is the soul alone without corporeal friend."[3]
Letters were as close as humans could come to divinity; with the winged
words of letters, we become almost angelic messengers. For Dickinson,
poems and letters were intimately related: she wove poems into her letters,
and considered her poems a form of letter writing: "This is my letter to the
World / That never wrote to Me."[4]

The route traveled by a letter to the world is always unpredictable.
Consider the strange journey of Emily Dickinson's letter-poem that begins
with the words "Alone and in a Circumstance." It began as a collage, carefully constructed with scissors, pasted objects, and a pencil. Then it made

its way, via knowledgeable letter carriers mindful of their mission, to precisely the one artist most likely to understand its supreme originality: the American surrealist and creator of magical boxes Joseph Cornell.

The manuscript of the poem is one of the oddest in all of Dickinson's writings. She constructed it around 1870, as she was coming to the end of her major harvest of poems. First, she used scissors to cut out some words from the "Editor's Literary Record" of the May 1870 issue of *Harper's Magazine*. The author of the column was concerned that the French novelist George Sand's *Mauprat* might prove "a dangerous book," despite its theme of the transformation of the brutish young man Mauprat through the influence of a noble woman.

> But the bitter conflict between base passion and the nobler nature is described with so great power, and the incidents which provoke the fiery temper within are wrought up with such consummate skill, that the youthful reader will be apt to find the devil in him more effectually raised than exorcised, the passion fired rather than extinguished.

Dickinson cut only a few words from the column. On one narrow clipping is the name "George Sand"; on the other is the title *Mauprat*. The words "of bandits a" are legible beneath *Mauprat*, part of a sentence describing the plot of the novel: "Mauprat is brought up among a company of bandits and robbers, relics of the feudal past."

The publisher of *Mauprat*, the first of Sand's novels to appear in the United States, was Roberts Brothers of Boston, which six years later included one of Dickinson's best-known poems, "Success is counted sweetest," in a volume of anonymous poems. It is unlikely, however, that Dickinson had read the novel when she made her collage. And in any case, it was George Sand's life as a writer that inspired her most, as when she wrote to her Norcross cousins, around 1861, of the suffocating childhoods of such literary heroines as Elizabeth Barrett Browning and George Sand: "Poor children! Women, now, queens, now!" She quoted Sand regarding how as a child she "must make no noise in her grandmother's bedroom," recalling Dickinson's own poem about how "They shut me up in Prose."[5]

The writer of the "Editor's Literary Record" described the relation of confinement and freedom in George Sand's life: "A wife at eighteen, a mother at nineteen, separated from her husband at twenty-seven, she began her literary life in the true style of the distinguished author of the novel and the melodrama, in a Paris attic, dressing in male attire, partly for economy's sake, partly for freedom."

George Sand was herself a famous writer of letters, one voice in perhaps the best-known exchange of love letters in nineteenth-century Europe. Her correspondence with the poet Alfred de Musset entranced readers, and demonstrated for a whole generation how a love affair could become a work of art.[6] It was a fantasy that Emily Dickinson herself had indulged in throughout her mature life. Her "master letters" seem, in retrospect, experiments in enacting a grand passion on the page, and so do her late letters to Judge Otis Lord, with her careful insistence that the real life of the affair was verbal, not "corporeal."

2.

The free woman in the Paris attic was on Emily Dickinson's mind as she affixed the two clippings from *Harper's* to the middle of a sheet of notepaper, using a sky-blue three-cent uncanceled postage stamp printed in 1869 to hold the clippings in place. It was as though she were sending a letter to George Sand, from her upstairs Amherst bedroom to Sand's attic room in Paris. Dickinson placed the stamp sideways, the top to the left side of the paper, with the clippings jutting out from the left-hand corners of the stamp. The resulting collage resembles a bird with wings outstretched.

The picture on the stamp, above the large "3," is a locomotive, with

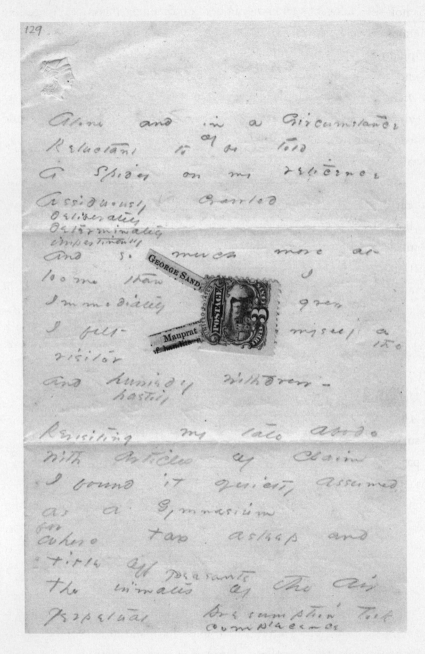

Dickinson manuscript of "Alone and in a Circumstance"
(Amherst College Archives and Special Collections)

smoke streaming from its pyramidal smokestack. Dickinson placed the stamp so that the train is traveling upward like a rocket, the smoke cascading down. One has to remember how unfamiliar trains were in the 1870s, and how fast, marking time with their "horrid—hooting stanza," as Dickinson wrote. The blue stamp in the middle of the page resembles a window, and through her own bedroom window Dickinson could actually see the locomotive—named for her father—arriving in Amherst; "I like to see it lap the Miles," she wrote of the train.[7]

Having placed the collage in the center of the page, Dickinson then drafted her poem around it, careful not to intrude upon the stamp or the clippings. The poem begins with four confident lines, all placed above the stamp with wings:

> *Alone and in a Circumstance*
> *Reluctant to be told*
> *A spider on my reticence*
> *Assiduously crawled*

Under the word *in* Dickinson wrote the alternative *of;* under the word *Assiduously* she wrote *deliberately, determinately,* and *impertinently.* Then she surrounded the stamp with four more lines, the last one extending across the page below the stamp:

> *And so much more at Home than I*
> *Immediately grew*
> *I felt myself a visitor*
> *And hurriedly withdrew*

In the twenty remaining lines of the poem—a very long poem for her—Dickinson develops a legal metaphor concerning her right to this "Home," as against the spider's competing claims. She returns to "my late abode" only to find it inhabited "As a Gymnasium." The gymnasts, whom she calls "inmates of the Air," have taken possession. For other offenses—an assault in the street, a theft—the statute is clear, but "what redress can be/ For an offence nor here nor there/ So not in Equity"? The poem concludes with a further characterization of the "offense":

> That Larceny of time and mind
> The marrow of the Day
> By spider, or forbid it Lord
> That I should specify.[8]

The spider, then, is not the only offender.

The whole poem is a puzzle, a rebuslike assemblage compounded by its interior collage. Readers have reached for simple solutions. Thomas Johnson, who edited the poems for the complete edition of 1955, thought the disturbance Dickinson describes was due to reading *Mauprat*; George Sand had robbed her of "time and mind." David Porter thought the setting of the poem was obvious, and intended to be funny: Dickinson was describing a visit to an outdoor privy, "a circumstance reluctant to be told," where a spider had disturbed her.

The development of the legal metaphor is certainly playful, but the poem seems less concerned with privies than with privacy. It is yet another of Dickinson's poems related to Byron's "The Prisoner of Chillon." Consider the key words *inmate* (Dickinson's "inmates of the air") and *home*, and the spiders and other inhabitants playing in their gymnasium. Here are Byron's lines, from the closing section of his Chillon poem, when the prisoner contemplates the prospect of freedom:

> These heavy walls to me had grown
> A hermitage—and all my own!
> And half I felt as they were come
> To tear me from a second home:
> With spiders I had friendship made
> And watch'd them in their sullen trade,
> Had seen the mice by moonlight play,

And why should I feel less than they?
We were all inmates of one place . . .

Inmates of one place; inmates of the air. Dickinson was back in her beloved Chillon. And she would have known that among the famous names inscribed on the columns of the dungeon of Chillon was that of George Sand. Perhaps in tribute to Sand's most famous theme—peasant life in the French countryside—Dickinson wrote an alternative word, *peasants*, above the word *inmates*.

3 ·

Who could be trusted to "deliver" Emily Dickinson's letter? By an amazing stroke of luck, the considerable job of sorting through Dickinson's manuscripts, in preparation for the landmark edition of her poems published in 1955, went to Jay Leyda. It was Leyda, a scholar and artist of remarkable range, who painstakingly unpacked the contents of Dickinson's desk, discovering along the way her own hoarding practices and constructed manuscripts. Leyda found a poem written on the back of a faded yellow Chocolat Meunier candy wrapper. He found a manuscript about a bird formed of two parts of an envelope pinned together to resemble a bird. He found a poem about a house written beneath the rooflike arc of another envelope.

And, of course, he found the Mauprat collage. A less imaginative cataloger might have simply described the oddities and left it at that, recording the text of the manuscripts so that the main editor, Thomas H. Johnson, could get on with the edition of Dickinson's poems. But Leyda, by temperament, training, and travel, was attuned to the visual and tactile allure of these manuscripts. From his own complicated trajectory, he knew exactly where Dickinson's originality might fit into the landscape of American art.

Leyda was born in Detroit in 1910 and moved to New York in 1930 to work for the photographer Ralph Steiner. He exhibited his own photographs and became interested in making films; on the strength of his apprentice work, he was accepted to the Moscow State Film School, where he studied directing under Sergei Eisenstein, thus initiating the defining relationship of his life. Leyda worked as Eisenstein's assistant and archivist before accepting a job as curator in the film department at the Museum of Modern Art in 1936. Four years later, amid rumors that he was a secret agent for the Soviet Union, Leyda was forced to resign and moved to Hollywood. There he began assembling documents relating to Herman Melville, a project originally planned as a birthday gift for Eisenstein. On the strength of the resulting landmark book, *The Melville Log,* Leyda was invited to join the team of scholars working on Emily Dickinson's literary legacy. In 1960, Leyda published two major works: *Kino: A History of the Russian and Soviet Film* and his marvelous documentary compilation *The Years and Hours of Emily Dickinson.*

With his deep familiarity with the montage effects of Eisenstein and Vertov—their radical juxtaposition of seemingly unrelated objects—Leyda immediately saw analogies between film montage and what he was looking at in Dickinson's late manuscripts. More important, he knew who among American artists would be most interested in Dickinson's own radical experiments.

During the early 1930s, Leyda had exhibited his photographs at Julien Levy's innovative art gallery in New York, where Joseph Cornell had shown his boxes as well. At the Museum of Modern Art, where Cornell had first exhibited one of his boxes—a "Soap Bubble Set," with lunar map, eggs, and a pipe for blowing bubbles—in 1936, Leyda followed the growing American interest in collage, which culminated in the 1961 survey "The Art of Assemblage." Leyda recognized an affinity between Emily Dickinson and Joseph Cornell—the "small, rickety infinitudes" of her poems and his boxes.[9] It was an affinity that Cornell himself had already begun to sense when he and Leyda began their exchange regarding Dickinson's radical manuscripts.

4 .

Joseph Cornell was born on Christmas Eve, 1903, in Nyack, New York, the same dilapidated Hudson River resort, clotted with old hotels, where Edward Hopper, another poet of loneliness and longing, was born a couple of decades earlier. Whatever promise Cornell might have shown during his stint as a science major at Phillips Academy in Andover, Massachusetts, was dashed in 1917 with the death of his father, a traveling salesman. When the family downscaled to New York City, Cornell supported his mother and younger brother, Robert (born with cerebral palsy), with a series of gloomy jobs, selling textile samples to companies and marketing door-to-door.

Cornell's idea of travel was to take long walks around lower Manhattan, scavenging in bookstores and record shops. He collected nineteenth-century guidebooks and cut out ads for modest Parisian hotels, which he liked to imagine as inhabited by aspiring divas and ballerinas. He haunted in particular the used-book shops along lower Fourth Avenue. Cornell was a "beachcomber in the city," as the art critic Jed Perl writes, "scavenging the used bookstores and print shops for the flotsam and jetsam of Europe and an earlier America, which had washed up on these shores."[10] Both Martin Johnson Heade and Emily Dickinson captured Cornell's attention during these forays.

One project that resulted from Cornell's collecting campaigns was titled "GC44," named for the Garden Center in Bayside, New York, a tree and plant nursery where Cornell worked as an assistant during the spring and winter of 1944. Cornell began assembling documents, notes, books, and illustrations for a sort of autobiographical "journey album . . . romantic museum . . . sanctuary, diary . . . "adventure or mystery novel."[11] What Cornell called the "apocalyptic realm of shining beauty" at the nursery reminded him of Alain-Fournier's evocative and nostalgic novel *Le Grand Meaulnes* (1913), known in English as *The Wanderer.* Cornell organized his documents into suggestive chapter headings reminiscent of Alain-Fournier's:

"The House on the Hill," "The Floral Still-Life," "The Little Dancer." Begun in 1944, "GC 44" became for Cornell "a lifelong pursuit."[12]

Under the rubric "Americana," Cornell placed an article he had clipped from the *Christian Science Monitor* about the dramatic rediscovery, in 1944, of Martin Johnson Heade. The writer of the article, identified only as "L. R.," began:

> Martin Johnson Heade (1819–1904) was an artist who gained popularity during his lifetime, but whose work later passed into almost total oblivion. For about forty years, he was ignored.

The large illustration for the article was Heade's *Summer Shadows,* a scene of salt marshes from the collection of the Brooklyn Museum. The author of the article mentions Heade's "taste for particularization," and specifically for "roses, magnolias, orchids, and hummingbirds." It is easy to imagine Cornell's self-identification with an artist, rescued from oblivion, and described as "not really either a romantic or a realist but a combination of both—and an individualist." Heade and Cornell also shared many of the same interests: birds, flowers, and the mood and atmosphere of romantic landscapes.

Cornell was also drawn to the ballerinas of nineteenth-century France. In a series of boxes, he evoked both their careers and the hotel rooms in which they took refuge, along with the French poets and artists Cornell— who had never been to Paris—imagined in these decrepit rooms. From old newspapers, Cornell clipped advertisements for hotels on the side streets of Paris, pasting them to the back of his memory palaces.

5.

Ballerinas—those seemingly weightless "inmates of the air"—first brought Emily Dickinson into Cornell's imaginative space. In 1944, he had assembled the contents for Lincoln Kirstein's magazine *Dance Index*, and included Dickinson's poem about her own interior ballet:

> *I cannot dance upon my Toes—*
> *No Man instructed me—*
> *But oftentimes, among my mind,*
> *A Glee possesseth me,*
>
> *That had I Ballet Knowledge—*
> *Would put itself abroad*
> *In Pirouette to blanch a Troupe—*
> *Or lay a Prima, mad.*[13]

Dickinson compared ballerinas to birds that "hopped for Audiences . . . One Claw upon the Air," a metaphor that would have particularly appealed to Cornell, whose boxes—invoking *Swan Lake* and other avian ballets—frequently made the same comparison. Some chance phrases on Dickinson in the artist Marsden Hartley's book *Adventures in the Arts* (1921) had also stayed with Cornell, such as "scintillant with stardust."

Cornell's interest in Dickinson intensified during the fall of 1952, a period he referred to the following year as "last Autumn's resurgence and rediscovery of E.D."[14] A year earlier, Cornell's mother had visited Amherst, and sent him a postcard with an engraving of the Dickinson house on Main Street. By the summer of 1952, Cornell was in touch with Jay Leyda.[15] Piqued by Leyda's work on Dickinson's manuscripts, Cornell in the first week of October borrowed two books on Dickinson from the Flushing library, the poet Genevieve Taggard's biography of 1930 and Rebecca Patterson's 1951 study, *The Riddle of Emily Dickinson*, which claimed to solve the "riddle" by identifying as Dickinson's secret lover a young woman named Kate Scott.

And then, on October 30, came one of those magical coincidences that Cornell waited for throughout his life. On one of his collecting forays, as he pored over books, photographs, and magazines along Fourth Avenue,

Cornell came across a reproduction of the single photographic portrait of Dickinson, the daguerreotype taken in Amherst in 1848, when she was seventeen. He wrote in his journal:

> first look at Emily Dickinson's daguerreotype in "Ancestor's Brocades" by Mabel Loomis Todd [actually by her daughter, Millicent Todd Bingham]—the impact in these surroundings the scene of so many countless browsings the background of all this for the E. D. photograph.

This discovery of Dickinson surrounded by the city she shunned pushed Cornell into even deeper research, as he acquired at least eleven books by or about Dickinson and inspected some of her manuscript poems on display at the Morgan Library.

Meanwhile, Cornell avidly questioned Jay Leyda about his findings, especially, as David Porter remarks, "Dickinson's penchant for cutting and pasting clippings and her own drawings and doodles."[16] Leyda sent Cornell lists of Dickinson's various combinations: valentines with images cut from New England primers; illustrations of children blowing bubbles (a favorite subject of Cornell's); an advertisement for a tombstone company; an engraving depicting a bird.[17]

By now, Cornell could discern manifold parallels between his own stay-at-home existence on Utopia Parkway and Dickinson's on Main Street. They were both armchair travelers, he felt, taking what he called "endless ecstatic" voyages in their narrow rooms by means of their accumulated clutter of books and clippings. Cornell confided this intuition to his journal:

> Before breakfast by kitchen stove—thinking about Emily Dickinson's "room" and the awakened significance via Rebecca Patterson's book—just now the poem beginning "Unto my books so good to turn"—what they must have meant in her torturous seclusion—a clue in the same kind of escape found in books on sunny mornings on Fourth Avenue ... E.D.'s foreign places, "Italy, etc." Is there a similar clue here in [my] own

feeling for the endless ecstatic "voyaging" through endless encounters with old engravings, photographs, books, Baedekers, varia, etc.?[18]

6.

But it was Dickinson's yellow *Chocolat Meunier* candy wrapper, with the firm's Paris address on Avenue de Choisy, that served as a magical sign for Cornell, proof of a spiritual affinity between the two artists. Cornell first came across a mention of the wrapper in Millicent Todd Bingham's introduction to the 1945 volume of poems *Bolts of Melody*. Many of the poems, Bingham wrote, "are written on the backs of brown-paper bags or of discarded bills, programs, and invitations; on tiny scraps of stationery pinned together; on leaves torn from old notebooks . . . on mildewed subscription blanks, or on . . . drug-store bargain flyers. There are pink scraps, blue and yellow scraps, one of them a wrapper of *Chocolat Meunier*."[19] Perhaps Cornell also knew through Leyda the enigmatic words that Dickinson scrawled on the back: "necessitates celerity."

In a series of eight extraordinary boxes, each with a Chocolat Meunier wrapper (the spelling on the wrappers Cornell discovered in his foraging trips), Cornell evoked Dickinson's own bedroom, and portrayed the poet herself as an absent songbird. Via the faded French wrappers, he inserted Dickinson into the nineteenth-century Parisian world of ballerinas and Romantic writers such as George Sand and Gérard de Nerval. In the first of these boxes, dated 1952, the poet is hidden behind a partition, a "warbling string" the only indication of her presence. In another, dated 1959, there is a small photograph of a solar eclipse on the upper bar—Cornell was a lifelong enthusiast of astronomy—and below the chocolate wrapper Cornell pasted a postage stamp from Ecuador. The image on the stamp is a hummingbird.

Cornell was predictably fond of hummingbirds. He clipped an article on hummingbird metabolism from a *Scientific American* of 1953, using its image of a bird perched in a bell jar as the basis of several collages.[20] In a collage he was working on in November 1956, at the height of his interest in Emily Dickinson, Cornell paired a hummingbird with Velásquez's Infanta in her white dress—so much like Dickinson's—giving the illusion that the bird is flying like a great brainstorm from the little girl's head. Behind them is a wire fence, a visual analogue of the fence around Dickinson's yard, and above is a beautiful blue sky with an orbiting gem, cut in the shape of a dodecahedron, the whole entitled *Observations of a Satellite.*[21] In other boxes and collages, Cornell often paired hummingbirds with stamps, and sometimes placed them in hotel rooms, transient inhabitants of a transitory world.

The stamp in the *Chocolat Meunier* box may allude to Dickinson's own self-portrait as hummingbird, "A Route of Evanescence," in which the hummingbird's vanished presence is perceptible only by the tumbled blossoms. The association of postage stamps and hummingbirds comes together in that poem's closing couplet: "The mail from Tunis, probably, / An easy Morning's Ride." The poem, as Porter notes, "intent upon the moment's enthralling aftermath, is in its own way a vacated space, a linguistic construction comparable to Cornell's empty bird habitats."[22]

In Cornell's work, the familiar romantic objects of Beecher and Stowe and Dickinson—birds and flowers and jewels and planets—reappear with a ghostly majesty and strangeness, "the fairer—for the farness—and for the foreignhood," as Dickinson wrote.[23]

7.

The most arresting of Joseph Cornell's tributes to Dickinson is also the most austere, his haunting *"Toward the Blue Peninsula" (for Emily Dickinson)* of 1953. In its visionary minimalism, the white box with its

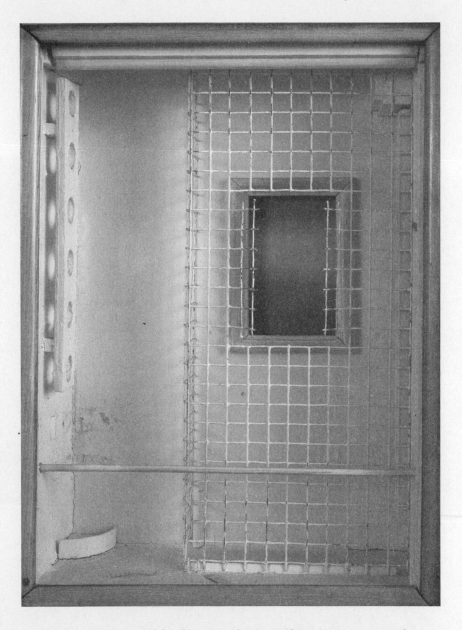

Joseph Cornell, Toward the Blue Peninsula (For Emily Dickinson), *ca. 1953, box construction , 14½ × 10¼ × 5½ in., The Robert Lehrman Art Trust, Courtesy of Aimee & Robert Lehrman Washington, D.C. Art © The Joseph and Robert Cornell Memorial Foundation/Licensed by VAGA, New York, NY*

central blue window sums up a whole cluster of themes that Cornell associated with Dickinson: birds and prisons, the transitory rooms of hotels and decrepit mansions, the starlit sky, and the escape and refuge provided by the voyaging imagination. *Toward the Blue Peninsula* is at once a deeply personal response to "the Dickinson experience" as well as the single most trenchant interpretive response, in all of American art, to the meaning of her life and work.

The box explicitly alludes to one of Dickinson's most moving Chillon-inspired poems:

> *It might be lonelier*
> *Without the Loneliness—*
> *I'm so accustomed to my Fate—*
> *Perhaps the Other—Peace—*
>
> *Would interrupt the Dark—*
> *And crowd the little Room—*
> *Too scant—by Cubits—to contain*
> *The Sacrament—of Him—*
>
> *I am not used to Hope—*
> *It might intrude upon—*
> *Its sweet parade—blaspheme the place—*
> *Ordained to Suffering—*
>
> *It might be easier*
> *To fail—with Land in Sight—*
> *Than gain—My Blue Peninsula—*
> *To perish—of Delight—*[24]

Cornell's box opens on a little room, painted white, with a framed window, slightly off center, that opens on a luminous blue sky. Out there somewhere is the "blue peninsula," which Rebecca Patterson and Cornell identified as Italy, the sun-drenched land of nineteenth-century longing. It is also the window of the prisoner of Chillon, where hope, the thing with feathers, sometimes visits.

A wire grid, symbolizing birdcage and prison, surrounds the space in front of the window. There is a perch for the bird. Two newspaper clippings lie on the floor, the usual materials for birdcages, but also closely matching the clippings of "George Sand" and "Mauprat" in Dickinson's manuscript collage of "Alone and in a Circumstance."

Now we can see how the blue window corresponds to the placement of the blue three-cent stamp in the center of Dickinson's collage. Each blue opening invites the "endless ecstatic voyaging" to George Sand's Parisian attic or the blue peninsula of Italy, or Florida.

Listen to the phrases. "The place ordained to suffering." "I am not used to hope." "It might be lonelier without the loneliness." "The inmates of the air."

The window is open. The perch is empty. The bird has flown.

ACKNOWLEDGMENTS

The initial impulse for this book came from Theodore Stebbins's *The Life and Work of Martin Johnson Heade*. I had picked up Stebbins's excellent study for distraction from a complicated memoir I was trying to write. Instead, in the pages about Heade's relations with Mabel Loomis Todd, I found the subject for my own next book. Some distraction! I want to thank Ted Stebbins, both for his pioneering work on Heade and for his steady encouragement of my own work.

My editor, Ann Godoff, and my agent, Melanie Jackson, have shared at every stage my excitement about this project. Lindsay Whalen at Penguin and Kayla Roufs at Mount Holyoke have helped with later stages of the manuscript and production.

I also want to thank several friends and colleagues who have helped me to see more clearly some of the topics and figures in this book: Sven Birkerts, Dan Czitrom, Nicola Courtright, Joe Ellis, Bob Herbert, Polly Longsworth, Mark Karpel, Frank Murphy, and Rosamond Purcell. At Mount Holyoke, Don O'Shea, dean of faculty, and Don Weber, chair of the English Department, have been steady supporters of faculty scholarship.

I am grateful to the helpful staffs of the following archives and libraries: Amherst College Special Collections, the Jones Library (Amherst), the John Carter Brown Library (Providence), the Harriet Beecher Stowe Study Center (Hartford), the Schlesinger Library (Harvard), the Houghton Library (Harvard), the Yale University Library, and the Mount Holyoke Library.

I first presented some of the material in chapters eight and nine as the Five College Jackie Pritzen Lecture in the spring of 2007, and some of chapter nine in different form at a symposium on "The Last Ruskinians," at the Fogg Art Museum, Harvard, in May 2007.

Mickey Rathbun and our sons, Tommy and Nicholas, have cheerfully indulged my passion for hummingbirds.

NOTES

PROLOGUE: A PLACE IN THE SKY WHERE A CLOUD HAS BEEN

1. Quoted in Ron Powers, *A Life of Mark Twain* (New York: Free Press, 2005), 459.
2. Mark Twain, *Life on the Mississippi*, in Twain *Mississippi Writings* (New York: Library of America, 1982), 491.
3. Martha Dickinson Bianchi, quoted in Judith Farr, *The Gardens of Emily Dickinson* (Cambridge: Harvard University Press, 2004), 219.
4. Thomas H. Johnson and Theodora Ward, editors, *The Letters of Emily Dickinson* (Cambridge: Harvard University Press, 2000), Letter 271. Subsequent letters are identified according to Johnson's numbering.
5. Theodore E. Stebbins, Jr., *The Life and Work of Martin Johnson Heade* (New Haven: Yale University Press, 2000), 139–140.
6. The passage is from Chateaubriand's novel *Atala*, first published in 1801. The translation is Irving Putter's, from Chateaubriand, *Atala/René* (Berkeley: University of California Press, 1952), 19.
7. Henry Adams, *History of the United States of America during the Administrations of Thomas Jefferson* (New York: Library of America, 1986), 86.
8. The quotation is from the tenth of Crèvecoeur's *Letters from an American Farmer*.
9. Judith Pascoe, *The Hummingbird Cabinet: A Rare and Curious History of Romantic Collectors* (Ithaca: Cornell University Press, 2006), 43. The Ruskin passage that serves as epigraph to this book also comes from Pascoe.
10. Pascoe, *Hummingbird Cabinet*, 43.
11. Hummingbirds figure in current debates about evolution as well. See, for example, Ethan J. Temeles and W. John Kress, "Adaptation in a Plant-Hummingbird Association," *Science* (April 25, 2003).

CHAPTER I: A TEA ROSE

1. Letter 235.
2. Higginson, *Army Life in a Black Regiment* (New York: Penguin, 1997), 79.
3. Higginson, *Army Life*, 78.
4. Higginson, *Army Life*, 79, 80.
5. Higginson, *Army Life*, 76.
6. Higginson, *Cheerful Yesterdays* (New York: Arno Press, 1968), 119, 120.

7. Higginson, "Why Back John Brown?" in *The Magnificent Activist: The Writings of Thomas Wentworth Higginson (1823–1911)*, ed. Howard N. Meyer (New York: Da Capo, 2000), 119.

8. Higginson, "Why Back John Brown?" in Meyer, *The Magnificent Activist*, 120–121.

9. Quoted in Edmund Wilson, *Patriotic Gore* (New York: Oxford University Press, 1962), 747.

10. Higginson, "The Life of Birds," in Meyer, *The Magnificent Activist*, 457.

11. Higginson, "The Procession of the Flowers," in *The Magnificent Activist*, 471. For the description of water-lilies see 481.

12. Higginson, *Cheerful Yesterdays*, 261.

13. Higginson, *Army Life*, 81–82.

14. Higginson, *Army Life*, 92.

15. Higginson, *Army Life*, 97.

16. *The Complete Civil War Journal and Selected Letters of Thomas Wentworth Higginson*, ed. Christopher Looby (Chicago: University of Chicago Press, 2000), 120.

17. Higginson, *The Complete Civil War Journal*, 284–85, 282–83.

18. Meyer, *The Magnificent Activist*, 530.

19. Meyer, *The Magnificent Activist*, 529.

20. Letter 18.

21. Letter 16.

22. R. W. Franklin, ed., *The Poems of Emily Dickinson* (Cambridge: Harvard University Press, 1998, 1999). Poem 202. All subsequent references to poems are from this source.

23. Poem 124.

24. Letter 260.

25. Letter 261. The quotations immediately following are from this letter.

26. Letter 280. For afuller account of Dickinson and her audience (from which this section is adapted), see Christopher Benfey, "The Mystery of Emily Dickinson," *New York Review of Books* (April 8, 1999).

27. Poem 370.

28. Letter 280.

29. Poem 234; Letter 282.

30. Higginson, *Army Life*, 116. All other quotations from "A Night in the Water" are from this edition.

31. Higginson, *Cheerful Yesterdays*, 263.

32. Letter 290.

33. Letter 294.

34. Letter 261.

35. Poem 1266.

36. Poem 910.

37. Letter 308.

38. For Higginson's tea rose, see *The Complete Civil War Journal*, 120.

39. Quoted in Wilson, *Patriotic Gore* 182.

40. Higginson, "The Life of Birds" 457.

CHAPTER 2: THE PRODIGAL

1. Poem 1488.

2. Henry Ward Beecher, *Norwood* (New York: Scribner, 1868), 489.

3. James M. McPherson, *Battle Cry of Freedom* (New York: Oxford University Press,

1988), 662.

4. Beecher, *Norwood,* 490.

5. Charles Stowe, *Life of Harriet Beecher Stowe* (Boston: Houghton Mifflin, 1889), 372.

6. Joan D. Hedrick, *Harriet Beecher Stowe: A Life* (New York: Oxford University Press, 1994), 307.

7. Details of Frederick Stowe's life can be found in James Tackach, "Frederick Stowe: In the Shadow of Uncle Tom's Cabin," *America's Civil War Magazine,* January 1999, at http://www. historynet.com/culture/social_history/3036401.html?featured=y&c=y.

8. Tackach, "Frederick Stowe."

9. Tackach, "Frederick Stowe." See also Charles Stowe, *Life of Harriet Beecher Stowe,* 366.

10. Tackach, "Frederick Stowe."

11. Hedrick, *Harriet Beecher Stowe,* 304–5.

12. Debby Applegate, *The Most Famous Man in America: The Biography of Henry Ward Beecher* (New York: Doubleday, 2006), 330.

13. Hedrick, *Harriet Beecher Stowe,* 306.

14. Harriet Beecher Stowe, *House and Home Papers* (Boston: J. R. Osgood, 1876), 78. The quotations immediately following can be found on pp. 83, 86, 90 (two passages), and 95 (the reference to Heade).

15. Stowe, *The Chimney Corner* (Boston: Ticknor and Fields, 1868), 246. The quotations immediately following can be found on pp. 254–55 (on Quakers), 229, 239, 206 (two passages), 207, 209 (four passages on "Humming-Bird"), 218, 210, 243, 217, 216, and 218.

16. This was not the first time that Stowe had compared a clothing-obsessed young woman to a hummingbird. In her second novel, *Dred: A Tale of the Dismal Swamp,* first published in 1856, she built a narrative around an escaped slave, modeled on Nat Turner, who takes refuge in the Dismal Swamp in Georgia. Stowe was among the first American writers and artists—Martin Heade was another—to find a new kind of beauty in the swamp:

> Evergreen trees, mingling freely with the deciduous children of the forest, form here dense jungles, verdant all the year round, and which afford shelter to numberless birds, with whose warbling the leafy desolation perpetually resounds. Climbing vines, and parasitic plants, of untold splendor and boundless exuberance of growth, twine and interlace, and hang from the heights of the highest trees pennons of gold and purple,—triumphant banners, which attest the solitary majesty of nature. A species of parasitic moss wreaths its abundant draperies from tree to tree, and hangs in pearly festoons, through which shine the scarlet berry and green leaves of the American holly.

On the edge of the swamp, Stowe sets a decayed plantation, with a young slave couple who will eventually join the fugitive slave leader Dred in the liberated "Switzerland" of the swamp. Lisette has both French and African descent, "producing one of those fanciful, exotic combinations that give one the same impression of brilliancy and richness that one receives from tropical insects and flowers." When we first meet her, she is welcoming her husband, Harry, back from an excursion and has discovered that he has a package of silk, destined, she assumes, for new dresses. "You are nothing but a humming-bird," Harry tells her, laughing, "made to live on honey!" When he playfully refuses to let her open the package completely, "the little sprite danced about the cottage floor, tearing the paper, and tugging at the string, like an enraged humming-bird." Finally, he cuts the cord and reveals "a gorgeous plaid silk, crimson, green, and orange"—colors fit for a hummingbird. In a common tangle of associations in American art and literature, hummingbirds are linked with the exoticism of the tropics, with freedom amid captivity, and with fashionable clothes, but also with anger and violence. See Stowe, *Dred: A Tale of the Dismal Swamp* (Boston: Houghton, Mifflin, 1856), 220.

17. Hedrick, *Harriet Beecher Stowe*, 307.

18. Hedrick, *Harriet Beecher Stowe*, 307–8.

19. Stowe, "Hum, the Son of Buz," in *Queer Little People* (New York: Ford, Howard, and Hulbert, 1867). The quotations that follow come from this brief story.

20. *Dunciad*, IV, 445–46.

21. *Hum* is also an archaic word for a strong drink. The OED gives examples: 1621, Fletcher: "Would I had some hum"; 1670, Cotton: "The best Cheshire hum he e'er drank in his life." Robert L. Herbert brought this citation to my attention.

22. Poem 207.

23. See George Monteiro, "Manzanillo," in *The Explicator*, vol. 43 (1985).

24. Hedrick, *Harriet Beecher Stowe*, 324, 325.

25. Stowe, *The Chimney Corner*, 94.

26. John T. Foster, *Beechers, Stowes, and Yankee Strangers: The Transformation of Florida* (Gainesville: University Press of Florida, 1999), 55.

27. Foster, *Beechers, Stowes*, 54.

28. Hedrick, *Harriet Beecher Stowe*, 329.

29. Stowe quoted in Hedrick, *Harriet Beecher Stowe*, 330.

30. Stowe quoted in Hedrick, *Harriet Beecher Stowe*, 330.

31. Quoted in Hedrick, *Harriet Beecher Stowe*, 329.

32. Hedrick, *Harriet Beecher Stowe*, 330.

33. Stowe to George Eliot, May 11, 1872, in *Life and Letters of Harriet Beecher Stowe*, ed. Annie Fields (Boston: Houghton, Mifflin, 1897), 339.

34. Hedrick, *Harriet Beecher Stowe*, 336.

35. Charles Stowe, *Life of Harriet Beecher Stowe*, 372.

36. Christine M. E. Guth, *Longfellow's Tattoos: Tourism, Collecting, and Japan* (Seattle: University of Washington Press, 2004), xi.

CHAPTER 3: BEECHER'S POCKETS

The epigraph is from Beecher's essay "Joys and Sorrows of Eggs."

1. Henry Ward Beecher, "My Pockets," in *Eyes and Ears* (Boston: Ticknor and Fields, 1862), 145. The quotations immediately following are drawn from this essay.

2. Lyman Abbott, *Henry Ward Beecher* (1903; New York: Chelsea House, 1980), 119–20.

3. It is possible that Thomas Hicks, who painted Beecher's portrait, had mentioned Heade's name to Beecher.

4. William C. Beecher and Rev. Samuel Scoville, *A Biography of Henry Ward Beecher* (New York: Charles L. Webster, 1888), 347.

5. Beecher and Scoville, *Biography of Henry Ward Beecher*, 650.

6. Beecher and Scoville, *Biography of Henry Ward Beecher*, 649–50.

7. Constance Rourke, *Trumpets of Jubilee* (New York: Harcourt, Brace, 1927), 167.

8. Debby Applegate, *The Most Famous Man in America*, 64–65. Cf. Paxton Hibben, *Henry Ward Beecher: An American Portrait* (New York: George H. Doran, 1927), 44: "For Henry Ward, the Greek was a Byron in the flesh."

9. Abbott, *Henry Ward Beecher*, 113.

10. Applegate, *The Most Famous Man in America*, 316–17. See also Harriet Prescott Spofford, "Rose Terry Cooke," in *Our Famous Women*, ed. Elisabeth Stuart Phelps Ward (Hartford: A. D. Worthington, 1883), 202.

11. Abbott, *Henry Ward Beecher*, 221, 210–12.

12. The invitation to Lincoln to speak in Plymouth Church was extended on October 12, 1859, the day before Beecher bought his Heade painting. Lincoln's famous and career-making speech was eventually moved from its original, smaller venue at Plymouth Church to Cooper Union. See Abbott, *Henry Ward Beecher*, 220.

13. Sarah Cash, *Ominous Hush: The Thunderstorm Paintings of Martin Johnson Heade* (Fort Worth: Amon Carter Museum, 1994), 43.

14. Quoted in Cash, *Ominous Hush*, 43. My analysis here is heavily indebted to Cash's observations.

15. For accounts of the commencement speeches by Lord and Beecher see Richard Sewall, *Emily Dickinson* (New York: Farrar, Straus and Giroux, 1980), 646–47. Sewall notes the similar phrases in Beecher's talk and Dickinson's poem (p. 647). See also Jay Leyda, *The Years and Hours of Emily Dickinson*, vol. 2 (New Haven: Yale University Press, 1960), 62.

16. Letter 256.

17. Stowe's painting of a snowy owl is in the Stowe House in Hartford. Lovell's stereoscopic photograph is in Special Collections at Amherst College.

18. Poem 728.

19. Susan H. Dickinson, "Magnetic Visitors," *Amherst* (publication of Amherst College, spring 1981), 13. Later quotations are from this article.

20. Poem 377.

21. Karen Dandurand, "New Dickinson Civil War Publications," *American Literature*, 56/1 (March 1984), 17. Dandurand discovered these important publications.

22. Poem 122.

23. Poem 95.

CHAPTER 4: TRISTES TROPIQUES

The epigraph is from Elizabeth Bishop's poem "Questions of Travel."

1. Theodore Stebbins Jr., *The Life and Work of Martin Johnson Heade*, 61. In the pages that follow, I rely heavily on Stebbins's account of Heade's sojourn in Brazil, as well as on Heade's manuscript journal, in the Museum of Fine Arts, Boston.

2. Stebbins, *Life and Work of Martin Johnson Heade*, 61.

3. Katherine Manthorne, *Tropical Renaissance: North American Artists Exploring Latin America, 1839–1879* (Washington: Smithsonian Institution Press, 1989), 125.

4. Heade, *Brazil-London Journal*, Museum of Fine Arts, Boston. Later quotations are drawn from this manuscript.

5. "Didymus" (Heade), "Pennsylvania Days," in *Forest and Stream* (January 7, 1892). See also Stebbins, *Life and Work of Martin Johnson Heade*, 2.

6. See Carolyn J. Weekley, *The Kingdoms of Edward Hicks* (New York: Abrams and Colonial Williamsburg, 1999), 94.

7. Walt Whitman, *Complete Poetry and Collected Prose* (New York: Library of America, 1982), 1234, 1232. Whitman compared Hicks's confidence in his own inner promptings to Emerson's concept of "self-reliance."

8. "Didymus" (Heade), "A Quaker Designation," in *Forest and Stream* (September 27, 1902). The anecdote recalls Emily Dickinson's well-known poem "My life had stood a loaded gun, in corners . . ." Both Heade and Dickinson liked the idea of guns stowed in corners, about to explode amid the propriety of their genteel surroundings.

9. Daniel Garber, cited in Robert G. McIntyre, *Martin Johnson Heade: 1819–1904* (New York: Pantheon, 1948), 4.

10. Stebbins, *Life and Work of Martin Johnson Heade*, 10.

11. Barbara Novak and Timothy Eaton, *Martin Johnson Heade: A Survey, 1840–1900* (West Palm Beach: Eaton Fine Art, 1996), 12.

12. See Stebbins, *Life and Work of Martin Johnson Heade*, 47.

13. All of these were hummingbird enthusiasts. Among the illustrations Hassam provided for Thaxter's *An Island Garden* of 1894 was one titled "Home of the humming-bird."

14. *Harper's New Monthly Magazine* (July 1875).

15. Stebbins, in *The Life and Works of Martin Johnson Heade* (New Haven: Yale University Press, 1975), mentions both Whitman and Thoreau in relation to these pictures. The quotation from Thoreau comes from his essay "Walking."

16. James Cooley Fletcher, *Brazil and the Brazilians*, (Boston: Little, Brown, 1878), 484.

17. Roderick J. Barman, *Citizen Emperor: Pedro II and the Making of Brazil, 1825–91* (Stanford, CA: Stanford University Press, 1999), 136.

18. Barman, *Citizen Emperor*, 186. My account of Pedro II is heavily indebted to this book.

19. Barman, *Citizen Emperor*, 187. See Maria Helena T. Machado, *Brazil through the Eyes of William James: Letters, Diaries, and Drawings, 1865–1866* (Cambridge: Harvard University Press, 2006).

20. Barman, *Citizen Emperor*, 195.

21. *Atlantic Monthly*, July 1867, 62.

22. Barman, *Citizen Emperor*, 56.

23. Stebbins, *Life and Work of Martin Johnson Heade*, 63–64.

24. Lawrence F. Hill, *Diplomatic Relations between the United States and Brazil* (Durham: Duke University Press, 1932), 162.

25. Hill, *Diplomatic Relations*, 167.

26. Stebbins, *Life and Work of Martin Johnson Heade*, 67–68.

27. "When it comes to courtship and 'marriage' I am afraid I can tell no tales of marital fidelity and 'growing old together.' Each male is a feathered Don Juan with interests limited to food, fighting, and courtship." See Crawford H. Greenewalt, *Hummingbirds* (Garden City, NY: Doubleday/American Museum of Natural History, 1960).

28. Cahill, "The Imperial Painting Academy," in Wen C. Fong et al., *Possessing the Past: Treasures from the National Palace Museum, Taipei* (New York: Metropolitan Museum of Art/Abrams, 1996), 171. The Emperor Hui-tsung's *Two Finches on Twigs of Bamboo* (John M. Crawford Jr. collection, Metropolitan Museum of Art, New York) is an excellent example. See Cahill, *Chinese Painting* (New York: Rizzoli, 1977), 73.

29. Stebbins, *Life and Work of Martin Johnson Heade*, 287.

30. Audubon "set as the main objective . . . the reconstruction of the complex matrix of intra- and interspecial relationships from which birds, along with all other life-forms, had traditionally been removed in scientific illustrations and texts." See Amy R. W. Meyers, "Observations of an American Woodsman: John James Audubon as Field Naturalist," 46.

31. William Bartram, *Travels and Other Writings* (New York: Library of America, 1996), 226-27.

32. Snake and hummingbird, as denizens of the earth and air, respectively, are paired in Letter X of Crèvecoeur's *Letters from an American Farmer*, "On Snakes; and on the Humming-Bird." Crèvecoeur was yet another sojourner in Quaker communities in Philadelphia.

33. Bartram, *Travels*, 124–25.

34. Heade, September 2, 1864, quoted in Stebbins, *Life and Work of Martin Johnson Heade*, 74.

35. Stebbins, *Life and Work of Martin Johnson Heade*, 74.

36. Stebbins, *Life and Work*, 74–75.

CHAPTER 5: THE PRISONER OF CHILLON

The epigraph comes from a description of the Castle of Chillon in an early travel article by Henry James.

1. Stowe, *Sunny Memories of Foreign Lands* (Boston: Phillips, Sampson, 1854), vol. II, 106–7.

2. Stowe, "Early Remembrances," in *Autobiography, Correspondence, Etc., of Lyman Beecher, D.D.*, ed. Charles Beecher, vol. 1 (New York: Harper, 1864), 529.

3. Stowe, "Early Remembrances," 531.

4. Stowe, "Early Remembrances," 529.

5. Harriet Beecher Stowe, *Three Novels* (New York: Library of America, 1982), 355.

6. Stowe, *Sunny Memories of Foreign Lands*, vol. II, 271.

7. Stowe, *Sunny Memories of Foreign Lands*, 274.

8. Stowe's article, originally published in the September 1869 issue of *The Atlantic*, was later expanded into book form as *Lady Byron Vindicated* (1870). See p. 328.

9. Hedrick, *Harriet Beecher Stowe*, 263.

10. Stowe, "The True Story of Lady Byron's Life," 313. The other quotations may be found on pp. 131, 195, 197, 302, 304, 306, and 311.

11. "It is likely that she took up Lady Byron's case out of her desire to regain the attention of a modern audience bored with her stories of New England life." Hedrick, *Harriet Beecher Stowe*, 363.

12. Quoted in Hedrick, *Harriet Beecher Stowe*, 365.

13. See Hedrick, *Harriet Beecher Stowe*, 365.

14. Van Wyck Brooks, *New England: Indian Summer* (New York: Dutton, 1940), 239.

15. One reason Stowe was drawn so insistently to the Byron flame may be that he had actually perpetrated a crime that had tempted her. Her proof of Byron's incest is based in part on extracts from his poetry—"internal evidence," in Oliver Wendell Holmes's phrase. But anyone reading Stowe's writings from this period might draw similar conclusions about her own incestuous fantasies about her brother Henry. The orphaned brother and sister in *Oldtown Folks* (1969; included in Stowe, *Three Novels* [New York: Library of America, 1982]) run away from their foster homes rather than enduring separation. They wander the marshland outside Boston, setting up house together in a haunted house, where Harry proposes marriage to his sister.

> "I'm *your* wife, ain't I?" said Tina, contentedly.
>
> "No. You're my little sister, and I take care of you," said the boy. "But people can't have their sisters for wives; the Bible says so."

"Well, I can be just *like* your wife; and I'll mend your clothes and knit your stockings when I get bigger." (p. 1029).

Oldtown Folks is a Christian fairy tale set in New England, where the witches belong to an older Calvinism of hatred and doom and the fairy godmothers practice the gospel of love. The one serious challenge to Tina's exclusive love for her brother is the arrival on the scene of Ellery Davenport, grandson of Jonathan Edwards. The dashing Davenport reads and speaks French "like a native"—a sure mark of dubious morals—and asks, rhetorically, "What is goodness but beauty, and what is sin but bad taste?" (p. 1172). He is described as "some beautiful but dangerous animal" and arouses in the narrator "a singular and painful contest of attraction and repulsion" (pp. 1172–73). Ellery Davenport is the Byron figure in the novel, conveying "that general interest which often pervades the female breast for some bright, naughty, wicked prodigal son." (p. 1168).

What exactly was Stowe saying about Jonathan Edwards, Davenport's grandfather and the most formidable Calvinist in the pantheon of later American Puritanism? Her implicit argument seemed to be that Edwards had gone so far in his insistence on "sinners in the hands of an angry God," dangling dangerously over the pit of hell, that later generations had fled in terror—finding an uneasy refuge not in salvation but rather in skepticism or outright disbelief. In her historical novel *The Minister's Wooing*, Stowe had enlisted Aaron Burr, a real-life grandson of Jonathan Edwards, to play the same Byronic part. Her point was the same one that Lady Byron had made of her husband: "the Calvinistic theology, as heard in Scotland, had proved in his case, as it often does in certain minds, a subtle poison. He never could either disbelieve or become reconciled to it, and the sore problems it proposes embittered his spirit against Christianity."

16. Letter 227.
17. Poem 235.
18. Poem 367.
19. Sewall, *The Life of Emily Dickinson*, 452.
20. Letter 178.
21. Habegger, *My Wars Are Laid Away in Books: The Life of Emily Dickinson* (New York: Random House, 2001), 330.
22. Michael F. Holt, *The Rise and Fall of the American Whig Party* (Oxford: Oxford University Press, 1999), 827, 829.
23. Holt, *Rise and Fall*, 231.
24. Letter 178.
25. Sewall, *Life of Emily Dickinson*, 449: "His popularity in Philadelphia has been compared to Henry Ward Beecher's in Brooklyn, and his preaching was ranked second only to Beecher's in the country."
26. Quoted in Sewall, *Life of Emily Dickinson*, 450.
27. Habegger, *My Wars Are Laid Away in Books*, 330–31.
28. Habegger, *My Wars Are Laid Away in Books*, 331.
29. Habegger, *My Wars Are Laid Away in Books*, 332.
30. Quoted in Habegger, *My Wars Are Laid Away in Books*, 704.
31. Sewall, *Life of Emily Dickinson*, 454; and Habegger, *My Wars Are Laid Away in Books*, 332.
32. Letter 182.
33. Poem 456.
34. Poem 466.

35. Poem 710.
36. Poem 445.
37. Poem 124.
38. Letter 248.
39. Poem 764.
40. Mark Twain, *A Tramp Abroad* (Leipzig: Tauchnitz, 1880), 143–44

CHAPTER 6: BIRDS OF PASSAGE

1. Poem 361.
2. Powers, *Mark Twain: A Life*, 45.
3. Mark Twain, *The Autobiography of Mark Twain*, chapter 11.
4. See Powers, *Life of Mark Twain*, 97–99.
5. Mark Twain, *The Innocents Abroad* and *Roughing It* (New York: Library of America, 1984), 887.
6. Powers, *Mark Twain*, 170–71.
7. Mark Twain, *Travels with Mr. Brown*, ed. Franklin Walker and G. Ezra Dane (New York: Knopf, 1940), 39.
8. Mark Twain, *Travels with Mr. Brown*, 40.
9. Fred Kaplan, *The Singular Mark Twain* (New York: Doubleday, 2003), 170
10. Mark Twain, *Travels with Mr. Brown*, 56.
11. Mark Twain, *Travels with Mr. Brown*, 47.
12. Mark Twain, *Travels with Mr. Brown*, 49–50.
13. Kaplan, *The Singular Mark Twain*, 170.
14. Kaplan, *The Singular Mark Twain*, 51.
15. My account of Twain's journey from Greytown to New York relies on the accounts by Ron Powers and Fred Kaplan.
16. Stebbins, *Life and Work of Martin Johnson Heade*, 78.
17. Stebbins, *Life and Work of Martin Johnson Heade*, 78.
18. Quoted in Stebbins, *Life and Work of Martin Johnson Heade*, 361.
19. Sanford Schwartz, "The Suspended Moment," *New York Review of Books* (February 10, 2000).
20. Mark Twain, *Travels with Mr. Brown*, 93.
21. Mark Twain, *Travels with Mr. Brown*, 94.
22. Dispatch to the *Alta California*, June 10, 1867, quoted in Ron Powers, *Mark Twain: A Life*, 190.
23. Mark Twain, *Travels with Mr. Brown*, 93–94.
24. Twain, *The Innocents Abroad* and *Roughing It*, 17.
25. See Powers, *Mark Twain*, 185; and Applegate, *The Most Famous Man in America*, 373.
26. Stebbins, *Life and Work of Martin Johnson Heade*, 239.
27. Stebbins, *Life and Work of Martin Johnson Heade*, 80.
28. Stebbins, *Life and Work of Martin Johnson Heade*, 239.
29. "The Arts. At the Studios," *Appleton's Journal of Literature, Science, and Art* (March 27, 1875), 410. Quoted in Stebbins, *Life and Work of Martin Johnson Heade*, 81.
30. Stebbins reproduces the photograph, *Life and Work of Martin Johnson Heade*, 270.
31. Twain, *Mississippi Writings* (New York: Library of America, 1982), 740.
32. For the quoted passages, see Mark Twain, *The Innocents Abroad and Roughing It*, 104, 123, 84.

33. See Powers, *Mark Twain*, 233; and Applegate, *The Most Famous Man in America*, 374–75.

34. "No constellation of relationships would ever mean more to him than the one centered on the bulky figure prowling the pulpit on [that] frigid Sunday morning. The adventures and the personal encounters influenced by Henry Ward Beecher would in time lead Sam [Clemens] to his first great book, his wife, his acceptance into the elite social and literary circles of the East, and to the nonesuch neighborhood that encompassed the twenty happiest years of his life." (Powers, *Mark Twain*, 182).

35. Heade, "The Doubting Didymus," *Forest and Stream* (January 3, 1903), 6.

36. Quoted in Sewall, *Life of Emily Dickinson*, 451–52.

37. See *Mark Twain's Letters*, vol. 2, 229.

38. Powers, *Mark Twain*, 260. Charles Jervis was a friend of Reverend Thomas Beecher in Elmira, New York.

39. Powers, *Mark Twain*, 261.

40. Powers, *Mark Twain*, 267.

41. Powers, *Mark Twain*, 267–68.

42. Mary Thacher Higginson, *Thomas Wentworth Higginson: The Story of His Life* (Boston: Houghton Mifflin, 1914), 260–62.

43. Jay Leyda, ed., *The Years and Hours of Emily Dickinson*, vol. 2, 184.

44. Annie Fields, ed., *Life and Letters of Harriet Beecher Stowe* (Boston: Houghton, Mifflin, 1897), 339.

45. Fields, *Life and Letters of Harriet Beecher Stowe*, 344.

46. Fields, *Life and Letters of Harriet Beecher Stowe*, 343.

47. Leyda, *Years and Hours*, vol. 2, 184.

48. Susan Dickinson, "Magnetic Visitors," 27.

49. Letter 342a.

50. Anna Mary Wells, *Dear Preceptor: The Life and Times of Thomas Wentworth Higginson* (Boston: Houghton Mifflin, 1963), 243–45.

51. Letter 330.

52. Higginson, "Emily Dickinson," reprinted in Meyer, *Magnificent Activist*, 543–64.

53. Letter 342a.

54. Letter 342b.

55. Higginson, *John Greenleaf Whittier* (New York: Macmillan, 1902), 100.

56. Mary Williams, *Dom Pedro the Magnanimous* (Chapel Hill: University of North Carolina Press, 1937), 206.

57. Williams, *Dom Pedro*, 247–48.

58. Williams, *Dom Pedro*, 195.

59. Quoted in Williams, *Dom Pedro*, 208.

Chapter 7: Covert Flowers, Hidden Nests

1. Poem 642.

2. Robert Shaplen, *Free Love and Heavenly Sinners* (New York: Knopf, 1954), 53. The picture itself has disappeared, but circumstantial evidence suggests that Beecher's passion for Martin Johnson Heade may have led him to purchase another painting by the master. Heade's work was becoming better known during the 1860s, and a Boston chromolithographer named Louis Prang approached him about making cheap prints of his works. Harriet Beecher Stowe and

Catherine Beecher greatly admired Prang's reproductions. Prang reproduced Heade's painting of trailing arbutus, titled *Flowers of Hope*, in 1870, but the painting has never come to light.

3. Poem 1357.

4. In his essay "The Procession of the Flowers," Higginson gave the flower's survival each spring an environmentalist twist; it was the Pilgrims, and their clearing of the land, that these flowers had to overcome: "Why can one recognize the Plymouth May-flower, as soon as seen, by its wondrous depth of color? Does it blush with triumph to see how Nature has outwitted the Pilgrims, and even succeeded in preserving her deer like an English duke, still maintaining the deepest woods in Massachusetts precisely where those sturdy immigrants first began their clearings?" Meyer, *Magnificent Activist*, 471.

5. Poem 1357.

6. In 1878, Heade gave his friend Frederic Church some arbutus plants for the garden of Olana, Church's flamboyant Hudson River estate. Stebbins, *Life and Work of Martin Johnson Heade*, 31.

7. Beecher, "Trailing Arbutus," in *Eyes and Ears* (Boston: Ticknor and Fields, 1862), 286.

8. Shaplen, *Free Love and Heavenly Sinners*, 35.

9. Shaplen, *Free Love and Heavenly Sinners*, 32.

10. My account of Elizabeth Tilton's response to *Norwood* relies on Shaplen's account in *Free Love and Heavenly Sinners*, 52–54.

11. Beecher, *Norwood* (New York: Scribner, 1868), 20, 21.

12. For the fate of the picture and the possible artist, see note 2, above.

13. Shaplen, *Free Love and Heavenly Sinners*, 4.

14. Beecher, *Norwood*, 82.

15. Altina L. Waller, *Reverend Beecher and Mrs. Tilton: Sex and Class in Victorian America* (Amherst: University of Massachusetts Press, 1982), 165 n27.

16. Shaplen, *Free Love and Heavenly Sinners*, 88. After a tour of Europe from 1845 to 1849, during which he studied with Thomas Couture in Paris, Hicks returned to New York in 1849. He had painted Heade's portrait around 1840–42. Both Hicks and Heade had worked under Edward Hicks, a cousin of Thomas Hicks. Plymouth Church, by the way, is on Hicks Street in Brooklyn.

17. Shaplen, *Free Love and Heavenly Sinners*, 133.

18. Richard Wightman Fox, *Trials of Intimacy, Love and Loss in the Beecher-Tilton Scandal* (Chicago: University of Chicago Press, 1999), 155.

19. Fox, *Trials of Intimacy*, 139.

20. The exchange is reproduced in Shaplen, *Free Love and Heavenly Sinners*, 233.

21. Applegate, *The Most Famous Man in America*, 454.

22. Shaplen, *Free Love and Heavenly Sinners*, 169.

23. Mark Twain, letter to Olivia Lewis Langdon, December 3, 1872, quoted in Powers, *Mark Twain*, 328.

24. Fox, *Trials of Intimacy*, 139.

25. Applegate, *The Most Famous Man in America*, 318, 365–66, 370–71.

26. Applegate, *The Most Famous Man in America*, 371.

Chapter 8: Foggy Bottom

The epigraph is from Edmund Wilson, on Oliver Wendell Holmes Sr., in *Patriotic Gore: Smtudies in the Literature of the American Civil War* (New York: Oxford University Press, 1962), 744

1. Adams, *Novels, Mont Saint Michel, The Education* (New York: Library of America, 1983), 1071–72.
2. James, "Pandora," in *Daisy Miller and Other Stories*, ed. Jean Gooder (Oxford: Oxford University Press, 1985), 135.
3. Polly Longsworth, *Austin and Mabel: The Amherst Affair and Love Letters of Austin Dickinson and Mabel Loomis Todd* (New York: Holt, Rinehart and Winston, 1984), 39. I have relied on Longsworth for many details of David Todd's life.
4. Stowe, *The Minister's Wooing*, ed. Susan K. Harris (1859; New York: Penguin, 1999), 20.
5. Cahill in Wen C. Fong et al., *Possessing the Past: Treasures from the National Palace Museum, Taipei* (New York: Metropolitan Museum of Art/Abrams, 1996), 165.
6. Mabel Todd's journal, from which these quotations are drawn, is in the collection of the Sterling Library at Yale University.
7. Robert G. McIntyre, in *Martin Johnson Heade:1819–1904* (New York: Pantheon, 1948), quotes the passage from a notebook that has disappeared.

CHAPTER 9: A ROUTE OF EVANESCENCE

The epigraph is from Keats's "Sleep and Poetry." I am grateful to Judith Pascoe for the citation.
1. Longsworth, *Austin and Mabel*, 25.
2. Mabel Todd, journal, March 2, 1882, Yale.
3. Heade to Loomis, June 18, 1882, in Loomis-Wilder family collection, Yale University Library.
4. Heade to Loomis, July 18, 1882, in Loomis-Wilder family collection, Yale University Library.
5. William McLoughlin, *The Meaning of Henry Ward Beecher* (New York: Knopf, 1970), 50, 51.
6. Stebbins identifies Beecher's sermon as "The Method of Creation." "Big Game vs. Birds" appeared in *Forest and Stream* (June 28, 1902).
7. The historian Peter Gay opens his magisterial study of sex and morality, *The Bourgeois Experience: Victoria to Freud* (New York: Oxford University Press, 1984), with a case study of Mabel Loomis Todd. For Gay, what is remarkable about Mabel is less her audacity in acting on her sexual desires than her care in recording them. "Mabel Loomis Todd's sexual self-portrait is exceptional in copiousness and candor," he writes; "not even George Sand descended, or rose, to such instructive detail."
8. Poem 1489.
9. The image was later used on the cover of the first selection of Dickinson's posthumously published poems and decorates Mabel's grave in the Wildwood Cemetery in Amherst.
10. Letter 769.
11. Jay Leyda dates the conversation September 1882. Cf. Habegger, *My Wars Were Laid Away in Books*, 590.
12. Letter 559.
13. Letter 751.
14. Letter 752.
15. Letter 444a.
16. Letter 476.
17. Letter 601a.

18. In which case "Head" could just possibly invoke "Heade," painter of hummingbirds.

19. Poem 1180.

20. Letter 261.

21. Letter 749b.

22. In *Emily Dickinson and Her Culture* (Cambridge, UK: Cambridge University Press, 1984), Barton Levi St. Armand discerned in poems such as "The Mountains stood in Haze" a "painterly method" that "approaches that of the native American school called luminism" (p. 242).

23. Judith Farr, *The Passion of Emily Dickinson* (Cambridge: Harvard University Press, 1992), 269.

24. Judith Farr, *The Gardens of Emily Dickinson* (Cambridge: Harvard University Press, 2004), 156, 320.

25. Susan H. Dickinson, "Magnetic Visitors," 9.

26. Heade, who was friendly with the Channing family, may well have known Higginson, whose wife was a Channing. Heade had once sought to paint a portrait of her father, a famous surgeon and pioneer in the use of ether in childbirth.

27. William Sheehan and John Westfall, *The Transits of Venus* (Amherst, NY: Prometheus Books, 2004), 288–91.

28. Longsworth, *Austin and Mabel*, 136–37.

29. Heade to Mabel Todd, December 9, 1882, Yale; Heade to Loomis, December 12, 1882, Yale.

30. *Amherst Record*, July 26, 1882.

31. Quoted in Habegger, *My Wars Are Laid Away in Books*, 623.

32. Letter 868.

33. Letter 781.

34. Poem 1491.

35. Letter 972.

CHAPTER 10: FLORIDA

The epigraph comes from Henry James's *The American Scene*.

1. Edward King, *The Great South* (Hartford: American Publishing Company, 1875), 386.

2. Stebbins, *Life and Work of Martin Johnson Heade*, 140. Heade's Letters to Loomis, quoted in the following pages, are in the Loomis Wilder Family papers at the Yale University Library, see also Stebbins, *Life and Work of Martin Johnson Heade*, chapter 5.

3. Longsworth, *Austin and Mabel*, 16.

4. Marie Caskey, *Chariot of Fire: Religion and the Beecher Family* (New Haven: Yale University Press, 1978), 328. Calvin Stowe, alert to the spirit world, had had visions from the other side since childhood; Harriet had used some of these in her novel *Oldtown Folks*.

5. Roberta Smith Favis, *Martin Johnson Heade in Florida* (Gainesville: University Press of Florida, 2003), 43.

6. King, *The Great South*, 387–88.

7. "Notes of Floridian Experience," *Forest and Stream* (May 24, 1883), 324, quoted in Favis, *Martin Johnson Heade in Florida*, 43.

8. Favis, *Martin Johnson Heade in Florida*, 45.

9. The letter is dated December 3. See Favis, *Martin Johnson Heade in Florida*, 45.

10. Favis, *Martin Johnson Heade in Florida*, 41.

11. Favis, in *Martin Johnson Heade in Florida*, suggests this date for the encounter (p. 47).

12. For parallels between Flagler and Heade, see Favis, *Martin Johnson Heade in Florida*, chapter 2, "Searching for the Fountain of Youth: Heade and Flagler in St. Augustine."

13. Field and Ralph, quoted in Favis, *Martin Johnson Heade in Florida*, 117, 116.

14. Sharf, quoted in Favis, *Martin Johnson Heade in Florida*, 65–67.

15. Longsworth, *Austin and Mabel*, 199.

16. Longsworth, *Austin and Mabel*, 197.

17. Longsworth, *Austin and Mabel*, quoting Mabel's summary of Molly's charges, 222.

18. Longsworth, *Austin and Mabel*, 216.

19. Letter 1004.

20. Letter 1031.

21. Letter 1037.

22. Letter 1046.

23. The cause of her death has long been assumed to be kidney failure, based on a diagnosis at that time, but the symptoms more closely resemble hypertension.

24. Longsworth, *Austin and Mabel*, 251.

25. Mabel did eventually settle in Florida, in a Japanese-style house built for her by another admirer in Coconut Grove.

26. Edward King, *The Great South*, 379.

27. James, *The American Scene*, ed. Leon Edel (Bloomington: Indiana University Press, 1968), 411.

28. On Heade's preference for flatness, see Favis, *Martin Johnson Heade in Florida*, 67 and chapter 4, "Poet of Wetlands/Prophet of Conservation."

29. Cf. Harriet Beecher Stowe on the Florida landscape: "The tops of the palms rise up round in the distance as so many hay-cocks, and seeming to rise above one another as far as the eye can reach," quoted in Favis, *Martin Johnson Heade in Florida*, 56.

30. Stebbins, *Life and Work of Martin Johnson Heade*, 145.

31. Stebbins, *Life and Work of Martin Johnson Heade*, 145, and Favis, *Martin Johnson Heade in Florida*, 111. See also King, *The Great South*, 384. "It is not grandeur which one finds on the banks of the great stream, it is nature run riot. The very irregularity is delightful, the decay is charming, the solitude is picturesque."

32. James, *The American Scene*, 451.

33. Stebbins, *Life and Work of Martin Johnson Heade*, 147.

34. James, *The American Scene*, 459. The quotations from James in the following paragraph may be found on 449, 408, 438, 439, 444.

35. On magnolias as "recognizable emblems of the South in general and of Florida in particular" see Favis, *Martin Johnson Heade in Florida*, 81–82.

36. Quoted in Favis, *Martin Johnson Heade in Florida*, 81.

37. Stowe, *Palmetto Leaves*, 162, quoted in Favis, *Martin Johnson Heade in Florida*, 115.

38. "Humming Birds as Pets," *Forest and Stream* (October 1, 1898), 264, quoted in Favis, *Martin Johnson Heade in Florida*, 118.

Epilogue: Toward the Blue Peninsnula

1. The epigraph is from a letter to John L. Graves, April 1856. Letter 184.

2. Poem 1672.

3. Letter 330.

4. Poem 519.

5. Letter 234.

6. See Dan Hofstadter, *The Love Affair as a Work of Art* (New York: Farrar, Straus and Giroux, 1996).

7. Poem 383.

8. Poem 1174.

9. The phrase is David Porter's from his article "Assembling a Poet and Her Poems: Convergent Limit-Works of Joseph Cornell and Emily Dickinson," *Word and Image*, vol. 10, no. 3 (July–September 1994), 199. My account of Cornell and Dickinson draws heavily on this important article, which itself makes use of Dore Ashton's pages on Dickinson in her *A Joseph Cornell Album* (1974). Porter is the first person, as far as I know, to identify Jay Leyda as the go-between.

10. Jed Perl, *New Art City* (New York: Knopf, 2005), 289.

11. Lynda Roscoe Hartigan, panel text in exhibition on Joseph Cornell at the Smithsonian Museum of American Art, Washington, D.C., fall 2006.

12. Lynda Roscoe Hartigan, "Joseph Cornell: A Biography," in Kynaston McShine, ed., *Joseph Cornell* (New York: Museum of Modern Art, 1980), 118 n105.

13. Poem 381.

14. Porter, "Assembling a Poet and Her Poems," 200.

15. Porter, "Assembling a Poet and Her Poems," 200.

16. Porter, "Assembling a Poet and Her Poems," 205.

17. Porter, "Assembling a Poet and Her Poems," 216.

18. Porter, "Assembling a Poet and Her Poems," 201.

19. Millicent Todd Bingham, *Bolts of Melody* (New York: Harper, 1945), xii, xvi, quoted in Porter, 208. Porter acknowledges Dore Ashton's discovery of the linkage here.

20. Pages from Oliver P. Pearson, "The Metabolism of Hummingbirds," *Scientific American* (January 1953), are included in the Joseph Cornell Collection, Smithsonian Institution, in the Archives of American Art. I wish to thank Lynda Roscoe Hartigan for alerting me to this material.

21. See Mary Ann Caws, *Joseph Cornell's Theatre of the Mind: Selected Diaries, Letters, and Files* (New York and London: Thames and Hudson, 1993), 221. In the entry for December 18, 1956, Cornell refers to this work as his "'Hummingbird' collage" (p. 224). Caws reproduces, after p. 192, another of Cornell's hummingbird works, *Forgotten Game. Box Construction. Observations of a Satellite I* is reproduced in Lynda Roscoe Hartigan, Walter Hopps, Richard Vine, and Robert Lehrman, *Joseph Cornell Shadowplay Eterniday* (New York: Thames and Hudson, 2003), 181.

22. Porter, "Assembling a Poet and Her Poems," 212. My colleague Karen Remmler suggests that the "mail from Tunis" may evoke the exotic stamps, often decorated with colorful birds, from foreign lands.

23. Poem 883.

24. Poem 535.

INDEX